THE ESSENTIAL TEACHINGS OF ISLAM

KU-666-049

THE ESSENTIAL TEACHINGS OF ISLAM

Edited by Kerry Brown and
Martin Palmer

ARROW BOOKS

Arrow Books Limited
20 Vauxhall Bridge Road, London SW1V 2SA

An imprint of Random Century Group

London Melbourne Sydney Auckland
Johannesburg and agencies throughout
the world

First published in Great Britain by Rider 1987
Arrow edition 1990

© International Consultancy on Religion,
Education and Culture 1987

Printed and bound in Great Britain by
Courier International Ltd, Tiptree, Essex

ISBN 0 09 973120 7

In the Name of Allah
Most Gracious, Most Merciful

Contents

Preface

The Essential Teachings Series

This book is the first in a series of readers which are intended to explore the great religious texts of the world and the faiths for which the texts are holy scripture. The books are designed to act as introductory volumes to the scriptures and to the fundamental teachings of the faiths. In all the major religious texts there are profound, beautiful, moving, disturbing, thought-provoking, calming and challenging words and insights. These are often able to speak across cultural and linguistic barriers, to those outside the faith itself, just as they speak across the centuries to those within the faith. There is therefore much to be gained personally by reading and reflecting on the scriptures. However, the scriptures do speak in a particular way to the faithful. In any selection of texts there is a 'theology' or 'philosophy' which informs their selection over and against other texts from within the same scriptures. It is this second level that we have sought to bring out through the commentaries which accompany each of the texts. What do these texts tell us about the core beliefs, teachings and ethics of the major faiths? Through the commentaries of contemporary believers we can enter into the world of the faith through its heart – the scriptures. By listening to what a believer hears in the words of the scriptures we are allowed access to the fundamental basis of the faith. By having the more obscure or complex parts of the texts explained to us, we can do more than read an interesting quote – we can come to understand more of the context of the faith from which it speaks.

This series has been designed to appeal to two sets of readers. Obviously the first group are those of the faith for whom the

series will come as a welcome source for personal reflection and
as a resource for teaching or study. The second group are those
who are not of the faith but who wish to open themselves to the
truths and insights which the faith has to offer. This encounter
will not always be an easy or comfortable one, for the message
which comes direct from the scriptures is often uncompromising
in its presentation of the choice facing humanity. In editing the
books our intention as editors is to allow each faith to speak with
its own integrity and with the particular force which is its
hallmark. We are not seeking some easy, syncretistic amalgam or
selection of 'nice' or 'safe' texts. In each book we follow the logic
of the faith in the selection of texts and the purpose or intention
behind the selection. As editors our task is to work with leading
scholars of the particular faith and to find a way of presenting the
message of that faith through the texts and commentaries which
will speak equally forcefully and authentically to the faithful as
well as to those outside the faith.

Introduction

The Essential Teachings Of Islam

The key figure in Islam is of course the prophet Muhammad .
While Muhammad  is considered to be only a human being,
and in no way divine, he is accorded great respect. Hence it is
customary to say 'Peace Be Upon Him' after mentioning his
name or one of his titles such as 'Messenger of Allah'. In the text
(excluding those taken from the Qur'an itself where this is not
recorded) we have used the Arabic words in the form of a 'seal'
(by courtesy of the Islamic Texts Society) to mark the use of this
phrase.

The Prophet Muhammad  was born in the year 570 CE.*
He was born at Makkah (Mecca) in what is now Saudi Arabia. In
610 CE, while meditating in a cave on Mount Hira, he received
the call to prophethood from the Angel Gabriel.

By the year 622 opposition to his teachings in Makkah had
become so strong that he and his followers took refuge in
Madinah (Medina). This journey, known as the Hijrah, marks
the start of the Islamic calendar.†

In 630 the Muslim forces conquered Makkah and from then
on Islam rapidly spread far to the north, east and west.

In 632 Muhammad  died. During his life, from 610
onwards, the Qur'an had been revealed to him. After his death
people collected well-authenticated stories about him and his
sayings. These are known as the Hadith and count as the second

*CE stands for 'Common Era', the term favoured by other Non Christian faiths
to the conventional AD with its specifically Christian overtones.
†The Islamic year is signified by the letters AH, which stands for 'After Hijrah'.
The year 1988 CE is 1409 AH.

most important source of Islamic teaching after the Qur'an. Both the Qur'an and the Hadith were first recorded in Arabic.

The Qur'an consists of 114 surahs or chapters. The ordering of the surahs is from the longest (Surah 2 has 286 verses) to the shortest (Surah 112 has four verses).

In the following text we have based our translation upon Abdullah Yusuf Ali's *The Meaning of the Glorious Qur'an*. At points we have drawn upon different translations by other scholars. Throughout we have modernized Ali's text, removing the 'thees' and 'thous' and simplifying some of the more convoluted sentences.

The book has been designed to provide a reading for each day of the year. You will therefore find there are 355 readings, as the year which we follow is the Muslim one, which is between ten and eleven days shorter than the Western year.

There have been many Muslims scholars who have worked with us on this book. Some wish to remain anonymous but some we wish to thank and name as our main contributors. They are Sheik Ismail Abdul Halim, BA, MA (Lecturer, The Muslim College, London). Maulana A.N. Beg (Chief Imam, Manchester Central Mosque) and Abdur Rahim (UK Islamic Mission, Manchester). Without these colleagues the book could never have been compiled.

1   The Faith

1: THE OPENING *(FATIHA)* 1:1-7

Praise be to Allah,
Lord of the Universe
Most Compassionate, Most Merciful
Master of the Day of Judgement
You alone do we worship
And to You alone do we pray for help.
Show us the Straight Way
The Way of those whom You have blessed
With whom You are not angry
And who have not gone astray.

This opening surah is a prayer which Allah has given for all who
sincerely wish to study His Book. It is as familiar to us as the
limbs He has given us, for it begins each of the prayers we recite
during the five daily prayer periods. It inspires us to study the
Qur'an, to recognize and worship the Lord of the Universe as the
source of all Knowledge and to pray for Guidance from Him
alone. Submission to Allah as the one and only God is the very
foundation of Islam. Indeed, the primary meaning of the word
Islam is 'submission to the Will of Allah'.

The surah addresses Him in the correct manner, acknowledg-
ing his supreme position, His blessings and His total authority
over us. A believer in Allah *(Muslim)* must never forget that we
will all be called to account on the Final Day and He will reward
or punish us justly.

Fatiha is a request to be shown the Straight Way, that is – His
Will – and His answer to us is the Holy Qur'an.

2: THE COW *(BAQARA)* 2:2–5

> *This is the Book (of Allah) without doubt. It is a guidance for*
> *God-fearing people who believe in the Unseen, keep up prayer and*
> *give from that which We have given them; who believe in the Book*
> *We have sent down to you as well as the Books We sent down*
> *before you; and who believe in their hearts in the life Hereafter.*
> *Such people are on the Path of their Lord and they shall prosper.*

This is the answer to the opening request for Allah's guidance.
Here is an end to doubt. The Divine Revelation of the Qur'an is
indisputable, so we know that it contains no mistakes. Here for
all who wish to turn to Allah is the Path of Islam: belief in the one
God; regular Prayer and Almsgiving; belief in the Holy Qur'an
and the other Holy Books revealed through the Prophets; and
belief in the Hereafter.

3: THE WOMEN *(NISAA)* 4:136

> *O you who believe, believe in Allah and His Apostle, and the*
> *Scripture which He sent to His Apostle and the Scripture which*
> *he sent to those before. And he who denies Allah, His Angels, His*
> *Books, His Apostles and the Day of Judgement has gone far, far*
> *astray.*

Islam begins with Faith. There are five Pillars of Faith *(Iman)*
which all Muslims must hold sincerely in their hearts: belief in
Allah, in the Scriptures which reveal His Word, in His Angels,
in His Prophet Muhammad 🕌 and all the Prophets before him
who had come to reveal His Word, and in the Hereafter. In fact,
anyone who believes in Allah and His Prophet Muhammad 🕌
is a Muslim, because, by definition, they must have accepted the
other three Pillars – the Prophet Muhammad 🕌 proclaimed
the Truth of these three Pillars, and a Messenger of Allah does
not lie.

4: HADITH *(BUKHARI)* 2:6

Allah's Messenger 🌼 *said: 'None of you has faith unless he loves for his brother what he loves for himself.'*

The love of Allah and His Prophet Muhammad 🌼 necessarily leads to the love of His Creation. When we have truly cast our gaze from material rewards and turned to Him, then our hearts will turn naturally to love of our fellow man. Love of this kind is not simply a matter of treating another as we would have him treat us, but of genuine empathy which goes beyond concern for our own lot.

5: FAITH *(IKHLAS)* 112:1–4

Say: He is Allah the One and Only, Allah the Eternal, Absolute. He does not beget, nor is He begotten. And there is none like Him.

The Oneness of Allah *(Tawhid)* is the essence of Islam. It means belief in the One God with all His glorious Names and Attributes. He is beyond our comprehension, for He is beyond time and space, the Truth before which all other truths pale into shadow. There is nothing comparable to Him. Nor can we ascribe mortal qualities to Him such as conception. He does not have children, nor does He have a father. He is the First and the Last, the One and Only Creator. We owe our existence to Him, our every breath. Declaration of belief in *Tawhid* is the first duty of every believer in Allah *(Muslim)*.

6: THE WINDS THAT SCATTER *(ZARIYAT)* 51:49

And of everything We have created pairs so that you may receive instruction.

Allah is unseen, so it is only through the Signs which He sends us that we can know Him. Everything in nature is a Sign of his Oneness *(Tawhid)*. The consistent division of Creation into male and female among the living, and matter and anti-matter among the non-living, is evidence of a balanced and coherent design. It is a sign that it is the Work of One God and a lesson to us of how we should live.

7: THE CONFEDERATES (*AHZAB*) 33:38

And the command of Allah is a decree determined.

Allah's plan is based upon universal principles which the arts and sciences have endeavoured to unveil throughout human history. This has been undertaken on the basis that there were obviously underlying rules, even if they could not be deciphered. The belief that Allah is the Absolute Controller and Regulator, with a predetermined course for all Creation, is a logical extension of *Tawhid*. Allah the All-Knowing must know the destiny of every creature.

8: THUNDER (*R'AD*) 13:2

It is Allah Who raised the heavens without any pillars that you can see, and it is He Who is firmly established on the Throne of His Kingdom. He has subjected the sun and the moon to His Law; each one runs its course to its fixed term. He regulates affairs, explaining the Signs in detail so that you may be convinced of meetings with your Lord.

Although there is nothing visible supporting the heavenly bodies, there is a constant and imperceptible power that holds them, including the Earth, in their orbits. The law of gravity is Allah's Law. Gravity and the other great forces of the Universe, such as electromagnetism, are unseen. They are a Sign in this Universe of the infinite Power of the Unseen God.

Allah is established on His Throne as the Creator and Ruler of the Universe. The people of Makkah to whom Muhammad 🕉 was preaching accepted this, while at the same time associating other gods with Allah. There are also, of course, atheists who deny Allah's existence altogether. The argument against both is clear. The whole Universe – the Earth, the moon, the sun and countless heavenly bodies – works as a perfect system under an All-Powerful Law that even now science continues to unravel. Therefore there must be an All-Powerful Lawmaker with perfect Judgement and Knowledge. For there can be no law without a lawmaker, no system without an administrator, no wisdom without a sage and no knowledge without a possessor of knowledge, and of course there can be no Creation without a Creator.

The system is also witness to the fact that there is nothing everlasting within it. Everything has a fixed term to run; therefore there must be a fixed term for the system as a whole. But, since Allah, His Will and His Purpose are eternal, there must be a Hereafter when the Universe has ended.

9: THE BEE *(NAHL)* 16:12–15

He has subjected the night and the day, the sun and moon to you; and the stars serve you by His command. Surely in this there are Signs for men of understanding.

And He has created all the things on the Earth in varying colours for you. Surely in this there is a Sign for men who praise Allah.

It is He who has subjected the sea to you, so that you may eat its fresh fish and take from it ornaments to wear. And you see the ships ploughing the waves so that you may benefit from the bounty of Allah and give thanks to Him.

And He has set mountains firmly on the Earth, lest it should shake with you, and rivers and roads so that you may guide yourselves.

The honour and duty which come to us as Allah's supreme Creation are apparent in the many signs which show that His Creation is designed to serve us in the best possible way. Out of His infinite Mercy Allah has given us the bounty of nature, its beauty and order. We, in turn, must serve Allah. His great gift must never be taken for granted, nor must its laws be contravened. To benefit from Allah's bounty is to reap the gifts of nature according to these laws. The unlawful use of nature inevitably rebounds on us as self-inflicted damage. We bring about hunger and deprivation in this life, and our own punishment in the next.

The balance of the world is fixed by the mountains, which like pegs keep the Earth maintained upon its axis. The natural passes, ravines and waterways Allah provided for us to find our way in the physical world, as a sign that he also provides the Guidance we need to find our way in the spiritual world.

10: MOST GRACIOUS (*RAHMAN*) 55:17–25

He is Lord of the two easts and Lord of the two wests.

Then which of the favours of your Lord will you deny?

He has let free the two bodies of flowing water, meeting together. Between them is a barrier which they do not transgress.

Then which of the favours of your Lord will you deny?

Out of them come pearls and coral.

Then which of the favours of your Lord will you deny?

And His are the ships sailing smoothly through the seas, lofty as mountains.

Then which of the favours of your Lord will you deny?

This surah, like Psalm 136 in the Book of the Prophet David, uses question and refrain to communicate the teachings. In *Rahman*, the question is asked no less than thirty-one times. The responses cite examples of Creation in pairs enhancing our sense of the mutual compatibility and balance of Creation. The two easts and two wests referred to here are the different points at which the sun rises and sets at the winter and summer solstice. The two waters are fresh water and salt water, and their ability to meet but not mix is a wonder of Allah. All bear witness to the Oneness of Allah and His design.

11: THUNDER *(RA'D)* 13:4

> *And in the Earth are tracts of land of different natures, even though they border on one another. And also vineyards, and seeds and palm trees springing from the same root or from separate roots. They are watered with the same water, yet some We make more delicious to eat than others. Surely these things are Signs for those who understand.*

All Creation is a Sign of Allah and His boundless Powers. In these examples we specifically see the diversity of Creation as a Sign that our own diversity is to be celebrated as His design. Just as neighbouring tracts of land differ, and plants irrigated by the same water differ, so do human beings differ. The Divine Wisdom has decreed diversity in all nature. Even in our own limited perception we can see the great benefit to human civilization through the interaction of diverse individuals and cultures.

The Earth with all its wonderful and purposeful Signs is clear proof that Allah is All-Wise, and that He would not create such a place for no reason, and certainly He must have had a purpose for his noblest Creation. We can be sure that we will be accountable to the Creator for the fulfilment of that Divine purpose.

12: GOLD ADORNMENTS *(ZUKHRUF)* 43:11

> *It is He Who sends down rain from the sky in due measure and thereby raises to life a land that is dead; even so will you be raised from the dead.*

In Allah's regeneration of the land each year, we can see His Power to give life to that which appears dead. So too, on the Day of Judgement, Allah will bring to life the dead to stand before Him. He is both Creator and Regenerator, as able to bring to life from nothing as to give back life to that which is lifeless. In the regeneration of the land we can see a Sign of our own Resurrection.

Here is evidence also of *Tawhid,* the unity of Creation by One God. The heavens providing the Earth with lifegiving rain is one of the endless examples of a universe that works as a single perfect whole. No universe that was merely a machine, or is run by a crowd of departmental gods, could be so simple yet intricate, and so perfectly integrated.

13: THE FAMILY OF IMRAN *(ALI-I-IMRAN)* 3:29

Say: 'Whether you hide what is in your hearts or reveal it, Allah knows it all, He knows what is in the heavens and what is on earth and Allah has Power over all things.'

The logical conclusion of *Tawhid* is total surrender to His Will, for indeed there is nothing that He does not know or control. With Submission comes self-assurance, for we know that we are the Creation of He Who is Perfect and it is to Him alone that we look for approval. We are also humble, for we know that everything we possess or achieve is by His Grace. We are brave, and fear less because we know that our life and our death are in His hands and cannot be changed by anything we do. We are outward-looking and socially responsible, because we know that everyone and everything is His Creation and must be cared for and respected. We endeavour to be righteous, because we know that He is Just and will punish he who is unjust.

14: PILGRIMAGE *(HAJJ)* 22:31

Be true in faith to Allah and never assign partners to Him. If anyone assigns partners to Allah, it is as if he had fallen from Heaven and been snatched up by birds, or the wind had swept him away to a far-away place.

The person who falls from belief in the One God has fallen from Heaven, to be snatched up by a passing cult of false gods that will carry him far away toward hell. These heavenly pretenders have nothing with which to hold him, and he will plummet down into hell.

15: HADITH
MUSLIM: Book of Remembrance of Allah (*Kitab Al-Dhikr*) 6475

Abu Huraira reported that Allah's Messenger ﷺ said: 'There are ninety-nine names of Allah; he who commits them to memory will get into Paradise. Truly, Allah is Odd (He is One) and He loves odd numbers.

The Ninety-Nine Names of Allah in the Qur'an and Hadith are:

1 Allah
2 The Compassionate (*al-Rahman*)
3 The Merciful (*al-Rahim*)
4 The King/Sovereign (*al-Malik*)
5 The Holy (*al-Quddus*)
6 The Source of Peace (*al-Salam*)
7 The Giver of Faith (*al-Mu'min*)
8 The Overall Protector (*al-Muhaimin*)
9 The Strong (*al-'Aziz*)
10 The Almighty (*al-Jabbar*)
11 The Majestic (*al-Mutakabbir*)
12 The Creator (*al-Khaliq*)
13 The Maker (*al-Bari'*)
14 The Fashioner (*al-Musawwir*)
15 The Great Forgiver (*al-Ghaffar*)
16 The Dominant (*al-Qahhar*)
17 The Bestower (*al-Wahhab*)
18 The Provider (*al-Razzaq*)
19 The Opener, The Reliever (*al-Fattah*)
20 The All-Knowing (*al-'Alim*)
21 The Restrainer, The Withholder (*al-Qabid*)
22 The Extender (*al-Basit*)
23 The Humbler (*al-Khafid*)
24 The Exalter (*al-Rafi'*)
25 The Empowerer (*al-Mu'izz*)
26 The Humiliator (*al-Mudhill*)
27 The All-Hearing, The Hearer (*al-Sami'*)
28 The All-Seeing (*al-Basir*)
29 The Judge (*al-Hakam*)

30   The Just (*al-'Adl*)
31   The Kindly One (*al-Latif*)
32   The Gracious, The Aware (*al-Khabir*)
33   The Clement, The Forbearing (*al-Halim*)
34   The Mighty (*al-'Azim*)
35   The Forgiving (*al-Ghafur*)
36   The Grateful, The Appreciative (*al-Shakur*)
37   The High, The Sublime (*al-'Aliyy*)
38   The Great (*al-Kabir*)
39   The Preserver (*al-Hafiz*)
40   The Protector, The Guardian, The Feeder, The Sustainer
     (*al-Muqit*)
41   The Reckoner (*al-Hasib*)
42   The Sublime One (*al-Jali*)
43   The Bountiful, The Gracious (*al-Karim*)
44   The Watcher, The Watchful (*al-Raqib*)
45   The Responsive, The Hearkener (*al-Mujib*)
46   The Infinite, The All-Embracing (*al-Wasi'*)
47   The Wise (*al-Hakim al-Mutlaq*)
48   The Loving (*al-Wadud*)
49   The Glorious (*al-Majid*)
50   The Resurrector (*al Ba'ith*)
51   The Witness (*al-Shahid*)
52   The True (*al-Haqq*)
53   The Advocate (*al-Wakil*)
54   The Most Strong (*al-Qawiyy*)
55   The Firm (*al-Matin*)
56   The Patron (*al-Waliyy*)
57   The Praiseworthy (*al-Hamid*)
58   The Numberer (*al-Muhsi*)
59   The Commencer (*al-Mubdi*)
60   The Restorer (*al-Mu'id*)
61   The Giver of Life (*al-Muhyi*)
62   The One Who Gives Death (*al-Mumit*)
63   The Living One (*al-Hayy*)
64   The Self-Subsisting (*al-Qayyum*)
65   The Perceiver (*al-Wajid*)
66   The One (*al-Wahid*)
67   The Independent (*al-Samad*)
68   The Powerful (*al-Qadir*)

69 The Dominant *(al-Muqtadir)*
70 The Giver *(al-Muqaddim)*
71 The Retarder *(al-Mu'akhkhir)*
72 The First *(al-Awwal)*
73 The Last *(al-Akhir)*
74 The Manifest *(al-Zahir)*
75 The Hidden *(al-Batin)*
76 The Governor *(al-Wali)*
77 The High Exalted *(al-Muta'ali)*
78 The Righteous *(al-Barr)*
79 The Relenting *(al-Tawwab)*
80 The Forgiver *(al-'Afuww)*
81 The Avenger *(al-Muntaquim)*
82 The Compassionate *(al-Ra'uf)*
83 The Ruler of the Kingdom *(Malik al-Mulk)*
84 The Lord of Majesty and Bounty *(Dhu'l-Jalal wa'l-Ikram)*
85 The Equitable *(al-Muqsit)*
86 The Gatherer, The Collector *(al-Jami')*
87 The Self-Sufficient *(al-Ghani)*
88 The Enricher *(al-Mughni)*
89 The Bestower *(al-Mu'ti)*
90 The Withholder *(al-Mani')*
91 The Propitious *(al-Nafi')*
92 The Distresser *(al-Darr)*
93 The Light *(al-Nur)*
94 The Guide *(al-Hadi)*
95 The Eternal *(al-Azali)*
96 The Everlasting *(al-Baqi)*
97 The Heir *(al-Warith)*
98 The Guide to the Right Path *(al-Rashid)*
99 The Patient *(al-Sabur)*

16: THE GATHERING *(HASHR)* 59:22–24

Allah is He besides whom there is no other god – who knows all, both secret and open; He Most Gracious, Most Merciful.

Allah is He besides whom there is no other god – the Sovereign, the Holy One, the Source of Peace, the Guardian of Faith, the

Preserver of Safety, the Exalted in Might, the Irresistible, the Supreme. Glory be to Allah, high above the partners they attribute to Him.

He is Allah, the Creator, the Evolver, the Bestower of Forms. To Him belong the Most Beautiful Names. Whatever is in the heavens and on Earth proclaims His Praises and Glory, and He is the Exalted in Might, the Wise.

These verses sum up the main Attributes of Allah, beginning with His essential uniqueness. This is repeated to emphasize that it is fundamental to our understanding of all His Attributes. The Attributes fall broadly into three categories – His Goodness, His Power and His continuous Creative Energy.

17: THE HEIGHTS *(A'RAF)* 7:180

The Most Beautiful Names belong to Allah, so call on Him by them, but shun men who use His name profanely. For what they do, they will soon be requited.

The ninety-nine Names of Allah are by no means comprehensive, but they are the Names relevant to us, for they cover all aspects of human life.

We address Allah by His different Names according to the specific needs of different occasions. If we wish for His forgiveness, we call upon Him as the Forgiver *(al-'Afuww)*, if we wish to see the Truth, we call upon Him as the Truth *(al-Haqq)*, if we wish to be esteemed among people we call upon Him as the Owner of Sovereignty *(Malik al-Mulk)*, and so on.

After we have realized, through logical reflection on the Universe, that there is One All-Powerful Creator (see p. 5–12), the next stage of coming to know Allah is through reflection on His Names and Attributes. The ninety-nine Names and Attributes are Allah's way of introducing Himself to His Creation. By reflecting on them we can build up a clear perception of Allah.

Memorizing the ninety-nine Names of Allah is the simplest form of appreciation of the Creator, but as our knowledge of Him grows so our reflection on these names will be deepened.

18: THE ROMANS *(RUM)* 30:30

> *So set your face steadily and truly to the Faith. Uphold Allah's handiwork according to the pattern on which He has made mankind. There can be no change made in God's Work – that is the standard religion but most among mankind do not understand this.*

We are all born in submission to Allah, that is our true nature. To set our faces 'steadily and truly to the Faith' carries the allegorical sense of a magnetic needle always true to the north pole. Both are in accord with the Laws of God. This is the good news of the Qur'an – that we are the handiwork of the Perfect God and as such we are created virtuous, obedient, pure and righteous. We do not begin tainted by original sin. Islam is our natural state – we do not discover it, we return to it, away from the corrupting forces of the Evil One established in superstition, ideology and lust. Thus Islam is the standard religion, not in the sense of a sectarian belief-system in conflict with other factions, but as the One True Way which includes all aspects of human life. It cannot be up-dated or reformed by popular demand, because it is the unchanging, eternal Law of the One God.

The Hadith record that before the Prophet 🕌 delivered this verse he said that every child is born in Islam and remains so until he has matured. It is his parents who make him a Jew or Christian or a polytheist. If his parents are Muslims then he will remain so (Muslim: Book of Remembrance of Allah, 6423–9).

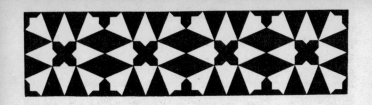

2 The Apostles

19: THE CATTLE (*AN'AM*) 6:82–87

It is those who believe and do not confuse their beliefs with wrong that are truly secure, for they are on the Right Path.

That was the reasoning We gave to Abraham to use against his people. We raise whom We will, degree after degree, for your Lord is full of Wisdom and Knowledge.

We gave him Isaac and Jacob – all three we guided. And before him We guided Noah, and among his progeny, David, Solomon, Job, Joseph, Moses and Aaron. Thus do We reward those who do good.

And Zakariya and John and Jesus and Elias, all in the ranks of the Righteous.

And Isma'il and Elisha and Jonas and Lot. And to all We gave Favour above the nations.

We chose them with their fathers and descendants and brothers, and We guided them to a Straight Way.

Since Creation, Allah has provided Guidance for humanity through selected people known as the prophets, who were not Divine themselves but who were the transmitters of the Divine Word. The above list spans the great prophets of the three Religions of the Book founded by the work of Moses, Jesus and Muhammad ﷺ.

The first Prophet spoken of is Abraham, who was the first

prophet known to have the Guidance revealed as a Book, although that is now lost. Then comes his son and grandson, who established the tribes of Israel. The other prophets mentioned in this verse were also men who became founders and leaders of nations.

In comparison to these very active men who were 'doers' in both the worldly and spiritual spheres, the next grouping is of the 'righteous' men. The Prophethood of Jesus was the focus of the Work of Allah performed through these four prophets, whose lifetimes all overlapped.

The last group of men 'favoured above the nations' all suffered because their nations were troubled (see 51), but they remained steadfastly in Islam and so survived. Included here is Isma'il, Abraham's older son, who founded the Arab nation out of which would come the Final Prophet of Allah ﷺ. Throughout time, there have always been those who were true Muslims – servants of Allah – appointed by Him to deliver the Revelation of His Will to those who will believe.

20: THE WOMEN (*NISAA*) 4:165

Apostles gave good news as well as warning, so that mankind after the Apostles should have no plea against Allah, for Allah is Exalted in Power and Wisdom.

All the Prophets had the same mission – to bring good news of Allah and everlasting Paradise to believers, and to warn disbelievers of the never ending punishment. Through their words and actions the Prophets spread Allah's Message. For those who ignored and those who still ignore His Message, there can be no plea of ignorance on the Day of Judgement. But for those who see and hear and believe, Paradise awaits them for having made the right decision.

21: JONAH (*YUNUS*) 10:47

To every people an Apostle was sent. When their Apostle comes before them, the matter will be judged between them with justice and they will not be wronged.

The Hadith state that 124,000 Prophets and Messengers have been sent to earth since the Creation. The Holy Qur'an mentions twenty-five of these by name. Once people have been sent a Prophet, they are responsible for their beliefs and no excuse will be accepted for not heeding the Message. This applies not only to the contemporaries of the Prophet, but also to those people whom the Message reaches in the centuries and millennia that follow. Because the Holy Qur'an continues to be published and taught all around the world, the people who follow the teaching given to the Prophet Muhammad 爨 are a growing international population. All who have been given the message of One Allah will be called to account for their beliefs on the Day of Judgement.

22: THE WOMEN (NISAA) 4:150–151

Those who deny Allah and His Apostles, and who wish to separate Allah from His Apostles saying 'We believe in some but reject others', and those who wish to take a course midway – they are in truth equally disbelievers, and we have prepared for disbelievers a humiliating punishment.

There can be no sincere belief in Allah that does not include belief in His Prophets. The eternal Message of Allah was with every Prophet, so to deny even one Prophet is to deny Allah's Message and therefore to deny Islam. Even Jews and Christians, who are People of the Book, that is People of Allah's Message, follow the path that leads to Hell. They declare faith in Allah and in the Prophet Abraham, but the former fall short by calling the Prophet Jesus an imposter, while the latter do so by calling him the son of Allah. Both peoples fail yet again by denying the Prophethood of Muhammad 爨.

23: HADITH
MUSLIM: Book of Faith (Kitab Al-Iman) 248

It is narrated on the authority of Abu Huraira that the Messenger of Allah 爨 observed: By Him in Whose hand is the life of

*Muhammad, anyone from the Jewish or Christian communities
who hears about me but does not affirm his belief in that with
which I have been sent and dies in this state (of disbelief) – he shall
be among those who dwell in hell-fire.*

This Hadith affirms that, while those who came before
Muhammad 爨 had their own Prophets with the Divine
Message, those who have been born since and have heard his
Message will have no excuse on the Day of Resurrection if they
have not accepted Muhammad 爨 as the last Prophet and the
Revelations sent to him. For this is the final and completed Word
of Allah. 'Today I have perfected for you your religion and
fulfilled my favour unto you' (Qur'an 5:3).

Of course, those who have not heard the Message of the
Prophet Muhammad 爨 , will not be blamed for their delusions.

24: THE FAMILY OF IMRAN
(AL-I-IMRAN) 3:33–34

*Allah chose Adam and Noah, the family of Abraham, and the
family of Imran above all people.*

*They all belong to the same line of descent. Allah hears and knows
everything.*

Two points are made here. First, Adam, Noah and the
descendants of Abraham and Imran are the chosen above all
people. That is to say, from among them will come the leaders of
all people. Secondly, they share the same lineage. In other words,
Jesus was not descended from Allah but from Abraham. Imran,
called Amran in the Bible, was Moses' and Aaron's father. He
was descended from Abraham on the side of Isaac and his son
Jacob (Israel). Mary and her son Jesus were descendants of
Imran.

These verses are the beginning of a revelation addressed to a
deputation from the Christian community of Najran, about 150
miles north of Sana'a (of Yaman), who themselves avowed belief
in the Prophets referred to here, but who persisted in
proclaiming Jesus as the son of Allah (see 53–56). The

deputation, which was lead by Abd Al-Masih, the chief of the Najran Christians, was one of many which visited the Holy Prophet after the conquest of Makkah. By then it was apparent that the future of Arabia lay with him.

25: THE COW (*BAQARA*) 2: 122–124

O Children of Israel, remember that special favour I bestowed upon you, and that I exalted you above all others. Then guard yourselves against a Day when one soul shall not avail another, nor shall any compensation be accepted from anyone, nor shall intercession profit any one, nor shall the offenders be helped from any quarter.

And remember that Abraham was tried by his Lord with certain Commands which he fulfilled. He said: 'I will make you an Imam to the Nations.' He pleaded: 'And also Imams from my descendants!'

Abraham's Prophethood marks the formal establishment of the eternal Message. This does not in anyway contradict the fact that Islam began the moment the world was created. We are all born Muslims, servants of Allah; it is human nature. But because humanity has the choice to go against its own nature, Allah in His Wisdom provided a line of Prophets formally to enshrine Islam in society.

Abraham began his mission in his own country, Ur – present-day Iraq – around 2100 BCE. Then he visited Syria, Palestine, Egypt and Arabia. Later, by the Will of Allah, he settled with his son Isaac in Palestine and his eldest son Isma'il settled in Arabia.

The two sons of Abraham were fathers of two peoples – the Isma'ilites and Israelites, who are identified respectively as the Arabs and Jews. The Israelites, who descended from Isaac's son, Jacob Israel, inherited Abraham's leadership of the world on the Path of Islam. This was the special favour that was bestowed upon them by Allah. They had many prophets born among them, including Joseph, Moses, David, Solomon, John and Jesus. All these prophets preached Islam, submission to Allah, but the Israelites strayed in their beliefs and left Islam.

26: THE BELIEVERS *(MU-MINUN)* 23:51–52

O you Apostles, enjoy all things good and pure and work righteously, for I am well aware of all that you do. And truly this Brotherhood of yours is a single Brotherhood and I am your Lord and Cherisher, therefore fear me and no other.

These verses are not meant as instructions for Apostles yet to come, for Muhammad 🕮 was the last Prophet (see 37–38). The Prophets are addressed as if they are all in one place at one time, because the Message of Allah is timeless and omnipresent. This is the bond that all Prophets share, as do all who follow the path of Islam. 'Without doubt, the nearest of kin to Abraham are those who follow him, as are also this Apostle and those who believe...' (The Family of Imran *(Al-i-Imran)* 3:68).

The instructions to the Prophets to live purely and righteously must also apply to us, for they were sent as perfect role models for us.

27: THE CATTLE *(AN'AM)* 6:48–50

We send the Apostles to give good news and to warn, so those who believe and mend their lives shall not fear or grieve. But those who reject Our Signs, Our punishment will touch, because they did not cease their transgressions.

Say: 'I do not tell you that the treasures of Allah lie with me. Nor do I know what is hidden, nor do I tell you I am an Angel. I merely follow what is revealed to me.'

Say: 'Can the blind be held equal to the seeing. Will you therefore not consider it?'

The difference between Muhammad 🕮 and those whom he addresses is that Allah has given him the Revelation. Therefore, he is an eyewitness to the Truth, whereas they can only speculate in the darkness of ignorance. The Prophet is the man with sight, the man with vision amongst those who are blind and must be guided if they do not wish to harm themselves.

28: THE ROCKY TRACT (AL-HIJR) 15:10–15

We sent Apostles before you among the religious sects of old.

But no Apostle ever came to them that was not mocked.

Even so do We let it creep into the hearts of the sinners:

That they should not believe in it; that has been the way of such people since ancient times.

Even if We opened out to them a gate from heaven and they were to continue ascending all day,

They would only say: 'Our eyes have been intoxicated, indeed we have been bewitched by sorcery.'

The wiles of Satan delude many, so they fail the test that Allah has set us. The Almighty allows the cynicism of Satan to creep into our hearts, and most are so willing to be misled they disbelieve no matter how obvious the evidence to the contrary. So blinded are they, that even if the Unseen were to be revealed to them they would still manage to talk themselves into evil lies.

29: THE CHILDREN OF ISRAEL (BANI ISRA-IL) 17:94–96

What kept men back from belief when guidance came to them was nothing but this: They said: 'Has Allah sent a man like us to be His Apostle?'

Say: 'If there were Angels on earth, walking about in peace and quiet, We should certainly have sent down to them from the heavens an Angel for an Apostle.'

Say: 'It is enough that Allah is a witness between me and you, for He is well acquainted with His servants and He sees all things.'

Disbelievers challenged Muhammad ﷺ by demanding to know

why he ate, drank and had a family like them. In their ignorance, they argued that if he was a Messenger of Allah he should have supernatural powers that could turn a mountain or a camel into an ant. But the Prophets do not come to dazzle us with magical powers, they come to guide us in the correct way of living. To serve this purpose, Allah, in His Infinite Wisdom, sends men, not supernatural beings, as living examples to teach us by their own actions as well as by His Words. As fellow men they understand our desires and temptations, our delusions and weaknesses. An Angel could no more understand and demonstrate how to overcome our human failings and live correctly, than we could understand and demonstrate how to live as Angels.

30: THE FAMILY OF IMRAN *(AL-I-IMRAN)* 3:79–80

It is not possible for a man who has been given the Book and Wisdom and the Prophetic office, to say to people: 'Be my worshippers rather than Allah's.' On the contrary he would say: 'Be worshippers of He Who is truly the Cherisher of all, for you have taught the Book and you have studied it earnestly.'

Nor would he instruct you to take Angels and Prophets for lords and patrons. What would he bid you to disbelieve after you have bowed your will to Allah?

No Prophet of Allah would ever claim Allah's Powers or Knowledge or, indeed, to have any part of Godhead. This would be a negation of the Absoluteness of the One Allah. Even though the People of the Book pay lipservice to *Tawhid* (the Oneness of God), the Christians among them deny it with their worship of Jesus Christ as the son and equal of Allah. It is obvious that the Prophet Jesus would never have claimed such a thing. These are the later distortions of misguided people.

31: THE CATTLE *(AN'AM)* 6:34–35

The Apostles before you were rejected, but with patience and constancy they bore their rejection and the wrongs against them until Our help reached them. There is none that can alter the Words of Allah. You have already received some account of those Apostles.

Although their spurning is hard on your mind, yet if you were able to seek a tunnel in the ground or a ladder to the skies and bring them a Sign, what good would it be? If it was Allah's Will, He could gather them together unto true Guidance. So do not be one of those who is swayed by ignorance (and impatience)!

The prophet Muhammad ﷺ suffered greatly under the persecution and ignorance of his countrymen. At times it must have seemed very hard for the Prophet to bear the insults and abuse. But he is told in these verses that all those who have been called to bear witness to the people have had to suffer in this way. Furthermore the desire of the Prophet ﷺ to have some mighty sign sent to stun the people into submission is dismissed by Allah. What good are such meaningless signs if the people already reject Allah's clearest signs – Creation and His Word.

32: THE CATTLE *(AN'AM)* 6:112–113

Likewise did We make for every Messenger an enemy – evil ones among men and jinns, inspiring each other with flowery discourses by way of deception. If your Lord had so planned they would not have done it, so leave them and their inventions alone.

Let the hearts of those who have no faith in the Hereafter incline to such deceits: let them delight in it, and let them earn from it what they may.

All Prophets have had to bear the burden of the insults of those around them. This is of the nature of Prophethood. But they will receive their punishment in the Hereafter. Those who have no faith in the future delight in the thought of the evil one. They see it as confirmation that there is no Lord Who will judge the world. Well, let them persist in their delusions if they wish. They will receive their answer on the Day of Judgement.

33: THE CITY OF SHEBA *(SABA)* 34:43–45

When Our Revelations are declared to them, they say: 'This is only a man who wishes to distract you from the religion of your forefathers,' and they say, 'This is only an invented lie.' And the disbelievers say of the Truth when it comes to them, 'This is nothing but obvious magic.'

But We had not given them Books which they could study, nor sent Apostles to them before you as warners.

And their predecessors rejected the Truth, although we granted them ten times what these people have. And when they rejected My Apostles, how terrible was My Rejection of them.

There were two groups who objected to the Message the prophet Muhammad ﷺ brought. The Arabs who had never had a Book revealed to them could not see why they should change from the ways of their fathers. Many saw the Book as a forgery. The other group were the People of the Book. They had been vouchsafed so many revelations yet they still refused to accept. They are ten times more to blame, for they have received ten times more than the Arabs in the time of their forefathers. They sought to abuse the Book by claiming it was superstitious magic.

34: THE FAMILY OF IMRAN *(AL-I-IMRAN)* 3:144

Muhammad is no more than an Apostle. There were many Apostles that passed away before him. If he dies or is slain, will you then turn back on your heels? If any does turn back on his heels, he will not do the least bit of harm to Allah, but Allah (on the other hand) will swiftly reward those who (serve Him) with gratitude.

This verse was revealed after the Prophet had been seriously wounded at the Battle of Uhud against the Quraish, the ruling tribe of Makkah. The cry went up that the Prophet had been killed, striking grief into the hearts of true Muslims, while the hypocrites were quick to talk of seeking amnesty from the

Quraish, and others even declared the Prophet to be an imposter for having died. Here, Allah admonishes the frail of faith, reminding them that Muhammad

 is a human being – the Messenger, not the Message. If their loyalty to Islam is in fact only loyalty to Muhammad, then it is a false Faith that will revert to disbelief and is unworthy of Islam.

According to tradition, on the morning eight years later when Muhammad

 died of natural causes, his companion Abu Bakr arrived at the mosque and found another companion declaring it a sin to say the Prophet was dead. When he discovered that the Prophet was indeed dead, Abu Bakr cried, 'As for him who worshipped Muhammad

, Muhammad

 is dead, but as for him who worships Allah, Allah is alive and does not die.' Then he recited the verse above as a reminder to the people.

This verse is also a reminder to us that as great and noble as the Prophet is, we must beware of placing him in a position that in any way vies with Allah.

35: THE ASSEMBLY PRAYER (FRIDAY) (*JUMU'A*) 62:2

> *It is He who sent amongst the illiterate an Apostle from amongst themselves to declare to them His Revelations, to purify them and to instruct them in Scripture and Wisdom – although they have been before in manifest error.*

The Prophet Muhammad

 could neither read nor write, nor was this necessary as the Qur'an is Allah's words. The Prophet was simply but gloriously His instrument. Mankind had been sent prophets before – Abraham, Moses, David, John and Jesus amongst others – but their message had been deserted as the people strayed from Islam and changed the Holy Writings accordingly. The final Prophet and Book was sent to bring them back to Allah.

36: THE HEIGHTS (*A'RAF*) 7:156–157

> *He said: 'My punishment comes to whom I chose, but My Mercy*

extends to all things. I will decree Mercy for all who act rightly and practise regular charity and those who believe in Our Signs –

'Those who follow the Apostle, the unlettered Prophet, who is mentioned in their own Scriptures – in the Torah and the Gospel – for he commands them to act justly and forbids them from evil; he permits as lawful what is pure and prohibits as unlawful what is impure; he releases them from their heavy burdens and from the yokes that are upon them, so it is those who believe in him, honour him, help him and follow the Light which is sent down with him – it is they who will prosper.'

Belief in the Prophet Muhammad 🕌 is one of the prerequisites for Allah's mercy. The Apostle Muhammad 🕌 , like the prophets before him, was sent to tell us Allah's Laws and guide us onto the Path of Righteousness. To deny him is to deny Allah's Laws.

These Laws are not onerous and oppressive; they benefit us both in this life and in the Hereafter. They are as coherent and perfectly designed as nature. They are not the complicated, burdensome laws devised by hair-splitting legislators, superstitious folk or political factions angling for personal power and wealth. By the time of the Prophet Muhammad 🕌 , Judaism had built around itself a great cage of ritual and restriction that resulted from the tampering of such interests. The Prophet came to clear away the worldly detritus which had accumulated on the Message of Islam and restricted the lives of the people.

There are numerous references in the earlier scriptures to the advent of the Prophet Muhammad 🕌 (see below).

37: FAMILY OF IMRAN (*AL-I-IMRAN*) 3:81-82

Behold! Allah took the Covenant of the Prophets, saying 'I give you a Book and Wisdom. Then an Apostle will come confirming the knowledge that is with you. Believe in him and help him.' Allah said: 'Do you agree to this and take My Covenant with you as binding?' They said: 'We agree'. He said 'Then bear witness, and I will bear witness with you.'

Anyone who turns back after this is a perverted transgressor.

The Talmud also refers to this Covenant, made when Allah brought Prophets from many different ages together on Mount Sinai. The Covenant was made before the time of the Prophet Muhammad ﷺ and at no place in the Qur'an does it say that he was party to the Covenant. Nor did he prophesy the coming of another Prophet as those before him had. This is, of course, because he was the Last Prophet spoken of in the Covenant. By rejecting the Prophet Muhammad ﷺ, the Jews and Christians were breaking the Covenant made with Allah by their prophets.

38: BATTLE ARRAY *(SAFF)* 61:6

And remember Jesus, the son of Mary, said: 'O Children of Israel! I am the apostle of Allah sent to you confirming the Law (Torah) which came before me and giving good news of an Apostle to come after me, whose name shall be Ahmad.' But when he came to them with Clear Signs, they said, 'This is obvious sorcery.'

Christ foretold the coming of the Prophet Ahmad (Muhammad) ﷺ, 'the Praised One'. However, the Christians deduce from Christ's promise, also reported in the Gospel of John, that a 'Comforter' who is the Holy Spirit will be sent. They further misunderstand, by imagining that the Holy Spirit is an alter-ego of Allah. The Holy Spirit is in fact Gabriel, but in this context there is no talk of the Angel or of a Comforter. The correct translation of the Greek word the Christians cite in the Gospel is not 'comforter' but 'advocate'. Certainly this is what the Prophet Muhammad ﷺ was. But the debate goes further, as our scholars believe the Greek word for 'advocate,' *paracletos*, is a corruption in the text of *periclytos*, which translates as Ahmad. We can see how easily Allah's Message is lost by men, if every word is not maintained assiduously, exactly as it was delivered.

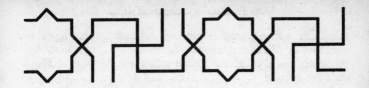

3   Abraham to Jesus

39: THE COW *(BAQARA)* 2:130

And who turns away from the religion of Abraham but those that debase their souls with folly? It is he We chose and rendered pure in this world. And he will be in the Hereafter in the ranks of the Righteous.

THE CATTLE *(AN'AM)* 6:74–79

Behold! Abraham said to his father Azar: 'Do you take idols for Allah? I see that you and your people are in obvious error.'

So also did We show Abraham the power and the laws of the Heavens and the Earth, that he might understand with certainty. When the night covered him over, he saw a star: he said: 'This is my Lord.' But when it set he said: 'I do not love those who set.' When he saw the moon rising in splendour he said: 'This is my Lord.' But when the moon set, he said: 'Unless my Lord guide me I shall surely be among those who go astray.' When he saw the sun rising in splendour, he said: 'This is my Lord; this is the greatest of all.' But when the sun set, he said: 'O my people, I am now free from your guilt of giving partners to Allah.'

For me, I have set my face firmly and truly toward Him Who created the heavens and the earth, and never shall I give partners to Allah.

The true nature of the world was revealed to Abraham by Allah, as it had been with Adam. But while Adam was told the names – in other words, the true nature – of all in Creation directly,

Abraham was required to use the rational powers given to mankind by Allah for our test on Earth. Using his mental ability, Abraham saw through the veil of nature the contours of Truth that lies beyond.

Tablets excavated at the city of Ur in Iraq, where Abraham lived around 2100 BC, mention the names of about 5000 gods. Each city in the kingdom had a chief god who was entitled to greater reverence than the others. In Ur, this god was the moon god. In Larsah, which later took over from Ur as the seat of government, the chief god was the sun god. There were also many minor gods, associated with the stars and planets, who were approached for worldly needs. There were idols for all these gods and goddesses, and rites of worship were performed regularly.

Through correct thought, Abraham dispelled the animist beliefs of his community and understood instead the Unseen Presence of Allah which lies behind. Even today, nature continues to be worshipped in place of the Unseen. Satan can use Allah's Signs against us if we are willing.

40: THE CATTLE *(AN'AM)* 6:80-82

> *His people argued with him. He said: 'Do you come to argue with me about Allah when He Himself has guided me? I do not fear the beings you associate with Allah. Unless my Lord wills, nothing can happen. In His Knowledge, my Lord comprehends all Things. Will you not be warned?*

> *'Why should I fear the beings you associate with Allah when you do not fear to give partners to Allah, without any authority having been given to you to do so? Which of our two parties has more right to feel secure? Tell me if you know.*

> *'It is those who believe and do not confuse their beliefs with* shirk *that are truly secure, for they are guided rightly.'*

As can be seen in these verses, the people of Ur, Abraham's home city, did not deny the existence of Allah the Creator. However, by denying Him exclusive Godhead – that is, by practising *shirk*

– they denied themselves a place in His Eternal Garden, no matter what good deeds they might have done. Again Abraham uses rational thought to reveal the Truth. Why should a believer, who knows that Allah's Will alone runs the Universe, fear any other beings? On the other hand, those who, without permission, assign associates to Allah, whose Will and Knowledge is absolute, have much to fear.

41: THE COW *(BAQARA)* 2:258

> *Have you not considered the case of the one who debated with Abraham about who was his Lord, because Allah had granted the disbeliever kingship. When Abraham said, 'My Lord is He Who gives life and causes death,' he answered, 'I give life and cause death.' Then Abraham said, 'But it is Allah who brings the sun from the east, can you bring it from the west?' At this, he who had rejected Faith (in arrogance), was confounded, yet did not believe, for Allah does not show the right path to unjust people.*

The king referred to in these verses is Nimrod (Namrud), King of Ur, the land of Abraham's birth. Abraham's father, a favoured chief officer of Nimrod, denounced his own son to the king for preaching the Oneness of Allah in defiance of Nimrod's claims of divinity. Nimrod did not deny the existence of the supernatural Allah, but claimed for himself the rank of royal god with absolute power over Iraq and all its inhabitants. Therefore he demanded that all his subjects acknowledge him as their supreme Lord.

Abraham would not do this, but declared: 'I acknowledge the Lord of the Universe exclusively as my Lord and God of worship, and I disown categorically the lordship and godhead of everyone else.'

He won the argument by pointing out that although Nimrod could sentence a person to death or reprieve them, he could not rule the sun's behaviour even in Ur. Allah alone has such ultimate power, and if only Nimrod realized it, even his royal powers were granted by Allah. Even so, Nimrod did not come out of the darkness of self-worship into the light of Truth. In his denial of Allah, he was unjust to himself, for it is our own souls that we imperil by such blindness.

Like the Prophet Abraham, we must stand fast in our exclusive obedience to Allah as Master of All. Although Allah commands us to obey our leaders and parents in worldly matters, this is only on the condition that it accords with His Will. Our obedience to others must never equal or override our submission to Allah. It is Allah's Will that the Message of Islam be given to everyone, so anyone, whether king or commoner, who stands in the way of this Message is a sinner and must be defied.

42: THOSE RANGED IN RANKS (*SAFFAT*) 37:90–96

So they turned away from him and departed. Then did he turn to their gods and said: 'Will you not eat of the offerings before you? What is the matter with you that you do not speak?' Then he turned upon them, striking them with the right hand. Then the worshippers came with hurried steps and faced him. He said: 'Do you worship that which you have carved? But Allah has created you and your handiwork!'

Having used logical argument, to no avail, with the disbelievers, Abraham now resorted to force. But this is not violence for the sake of violence. That is not the Way of Islam. Violence can only be used on two occasions: in self-defence, and to eliminate an obstruction to Islamic teachings. Abraham's action not only physically demolished the idols blocking the people's submission to the One Allah, but more importantly demolished any argument for worshipping the idols by demonstrating to the people the total impotence of their gods. It may seem extra-ordinary that they could not see, when it was pointed out, the absurdity of worshipping their own easily broken creations rather than their Creator. Logically, the former can have no power over them, while the latter must by definition have total power. However, the priestly and royal classes benefited politically and economically from a society based on the worship of these false gods. The people were fooled into believing that these gods could bring them wealth and long life. When vision is clouded by greed, the mind and heart can shut out even the most lucid argument.

43: THOSE RANGED IN RANKS *(SAFFAT)* 37:97–98

> *They said: 'Build a furnace and throw him into the blazing fire!'*
> *They attempted to harm him, but We made them the ones most*
> *humiliated!*

The physical laws of nature cannot bind their Creator. Fire loses
its property of heat, when Allah Wills it. He said: 'O fire, be cool
and a means of safety for Abraham!' (The Prophets *(Anbiyaa)*
21:69), and so Abraham stood as in a cool wind. Anyone who
stands by the principles of Allah may seem to be in great danger,
but in the end these dangers will be defeated, for the Will of Allah
prevails. After the emigration of Abraham, the ruling Nammu
dynasty was beset by disasters and defeated first by the people of
Elam and then by the dynasty of Babylon.

44: THOSE RANGED IN RANKS *(SAFFAT)* 37:99–102

> *He said: 'I will go to my Lord! He will surely guide me!'*

> *'O my Lord! Grant me a righteous son.' So we gave him the good*
> *news of a boy ready to suffer and forbear.*

> *Then when the son reached the age of responsibility, he said: 'O*
> *my son, I see in a vision that I offer you in sacrifice. Now what is*
> *your view?' The son said, 'O my father, do as you are*
> *commanded. You will find me, if Allah wills it, patient and*
> *constant.'*

Abraham was set one of the greatest trials a man could undergo.
He was asked to take the life of the righteous son, Isma'il, whom
Allah had given to him. Their mutual affection and respect is
apparent in the exchange between father and son. Abraham does
not order his son to give up his life, he asks him his view. It is not
for one human being to order another about on behalf of Allah.
Obedience is owed only to Allah. Nor does the boy reply that he
will follow his father's will. He advised his father to follow
Allah's Will, and says he will do so also.

In this short story, we should remember there would have been a long and deep struggle within both father and son. Prophethood does not exempt any human being from the doubts and temptations that are Satan's armoury, aimed at us most particularly when our frail will is called to a great trial. Indeed the Hadith report that Satan tempted Isma'il on the way to the sacrifice with thoughts of disobeying his father. Like all humans, the boy had to turn to Allah for protection against our sworn enemy (see 188).

45: THOSE RANGED IN RANKS *(SAFFAT)* 37:103–107

> *So when they had both submitted their wills to Allah and he had laid him flat on his forehead (for sacrifice), We called out to him: 'O Abraham! You have already fulfilled the vision.' So indeed do We reward those who act rightly. For this was obviously a trial – and We ransomed him with a momentous sacrifice.*

It was necessary for the Prophet Abraham to undergo a test of great sacrifice, because the gift of Prophethood is most certainly a call to a life of sacrifice. The Prophet must give up all his worldly lusts and attachments in pure obedience to Allah. But God, in His Great Mercy, did not take the test any further than necessary. Once Abraham had shown sincere submission in his heart, Allah accepted a sacrificial animal in place of Isma'il.

46: THOSE RANGED IN RANKS *(SAFFAT)* 37:108–12

> *And We left this blessing for him among generations to come. 'Peace and salutation to Abraham!' So indeed do We reward those who act rightly. For he was one of Our believing Servants and We gave him the good news of Isaac – a Prophet – one of the righteous. We blessed him and Isaac. But from their offspring came those who did right and those who went wrong.*

As Allah's trials are great, so are His rewards, whether in this life

or the next, for he is the Judge and the Beneficent (see 15).
Abraham was rewarded with a second son, the Prophet Isaac,
father of Jacob, and their descendants were promised Allah's
favours. However, to be of the line of Abraham does not
exonerate anyone from following the path of Islam or from just
retribution if they do not.

47: WINNOWING WINDS (*ZARIYAT*) 51:24-30

> *Has the story reached you of the honoured guests of Abraham?
> Behold, they came to him and said: 'Peace!' He said, 'Peace!' and
> thought, 'These seem unusual people.' Then he turned quickly to
> his household, brought out a fatted calf and placed it before them
> saying: 'Please eat.'*

> *(When they did not eat) he became afraid of them. But they said:
> 'Do not fear,' and gave him good news of a son endowed with
> knowledge. But his wife came forward laughing aloud. She struck
> her forehead and said: 'A barren old woman!' They said: 'Even
> so, your Lord has spoken and He is full of Wisdom and
> Knowledge.'*

Here again is an example of Allah's power to create as He wills.
Abraham and his wife Sarah were old (the Bible says he was a
hundred and she ninety at the time) and Sarah was also barren,
and yet when Allah willed it they had a son. This was Isaac who
was given a Prophet's knowledge. Abraham already had one son,
Isma'il, by his wife Hajar.

The honoured guests who came were Angels, who naturally
did not need food. Although the main point here is the Signs
Allah sends, it is important to note the details of Abraham's
treatment of his unknown guests. He greets them as a Muslim
and does not hesitate to arrange the best hospitality for them.
Thus we know from his example that it is incumbent on all
Muslims to offer hospitality without desire for personal profit.

48: THE PROPHET HUD (*HUD*) 11:74-76

> *When fear had passed from Abraham and the good news had*

reached him, he began to plead with Us for Lot's people. For Abraham was without doubt tolerant, compasionate and given to look to Allah.

O Abraham, do not seek this. The Will of your Lord has been decreed. For them there is a Penalty that cannot be turned back.

The surah which includes these verses was delivered by the Prophet at a time when the ruling aristocracy of Makkah, the Quraish, were doing their best to crush the Message of Islam. In their arrogance, the Quraish believed that because they were descendants of Abraham and guardians of the Ka'aba (see 184) they were protected from the Just Wrath of Allah. This story of Abraham's intervention on behalf of the people of his nephew is a lesson to them that neither kinship with Abraham nor even his pleas for a reprieve can change the course of Divine Justice. There is no special dispensation for the wicked.

The timing of the giving of the story of Abraham and his nephew Lot reinforces this lesson. On the one hand, Abraham, exiled and apparently powerless, was rewarded by Allah for his righteousness by a son and descendants who would for centuries rule the land of Palestine where Abraham lived as an exile. On the other hand, Lot's people, prosperous and apparently powerful in their own land, were to be punished for brazenly flouting the Laws of Allah.

49: THE HEIGHTS (A'RAF) 7:80–81

We also (sent) Lot: He said to his people: 'Have you become so shameless that you commit indecent acts such as no one has done before you?

'For you satiate your desires on men instead of women. You are certainly transgressors of all limits.'

The Prophet Lot was a nephew of Abraham who left Ur with his uncle. Together they travelled to Syria, Palestine and Egypt. Lot was then appointed as a Messenger by Allah to reform the tribe living between present-day Iraq and Palestine, in what is now called Trans-Jordan. The Bible records its capital as Sodom, and the Talmud says there were four other large cities.

Lot's tribes committed many crimes, but were most notorious for their homosexuality, a detestable sin against Allah's creation and laws of nature, their own bodies and their society. Allah created life on Earth in pairs of male and female, to complement each other and to perpetuate the Creation. Homosexuality is both a contravention of this natural law and a misuse of the bodily organs for pleasures which do not fulfil the duties of every human to their species and society. Not only do such acts spell long-term doom for a civilization, but they immediately threaten its moral and social fabric by attacking the institution on which all societies are based – the family. This is the first and enduring bond of all social systems.

50: THE PROPHET HUD *(HUD)* 11:77–79

When Our Messengers came to Lot, he was grieved on their account and felt himself powerless to protect them. He said: 'This is a day of distress.'

And his people came rushing towards him; these habitual sexual offenders. He said: 'O my people! Here are my daughters. They are purer for you if you marry. Now fear Allah and do not cover me with shame in front of my guests. Is there not one right-minded man among you?'

They said: 'You know well we have no need of your daughters. Indeed you know quite well what we want!'

He said: 'If only I had the power to control you or that I could draw on some powerful refuge.'

It is apparent from these verses that when Allah's Messengers came to Lot in the form of young men, Lot was concerned on their behalf because of the homosexual practices of his people. Lot begged them to turn to his daughters in righteous marriage. He was probably referring to all the women of the tribe, as the role of the Prophet is like a guiding father. But the men were so depraved that not only did they sin, but they flaunted their sins with glee.

51: THE PROPHET HUD (HUD) 11:81-82

The Messengers said: 'O Lot, We are Messengers from your Lord. By no means will they reach you! Now travel with your family while a part of the night remains, and do not let any of you look back except your wife, who will stay behind with the people. Morning is their appointed time. Is not the morning near?'

When what We had decreed took place, We turned the cities upside down and rained down on them brimstone hard as baked clay, spread, layer on layer.

Lot's people had gone too far in their depravity, not only sinning, but revelling in their wickedness. They brought upon themselves Allah's retribution, which on the description here, and the geological evidence, was likely to have been an earthquake and volcanic eruption. The Bible and the Talmud speak of the rich and fertile land of Sodom. Now most of that land is covered by the Dead Sea which is also known as Lot's Sea.

Lot's wife was related to the tribe and had chosen to side with them in their evil ways. She is a reminder that no relationship can deliver an individual from the Retribution they have earned.

52: THE HEIGHTS (A'RAF) 7:143-145

When Moses came to the place appointed by Us, and his Lord addressed him, He said: 'O my Lord show Yourself to me, so that I may see You.' Allah said: 'By no means can you see Me (directly), but look to the Mount if it abides in its place, then you shall see Me.' When his Lord manifested His glory on the Mount He made it as dust, and Moses fell down in a swoon. When he recovered his senses he said: 'Glory be to You. To You I turn in repentance, and I am the first to believe.'

Allah said: 'O Moses, I have chosen you above men, by the mission

I have given you and the words I have spoken to you. Take, then, the Revelation which I gave you and be of those who give thanks.'

And we ordained laws for him in the Tablets in all matters, both commanding and explaining all things: 'Take and hold to these steadfastly and enjoin the people to remain steadfast by the best in the precepts.'

Moses was the only Prophet to whom God has spoken directly, rather than through the Angel Gabriel. He was also the one given the first Book which would survive, albeit in corrupted form, for Moses was given the Torah. These Tablets of the Law contain the essential Truth on which all religion is based. He was the first to believe, not as the first man ever to adopt Islam, but the first in the strength and zeal of his Faith. By the Will of Allah, Moses had brought his people safely out of Egypt, but even as he received Divine Instruction on the Mount, the people had forgotten Allah and were making a golden calf to worship. The human race has plagued itself with ingratitude to Allah.

53: MARY *(MARYAM)* 19:16–21

Relate in the Book the story of Mary, when she withdrew from her family to a place in the East.

She placed a screen between them; then we sent Our Angel to her and he appeared before her as a man in all respects.

She said: 'I seek the protection of Allah Most Gracious from you. If you fear Allah do not come near.'

He said: 'No, I am only a messenger from your Lord, to announce to you the gift of a holy son.'

She said: 'How can I have a son when no man has touched me and I am not unchaste?'

He said: 'So it will be. The Lord says: "That is easy for Us, and We wish to appoint him as a Sign for men and a Mercy from Us. It is decreed."'

After the people had strayed from the Message delivered by Moses, Allah again sent prophets to the Israelites. Jesus was the son of Mary, a member of the family of Imran which Allah had promised would have many leaders of men amongst its descendants (see 24). The Qur'an reports that Mary's piety and favour in the eyes of Allah were apparent to her family from a young age, and it appears she may have retreated to an eastern chamber to pray when the Angel Gabriel appeared to her. She was to bear a child without a father, for Allah is not bound by the laws of His own Creation, and can add to it as He pleases. The nature of his Mission was twofold – to be a Sign of Allah by virtue of his miraculous birth and life, and to be the vehicle of Allah's Mercy coming to turn men back to the Straight Path at a time when many had gone astray.

54: MARY (*MARYAM*) 19:27

At length she carried her baby to her people. They said: 'O Mary, this is truly an amazing thing.'

'O sister of Aaron, your father was not a man of evil, nor your mother an unchaste woman.'

But she pointed to the baby. They said: 'How can we talk to one who is a child in the cradle?'

He said: 'I am indeed a servant of Allah. He has given me Revelation and made me a Prophet.

'And he has made me blessed wherever I am and has enjoined on me prayer and charity as long as I live.

'He has made me kind to my mother and not overbearing or miserable.

'So peace is on me the day I was born, the day that I die and the day that I shall be raised up to life.'

Jesus's first act in his short but miraculous life was to speak out in defence of his mother against those who declaimed in horror when the young unmarried woman appeared with a baby in her arms. They were quick to remind her of her priestly family. Aaron, the brother of Moses, was the first in the line of Israelite priests, and as a descendant of this family Mary was a 'sister of Aaron'. Thus the people reproached her for disgracing her priestly lineage as well as her own impeccably virtuous parents.

In his preaching, the baby Jesus explained his relation to Allah as servant – he never, then or later, laid claim to being the son of Allah. The message of Islam was with him as with all who surrender their will to Allah. The nature of his Mission as one of prayer and charity is aptly foretold, as is his own gentle temperament.

The early start to a miraculous and prophetic life is unusual among the Prophets, as is its short and ascetic nature. Most of those appointed by Allah married and had families, assumed Prophethood around the age of forty and lived to a good age. Jesus remained unmarried, and his Mission lasted for only three years from the time he was thirty.

55: THE TABLE SPREAD *(MA'IDA)* 5:110, 116, 117

Then will Allah say: 'O Jesus, the son of Mary, remember My favour to you and to your mother. I strengthened you with the holy spirit so that you spoke to the people in childhood and in maturity. Behold, I taught you the Book and Wisdom, the Torah and the Gospel, and behold you made the figure of a bird out of clay by My leave, and you breathed into it and it became a bird by My leave, and you healed those born blind and the lepers by My leave. And behold, you brought forth the dead by My leave. And behold, I restrained the Children of Israel from harming you when you showed them the Clear Signs, and the disbelievers among them said: "This is obviously magic."'

And behold, Allah will say: 'O Jesus, the son of Mary, did you say unto men: "Worship me and my mother as gods besides Allah?"' He will say: 'Glory to You, never could I say what I had no right to say. Had I said such a thing, You would indeed have known it. You know what is in my heart, though I do not know what is in Yours. For You know in full all that is hidden.

'I never said anything to them except what You commanded me to say, that is: "Worship Allah my Lord and your Lord," and I was witness over them while I dwelt among them. After You took me up You were the guard over them, and You are a witness to all things.'

Jesus was sent as a Prophet to the Israelites, when they had strayed from the Book or Law (Torah) sent to Moses. His cousin John was his immediate predecessor, paving the way for him. This verse is part of a description of a court scene at the Day of Judgement when Jesus is asked by Allah to recount all the favours shown to him. Jesus is bearing witness against those who corrupted the Message by denying that the miracles happened, or by ascribing them to him, rather than to Allah. Jesus was either defiled as an imposter or hailed as the son and partner of Allah. In both cases, the purity and truth of his Prophethood was sadly abused.

56: THE WOMEN *(NISAA)* 4:157–158

They boasted: 'We killed Jesus Christ, the son of Mary, the Apostle of Allah,' but they did not kill him or crucify him, but so it was made to appear to them, and those who differ on this are full of doubts with no facts but only conjecture to follow, for certainly they did not kill him.

No, Allah raised him up to Himself and Allah is Exalted in Power, Wise.

The end of the life of Jesus Christ on earth has been cause of much conjecture, not least among the Christians themselves in the early days of the Church. But here Allah tells us that he definitely was not crucified. Although no further details are given in the Qur'an, the Hadith indicate that one of Jesus's followers volunteered to go in his place, and so Allah made him look like Jesus. Such devotion may seem surprising, but it is not uncommon among the followers of the prophets. When the

Prophet Muhammad ﷺ was preparing for the first battle against the Makkans, the head of the Madinians came to him and said: 'We want to keep you away from the battlefield. We can do without ourselves but we can't do without you.'

There are two schools of thought as to what happened to Jesus after the aborted crucifixion. Some maintain that 'God raised him up to Himself' means that Jesus did not die a normal human death but was taken up into Heaven still in his body. Others maintain that the reference is to Jesus being raised to a state of Prophethood in the eyes of the people, instead of being slandered as a dissident.

4 The Book

57: THE ANTS (NAML) 27:1–6

These are the verses of the Qur'an, a book which makes things clear;

A guide and good news for the believers,

For those who establish regular prayers (salat) and give alms regularly (zakat), and who believe wholeheartedly in the Hereafter.

As to those who do not believe in the Hereafter, We have made their actions pleasing in their own eyes and they wander about in distraction.

They are the ones for whom a grievous Penalty awaits, and theirs will be the greatest loss in the Hereafter.

As to you, the Qur'an is bestowed upon you from the One who is Wise and All-Knowing.

The Qur'an is the Book of Allah bestowed upon the Prophet Muhammad ﷺ so that he might deliver it to humanity. The Book reveals Allah's purpose for us, explains how to fulfil this purpose and brings the good news of Allah's infinite Wisdom and Justice. But the great blessings of the Qur'an are conditional. To benefit from it, we must be upholders, first, of the Five Pillars of *Islam* (Submission) and, secondly, of the Five Pillars of *Iman* (Faith). Obligatory prayers and obligatory charity (*zakat*) are cited here, for these first two Pillars of Islam indicate that a person has adopted a life of submission.

Belief in the Hereafter receives particular mention because if a person does not believe in the Day of Judgement he will never be able to accept Divine Guidance – even if he believes in the One God. Allah has given humanity a nature such that once we turn away from belief in an ultimate and just requital for our deeds, we will latch onto material rewards and then, blinded to any other purpose, will be absorbed by our own obsession.

58: THE HORDES *(AL-ZUMAR)* 39:41

Certainly, We have revealed the Book to you in Truth for instructing mankind. He that receives guidance benefits his own soul, but he that strays injures his own soul. Nor are you sent to stand over them and arrange their affairs.

The Qur'an was sent by Allah to teach us knowledge that has been lost through wrongdoing and degenerate thought. It is sad but true that although we are all born full of the knowledge of Allah, we lose this, even though the created world is full of Signs of the Creator. It is because of His great Mercy that Allah has also sent the Holy Qur'an.

The Qur'an has been revealed in Absolute Truth, so to deny or ignore any of it is to condemn our own souls to hell-fire. Similarly, by the simple and sincere acceptance of all within its pages we are assured of everlasting Paradise.

Allah relieves the Prophet Muhammad ﷺ of any responsibility for the souls of others. His task is simply to convey the Message. Here is a warning to us that our future in this world and the next cannot be blamed or laid upon another.

59: THUNDER *(R'AD)* 13:38–39

It was never the part of an Apostle to bring a Sign except as God permitted. A book is revealed for each period.

Allah blots out or confirms what He pleases. With Him is the Mother of the Book.

> *Whether We show you within your lifetime what We promised them or take your soul to Ourself (before it is all accomplished) – your duty is to make the Message reach them. It is Our part to call them to account.*

The Qur'an is one of the Signs of Allah, as are all his Books. The disbelievers denied the Qur'an as Revelation, saying there were already revealed books, the Torah and the Gospels, so what need was there for another, especially one which differed in parts from these books. But parts of these books have been corrupted. The discrepancies between the earlier books and the Qur'an are due to the changes made by men to the former. Allah has the Power to correct these corrupted versions through new Revelations of the Original Book which expresses His Eternal Will.

60: GOLD ADORNMENTS (*AL-ZUKHRUF*) 43:2-4

> *By the Book that makes things clear, we have made it a Qur'an in Arabic so that you can understand and become wise. And truly it is transcribed from the Mother of the Book, that is kept with Us, sublime and full of wisdom.*

The Qur'an was written in Arabic because it was from Arabia that God, Who Knows All, chose to launch the Final Book – the Book which has since spread throughout the world. It is a transcript of the Mother Book, the Original Message of God's Will, which is eternal and unchanging, written in the language of those who were to pass it on. But the Qur'an is not, in any sense, a parochial text. Its Divine language is deeply human, transcending cultural, class and temporal barriers to accommodate the worldwide audience for which it was spoken. This can be seen in the presentation of its ideas to accord with common human experiences and dilemmas, its simple but profoundly moving parables and its beautifully allegorical descriptions.

61: REVELATIONS WELL EXPOUNDED (*FUSSILAT*) 41:41-43

> *Those who reject the Message when it comes to them are not hidden*

from Us. And indeed it is a Book of exalted power.

No falsehood can approach it from before or behind it. It is sent down by One Full of Wisdom, worthy of all praise.

Nothing is said to you that was not said to the Apostles before you. Your Lord has at His Command all forgiveness, as well as a most Grievous Penalty.

In these verses is the assurance that no distortions can ever blur the pure Message of the Qur'an. No errors can be imposed from those adulterated Scriptures that came before, nor will degenerate ideas that come after it succeed in sullying the Holy Word. And time has proved this true, for the Arabic Qur'an, as dictated to Muhammad ﷺ, remains intact and unaltered to this day. The Message given to the Prophet Muhammad ﷺ is the same as was given to those who came before – that God is the controller of fate, that He is the rewarder and the Punisher.

62: THE FAMILY OF IMRAN *(AL-I-IMRAN)* 3:7

It is He Who has sent down to you the Book. In it are fundamental verses of established meaning. They are the foundation of the Book. Others are allegorical. But those whose hearts are perverse, follow the part that is allegorical, seeking discord and searching for its hidden meanings, but no one knows its hidden meanings except God and those who are firmly grounded in knowledge. Say: 'We believe in the Book; the whole of it is from our Lord, and none will grasp the Message except men of understanding.'

The precise and clear verses of the Qur'an constitute its fundamental objectives. They invite everyone to Islam; enumerate the Pillars of Belief *(Iman)* and the Pillars of Submission *(Islam)* (see 3 and 132); teach the Right Path in social, economic and political matters; and refute and warn against false beliefs and practices. All the Knowledge a person needs to live as a Muslim is contained in these verses.

The verses which contain allegorical meaning are intended to convey something of the mysteries of the Universe – its

beginning and end, and our status within it. Of course, these
great mysteries defy the limits of our sensory perception,
intellect and imagination, and therefore are also beyond the
bounds of our language. For this reason, metaphor and parable
are used to provide a glimpse of the Unseen. Clearly to try to pin
down a precise meaning by analysing the verses in detail can lead
to controversy and confusion. It is akin to trying to see a painting
by pulling apart its colours and brushstrokes. The Qur'an can
only be understood fully when it is accepted as a whole.

63: THE BEE *(NAHL)* 16:101–102

*When We substitute one revelation for another – and Allah knows
best what He reveals in stages – they say: 'You are nothing but a
forger.' But most of them do not understand.*

*Say, the Holy Spirit has brought the revelation from Your Lord in
Truth in order to strengthen those who believe, and as a Guide and
Glad Tidings to Muslims.*

Disbelievers, grasping at straws, repudiated the Qur'an on the
grounds that Allah should be able to deliver His Message in one
single argument, without gradually thinking out details or giving
several versions to explain the same thing. Of course, even a
second thought makes it obvious that it is men, not the Almighty,
who are limited and would therefore be unable to assimilate and
understand all the themes and instructions if they were relayed at
once.

Allah, in His Wisdom, sent His Message so complete that it
could be comprehended by any human being. It is unfolded and
elaborated upon so as to meet vast differences in intellectual
ability and culture. Again, time has shown Allah's Wisdom, for
no educational or cultural barriers have blocked the spread of
Islam.

Furthermore, as is seen over and over again, Allah ties Words
to deeds so that His Guidance will be better understood. The
people who first heard the Qur'an found it directly relevant to
the events in their lives. In this way, the Message was firmly
rooted, so that it might grow and flourish well amongst all
people.

The Holy Spirit referred to is the Angel whom Allah sent down with the Qur'an, and is a reminder that the Qur'an cannot contain errors because Angels are incapable of deceit or lies.

64: THE SPIDER *(ANKABUT)* 29:48–51

And you were not able to read a Book before this Book, nor were you able to transcribe it with your right hand. In that case, certainly, the cynics would have doubted.

Indeed, here are self-evident Signs for those endowed with Knowledge, and none but the unjust reject Our Signs.

Yet they say: 'Why aren't the Signs sent down to him from his Lord?' Say: 'The Signs are indeed with Allah: and I am indeed a clear Warner.'

And it is not enough for them that We have sent down to you the Book which is related to them? Truly, in it is Mercy and a Reminder to those who believe.

It is a historical fact that the Prophet Muhammad ﷺ was known by his family and friends to be totally illiterate. What clearer Sign of the Divine Presence could there be than that of an uneducated man suddenly revealing a vast knowledge of the Holy Books, the past Prophets, the history and beliefs of ancient peoples and the issues of social, moral, political and economic life? On top of that, he delivered this knowledge in language that not even the great extempore poets of his time could match. Obviously this was not a case of a great man arising out of the right social conditions, for the Prophet's abilities bear no relation to his background. It is sure proof that they were in fact Allah's Abilities. The recitals of the Qur'an were Signs themselves, for those who would see, as was the blessed personality of the Prophet ﷺ.

65: THE TABLE SPREAD *(MA'IDA)* 5:68–69

Say: 'O people of the Book, you have no ground to stand upon unless you stand fast by the Law, the Gospel and all the revelation that has come to you from your Lord.' It is the Revelation that comes to you from your Lord that increases in most of them their obstinate rebellion and blasphemy. But do not grieve over people without Faith.

Those who believe (in the Qur'an), those who follow the Jewish (Scriptures) and the Sabians and the Christians – and who believe in Allah and the Last Day, and live righteously – they shall have no fear nor grief.

Allah instructs the Prophet ﷺ to challenge the Christians and Jews on their own terms – that is, according to the Books that Allah sent to them previously. Although parts of the Torah and Bible have been tampered with, the Truth nevertheless survives in parts, notably the Commandments and the words of the Prophets. If the Jews and Christians of Madinah, where this surah was revealed, had been following these teachings, they would immediately have recognized the Qur'an as the same Message, and the religion of the Prophet ﷺ as a continuation of the one they claimed to follow. But because they had in fact broken their Covenant with Allah and deserted their Faith, the Revelation sent through Muhammad ﷺ only hardened their blasphemous resolve. Once we have turned from Allah, everything becomes justification for further wrongdoing and fuel on the path to hell. Allah chooses not to guide disbelievers, so we should not grieve for what is His Will.

66: THE BEE *(NAHL)* 16:98–100

When you read the Qur'an, seek Allah's protection from Satan the rejected one.

He has no authority over those who believe and put their trust in their Lord.

His authority is only over those who take him as patron, and who associate others with Allah.

Even the Holy Message of the Qur'an can be twisted by the Evil One's suggestions if we do not read with sincere desire for the Truth. Satan will attempt to plant doubts and suspicions, misguided theories and fantasies in our heads to prevent us receiving Guidance. This is his sworn aim (see 209), and the Qur'an is the source of all Guidance. Allah will help and protect honest seekers, but those who approach carelessly or cynically will be easily blinded by Satan.

67: THE RESURRECTION *(AL-QIYAMA)* 75:16–19

Do not move your tongue hastily to recite this Qur'an.

It is for Us to collect and to proclaim it.

But when We have proclaimed it, follow its recital as proclaimed.

What is more, it is for Us to explain it.

On one level, these verses are simply addressed to Muhammad ☙ , assuring him that he need not babble hurriedly the Words Allah sends. They will not slip away from his mind before he has had time to communicate them, as they are under the complete control of Allah. But these verses also apply to all Muslims, as we should follow the Prophet's example as much as possible. We should not hurry over the verses at daily prayers simply to have them said, and we should be meticulous in the correct repetition of the words as proclaimed in Arabic. By so doing, we will find that all we need to know is there, explained by Allah.

68: THE ANTS *(NAML)* 27:76–81

Truly this Qur'an explains to the Children of Israel most of the matters in which they disagree.

And it certainly is a guide and mercy to those who believe.

Without doubt, your Lord will decide between them by His Decree and He is exalted in Might, All-Knowing.

So put your trust in Allah, for you are on the Path of Manifest Truth.

Truly you cannot cause the dead to listen nor the deaf to hear the call, especially when they turn back in retreat.

Nor can you be a guide to the blind to prevent them straying. Only those who believe in Our Revelations will listen, and they will bow in Islam.

The tribes of Israel and their scholars quarrelled amongst themselves as they strayed further and further from the teaching handed down to them. The Qur'an resolves all these disagreements except those which are purely in the realm of material and circumstantial conflict.

These verses are also a promise that the Qur'an will settle the differences the Children of Israel maintained with the Prophet Muhammad ﷺ and his followers. And, in fact, within a few years of this surah being revealed the Prophet was acknowledged throughout Arabia as Allah's Messenger.

69: THE ANTS (*NAML*) 27:82

And when the Word is fulfilled against the unjust, we shall produce from the Earth a beast to face them. He will speak to them of their disbelief in Our Revelations.

The warnings of the Qur'an against those who deny its teachings will be fulfilled on the Day of Judgement. It is understood that a beast will come when this Day is nigh and, by the Power of Allah, it will speak to men in their own tongue. The details on this, given in secondary sources, vary, but a saying of the Prophet ﷺ, on the authority of Abu Sa'id Al-Khudri, reports that the beast will appear when all men have ceased fulfilling their duty to teach one another to live righteously and reject evil.

70: GOLD ADORNMENTS *(ZUKHRUF)* 43:31-32

Also, they say: 'Why isn't the Qur'an sent down to some leading man in either of the two cities?'

Do they portion out the mercy of your Lord? It is Us Who portion out between them their livelihood in the life of this world, and We raise some of them above others in ranks so that some may command work from others. But the Mercy of your Lord is better than the wealth which they amass.

The foolishness of the people of the Prophet's time is here shown clearly. They could not believe that such an ordinary, humble individual could be chosen by Allah as His Messenger. They felt that such an honour should have been given to a leading person from either Makkah or the garden city of Taif. But who knows the true worth of a person if not Allah? The vanity of the people in thinking that they know from outward appearances and status who is worthy!

To be sure, there are those whom Allah has blessed with worldly goods, but these are as nothing in comparison with the wealth of Paradise which will be given by Allah to those whose lives, wealthy or poor, have been lived according to His Will.

71: THE BEE *(NAHL)* 16:64

And We sent down the Book to you for the express purpose that you should make clear to them those things in which they differ, and that it should be a guide and a mercy to those who believe.

The responsibility of the Prophet was made very clear. All the disputes which have arisen between the various Peoples of the Book about how to understand the Message can now be answered through the complete harmony of the Holy Qur'an. With this unity, all humanity can now, if they will accept the Qur'an, be united. The path to this unity is to act as Allah requires and to seek His Mercy by repenting and asking his forgiveness. This is the way for those who will listen to the Message.

72: REVELATIONS WELL EXPOUNDED (FUSSILAT) 41:44–45

Had We sent this as a Qur'an in other than Arabic, they would have said: 'Why aren't the verses explained in detail? What, not in Arabic and a Messenger an Arab?' Say: 'It is a guide and a healing to those who believe, and for those who do not believe there is a deafness in their ears and a blindness in their eyes. They are being called from a place far distant.'

We certainly gave Moses the Book before, but dispute arose about it. If not for a previous decree of Your Lord their differences would have been settled, but they remained in suspicious disquieting doubt.

It is only natural that the Qur'an should have been given in Arabic. Of what use would it have been to Muhammad's people if it had been in Chinese!

Muhammad 🌟 was an Arab, hence the text was given in Arabic. To those who say, why one language and not another? we reply that those who wish to hear the Message will hear it whatever language it is in. Those who wish to remain deaf to its truth will ignore the Truth, no matter what language it is given in.

Look at the Jews, who had the Message in their own language, but who chose to spend their time in pointless dispute about this word or that letter. Although they had the Message, they were able to deafen themselves to the Truth by dispute.

73: MIST (DUKHAN) 44:3–6

We sent it down during a blessed night, for We (always) wish to warn (against evil).

In that (night) all matters of wisdom are made clear.

By command from Our Presence, for We (ever) send (Revelations).

As a Mercy from your Lord. For He hears and knows all.

The night of *Qadr*, meaning 'Power', 'Honour', 'Dignity' and also 'Divine Decree', is exalted above all other nights of the year. On this night the complete Qur'an was sent down from the Mother Book to the lowest Heaven. From there the Holy Spirit, Gabriel, revealed it to Muhammad 🕮 piecemeal as was appropriate, with the first Revelation arriving on that same night when the Prophet was forty years old.

74: CONSULTATION *(SHURA)* 42:51

It is not fitting for any mortal to be spoken to by Allah except by inspiration, from behind a veil or by sending a Messenger to reveal with Allah's permission what Allah wills, for He is Most High, Most Wise.

These are the three modes by which Allah speaks to His Prophets. The first is when Allah conveys an idea or realization to the mind of a individual so that it is experienced rather like a flash of lightning or a pebble being thrown in a still pond. The second mode refers to dreams and visions experienced while sleeping or in a trance. The third mode, 'Revelation that is recited', is the highest form. This is when the Angel Gabriel appears to deliver the Divine Message in specific words to the Prophet.

75: HADITH
BUKHARI 1:1

The first that came to the Messenger of Allah of Revelations were good dreams, so that when he had a dream it came true as the dawn of the day.

The Prophets are the only ones to experience the different modes of Revelation. Not only do the Hadith report that Muhammad 🕮 was sent visions, and at times voices, by Allah, which fall into the second category of Revelation, but he was also sent inspiration by Allah. This is the method by which he was able to supply the details of Law as reported in the Hadith.

76: HADITH
BUKHARI 1:1

Then he (the Angel) took hold of me and he pressed me so hard that I could not bear it any more, and then he let me go and said, Read.

While realization and dreams from Allah bring little change to the recipient's normal condition, the Revelation that is recited brings dramatic changes felt by both the Prophet and observers as he is transported from one world to another. This description of the Prophet Muhammad's experience when the first Revelation of the Qur'an came to him, in the cave of Hira, conveys some idea of the ordeal that the prophets underwent.

There are disbelievers who, in their determination to deny the Truth, attempt to dismiss the Qur'an as the product of physical fits. It requires the most breathtaking denial of commonsense to claim that a man's epileptic fits could purify and inspire first him, then his followers and then an entire nation to obey meticulously the Message that would be the fastest growing religion in the world by the last quarter of the twentieth century.

77: HADITH
BUKHARI 1:1

It comes to me sometimes as the ringing of a bell and this is hardest on me, then he leaves me and I remember from him what he says, and sometimes the Angel comes in the shape of a man and he talks to me and I remember what he says.

In this hadith the Prophet Muhammad ﷺ explains two ways in which he received the Revelation of the Qur'an, one being more of an ordeal than the other. However, in both cases the Revelation was delivered by the Angel, as this is always the way in which the Book was revealed to the prophets. In the first instance, the form of the Angel is not specified but the words he delivered had the clanging metallic quality of a bell. In the second instance, the Angel appeared as a man and spoke in softer, human tones. Because the Prophet was in effect transported to another world beyond the senses of ordinary men, no one with him at the time of Revelation could hear the Angel.

5 The Angels

78: THE ANGELS (MALAIKA) 35:1

Praise be to Allah, Who created (out of nothing) the heavens and the earth, Who made the Angels messengers with wings – two, three or four pairs.

The third Pillar of *Iman*, belief in the Angels, is not based on sensory evidence as they are spiritual beings free from the needs, desires and instincts which come with bodily existence. Faith can have no reality unless we sincerely believe in that spiritual world.

A tradition of the Prophet reported by his wife Aisha explains that the Angels were made out of light, as the jinns were made from fire and man from clay. Nevertheless, the Angels can assume bodily forms when Allah wills it. There are numerous instances of this, from the Angels who appeared to Abraham and Lot (see 47 and 48), to Gabriel's visit to Mary (see 53), and of course those occasions when Gabriel appeared to the Prophet (see 76 and 77).

79: THE PROPHETS (ANBIYAA) 21:26–28

And they say: 'Allah Most Gracious has begotten children.' Glory to Him, they are but servants raised to honour.

They do not speak before He speaks, and they act by His Command.

He knows what is before them and what is behind them, and they offer no intercession except for those who are acceptable, and they stand in awe and reverence of Him.

The Angels are creations of Allah, and are therefore His servants, just as we are – with the difference that their obedience is perfect, unquestioning, and without intermission, because of the nature Allah has given them. These verses were particularly addressed to those Arabs who believed that the Angels were the daughters of Allah and treated them as deities, making supplication to them to intercede on their behalf with Allah. But not only does Allah have no descendants (see 5), but no one can intercede on another's behalf without the prior permission of Allah. For only He has All-Encompassing Knowledge.

80: THOSE RANGED IN RANKS *(SAFFAT)* 37:164–165

(Those ranged in ranks say): 'Each of us has a place appointed;

'And we are truly those who declare Allah's glory.'

The Angels have been arranged in a hierarchy, like all servants of Allah. Just as human beings have individual talents and abilities which differentiate the nature of their work for Allah, so do the Angels. They are equal in rights, but they each have a prescribed duty to fulfil in the heavenly realm and in the earthly realm. In the spiritual world an Angel worships Allah through an allotted task and place, such as Thronebearing, Gatekeeping or Fire Supervision (see below). And in the physical world he worships Allah through supervision of an assigned sphere, which is the limit of his knowledge and influence. This may be care of the rain, wind or stars, or it may be as a recorder of men's deeds or as bearer of the Revelation (see below).

81: HADITH
BUKHARI: Book of Commentary *(Kitab Al-Tafsir)*

Allah's Messenger said: 'Surely Satan has certain signs in his relationship with men, and surely the Angels have a certain sign in their relationship with men. The Sign of Satan is to whisper that which is bad and to disbelieve in the Truth. The Sign of the Angel is to whisper that which is good and to believe in the Truth, so whoever amongst you finds these things which are good, let him know that they are from Allah and let him thank him for that. And if it is the other, let him know they are from Satan and let him seek refuge with Allah.

The Angels are Allah's Messengers to us – not only to bring Revelations to the prophets but to strengthen directly the spiritual dimension of every man and woman by inspiring what is good. Neither they nor Satan are perceived by the senses of ordinary people, but we know they exist just as we know our own soul exists although we cannot experience it physically. We experience our soul as an intangible integrating and motivating force within ourselves. The Angels are experienced by us as intangible but unmistakable beings in the sense of shame that comes to us when we are about to act wrongly, and also as that flash of understanding when we dwell on godly thoughts or that sense of joy that accompanies a righteous act.

This hadith was said by the Prophet ﷺ immediately before he received the Revelation: 'The Evil One threatens you with poverty and calls you to unseemly conduct. Allah promises you His forgiveness and bounties and Allah cares for all and He knows all things' (2:268).

82: THE COW (*BAQARA*) 2:97–98

Say: 'Whoever is an enemy to Gabriel' – for he brings down to your heart, by Allah's Will, the Qur'an to confirm what came before it and Guidance and good news for those who believe –

'Whoever is an enemy to Allah and His Angels and Apostles, to Gabriel and Michael – lo, Allah is an enemy to those who reject Faith.'

The Prophet Muhammad's revelation was through the inter-mediary of Gabriel, the Angel who had brought all the Revealed Books to the prophets of the past. This is the greatest task for an

Angel, given by Allah to his highest Angel. Gabriel is also called the Holy Spirit (16:102), the Spirit of Faith and Truth (26:193) and the Most Honourable Messenger (81:19), to emphasize that he brings the Divine Revelation, exactly as decreed by Allah, for Gabriel is His incorruptible Messenger.

Michael was an Angel revered by a party of Jews, who disliked the notion of Gabriel coming to the Prophet and declared him an Angel of ill-omen anyway. Both Angels appear in the Torah, and Allah here warns that we cannot pick and choose the Apostle or Angels we wish to believe in – to reject even one is to set ourselves against Allah.

83: MARY (*MARYAM*) 19:64

The Angels say: 'We descend only by the command of your Lord. To Him belongs what is before us and what is behind and what is between; and your Lord never does forget.'

This verse came in reply to a request from the Prophet to Gabriel: 'Can't you come more often than you come nowadays?' (Bukhari). Even the Prophet Muhammad 鄭, a man renowned for his patience and forbearance, felt at times the need for quicker results. How much more impatient we ordinary men and women become when it seems that the Will of Allah is not working as quickly as we might like. But Allah never forgets us or becomes sidetracked. And it is He, not His Angels, who decide the timetable, for their authority in this world is by His permission. The Qur'an took twenty-three years to deliver, and this was appropriate to the capacity for the community to absorb it and expand so that it might become the world force it is today.

84: QAF 50:17–18

Behold, two (Guardian Angels) appointed to learn his deeds and note them, one sitting on the right and one on the left.

Not a word does he utter but there is a sentinel by him ready to record it.

The Angels are the recorders of our every action, and this record will be brought before us on the Day of Judgement to bear witness to our lives. It is understood from these verses that it is our words and actions, not our thoughts, which are being recorded. Naturally Allah knows our thoughts, but these are forgiven if they are not given form through the action of speaking. On the other hand, a good thought is recorded by the Angels if it has at least prompted speech, if not a more positive action.

85: HADITH
BUKHARI: Book of Commentary *(Kitab Al-Tafsir)* 241

The Angels of the day and the Angels of the night are assembled at the time of the morning prayer.

Some of the Angels spend half their sleepless existence serving Allah on Earth and half in Heaven, close to Him. The crossover between those coming onto earthly duty and those returning to Heaven comes at dawn, so it is at this prayer that a person's two Angels of the night and two Angels of the day are all present. This hadith explains verse 17:78, which particularly emphasizes the importance of morning prayer: 'for the prayer and reading in the morning carry their testimony'. A further tradition explains that the evening prayer is also important, for the Angels may then report to Allah: 'We reached them while they were praying and left them while they were praying' (Bukhari, Book of Prayer, 16).

86: THE BELIEVERS *(MU-MIN)* 40:7–9

Those who carry the Throne and those around it sing glory and praise to their Lord, believe in Him and implore forgiveness for those who believe: 'Our Lord, Your Reach is over all things, in Mercy and Knowledge. Forgive, then, those who repent and follow your Path and save them from the penalty of the Blazing Fire.

'And grant our Lord that they enter the Gardens of Eternity which you have promised to them and to the righteous among their fathers, their wives and their descendants, for You are the Exalted in Might, full of Wisdom.

'And save them from ills – and any whom You do save from ill that Day, on them will you have bestowed Mercy indeed, and that will truly be their highest achievement.'

The Angels who carry the Throne of Allah and surround it in Heaven plead on our behalf that we may be guided and forgiven for our sins. To carry the Throne of Allah is to be the closest to Allah, to be the most perfect in righteousness and obedience, so the Angels do not ask for anything that is against His Will. No one can sway the Divine Justice from its determined course, but it is Allah's Will that his Angels and indeed all worshippers of Him should pray for the good of others.

87: CATTLE (AN'AM) 6:61

At length, when death approaches one of you, Our Angels take his soul, and they never fail in their duty.

The infallible servants of Allah are the ones who will take our souls at the time appointed by Allah. There is no evading them, nor should we wish to, for they are returning us to our Lord. They have watched over us in life, protecting us from evil and leading us onto the Straight Path as Allah wills, and they bear us only goodwill.

88: THUNDER (R'AD) 13:23–24

And Angels shall welcome you from every gate:

'Peace unto you, for you persevered in patience. Now how excellent is the Final Home.'

The Angels, who know each man and woman better than their

own families know them, will greet the righteous at the gates of Heaven, welcoming them into the Final Home where there is no suffering or distress. It will be a joyful departure for those who have kept us in their gaze throughout our lives and tended the elements so that Allah's bounties may benefit us as He wills.

89: PROHIBITION *(TAHRIM)* 66:6

> *O believers, save yourselves and your families from a fire whose fuel is men and stones overseen by stern and severe Angels who do not balk at the commands they receive from Allah, but do exactly as they are commanded.*

We think of the Angels as kind and gentle, as indeed they are, but being the perfect executors of Allah's Will they do not misrepresent Divine Justice, which is the natural complement of kindness. It would be unjust for any ruler to allow his subjects to break laws or harm or benefit whomever they pleased. It is a sign of Allah's Mercy to all Creation that He assigns Angels to carry out the punishment of those who wreak evil and chaos. We should also note that the warning here is to save not only ourselves but our families. To act justly ourselves we should do everything in our power to ensure those who are dependent on us do not suffer at the hands of their own wrongdoing.

6   The Hereafter

90: THE INEVITABLE EVENT (WAQI'A) 56: 57-73

It is We who have created you: why will you not bear witness to the truth?

Do you understand? Who creates the seed which comes from you – is it you or is it We, the Creator?

We have decreed death to be your common lot, and there is nothing that can stop Us from changing the form you now have and creating you again in forms unknown to you.

And you certainly know already the first form of Creation: why then do you not celebrate His praises?

Do you see the seed that you sow in the ground?

Is it you that cause it to grow, or are We the cause?

Were it Our will, We could crumble it to dry powder, and you would be left astonished, saying: In reality we have done nothing and are indeed in debt; we are shut off from the fruits of our labour.

See you the water that you drink?

Do you bring it down (in rain) from the clouds, or do We?

Were it Our will, We could make it salt: then why do you not give thanks?

See you the fire which you kindle?

Is it you who grow the tree which feeds the fire, or do We grow it?

We have made it a sign of Our handiwork, and a symbol of comfort and convenience to those who dwell in the deserts.

Allah is the beginning and the end of all life. He has created all life and so surely can He end all life. Does anything come to be because man wills it to be? No, only Allah can do this. So it will be after death. He will bring us to life in whatever shape He wills, just as He has given us body and form in this life. If we will only look on what Allah has already made for us, then we shall know that He is Lord and Master of not only our beginning but also our end.

91: THE COW (*BAQARA*) 2:28

How can you reject Faith in Allah? For you know you were without life, and He gave you life; He will cause you to die, and will again bring you to life, and again to Him will you return.

Why are men so blind? If it is Allah who brings you to life and who will end your days in this life, then why can He not also bring you to life again at the Day of Resurrection? We come from Allah, and to Him we will return to be judged and rewarded or punished.

92: THE CRITERION (*AL-FURQAN*) 25:47–50

And it is He who makes the Night as a robe for you and sleep as repose and makes the Day as it were a resurrection.

And it is He who sends the winds as heralds of glad tidings, going before His Mercy, and We send down purifying water from the sky

So that We may give life to a dead land and quench the thirst of men and beasts We have created in great numbers.

And We have distributed the water amongst them so that they may take heed, but most men are averse to anything but disbelief and ingratitude.

Through the harmony, beauty and purpose of all God's Creation, we are both blessed and reminded of the greater purpose in His Creation. For instance, the night comes as a companion for our sleep, which is both a blessing and an act of worship according to God's Laws. At the same time night and sleep are reminders of the darkness and the end to activity that comes with death. Similarly, in the daily rising of the sun the earth is blessed with new energy, and we see in the new light and our own awakening a Sign of our resurrection on the Day of Judgement.

These verses were also revealed to answer criticisms of the Qur'an by the Holy Prophet's contemporaries. Metaphorically the verses remind us of the purifying effects of Prophethood. Like water to a parched land, the Prophets have been sent so that people might have life. Yet most have turned away from their refreshing, life-giving message and have remained like a land smitten with drought.

93: THE WOMEN *(NISAA)* 4:136

O you who believe! Believe in Allah and His Apostle, and the Scripture which He has sent to His Apostle and the Scripture which He sent to those beforehand. Those who deny Allah, His Angels, His Books, His Apostles, and the Day of Judgement, have gone far, far astray.

The Will of Allah has been made known. The Prophet Muhammad 🕌 was sent to bring the Holy Qur'an to all people. Before the Prophet 🕌 there came other prophets, also sent to bear witness to Allah and to bring the Word of Allah to all people. Yet still people turn away and reject the Holy Word, the prophets and even the very idea that there will be a Day of Judgement. Yet the prophets and the Scriptures have borne witness to this Day. Therefore those who reject these truths will be lost, for they have gone far from the revealed Will of Allah.

94: MYSTIC LETTERS TH (TA-HA) 20:124

'But whosoever turns away from My Message, for him is a life narrowed down, and we shall raise him up blind on the Day of Judgement.'

The message of the Qur'an has been made known. Those who hear it or know of it and yet still turn from Allah will not only suffer in the life Hereafter, but even in this life they will not experience happiness. A 'life narrowed down' means a life which, even if it contains wealth and comfort, is still restless and discontented. Life cannot be fulfilled unless in the service of Allah, in submission to His Will. Therefore any life which is not in submission to Him is bound to be a lesser life, an unsatisfactory life, a life which is not fulfilled. This is why on the Day of Judgement Allah will raise such people up blind, for this shows how they have been blind to His Truth and how impaired their earthly life has been.

95: TIME OR MAN (DAHR OR INSAN) 76: 5–10

As to the righteous, they shall drink of a cup of wine mixed with Kafur, from a fountain where the devotees of Allah drink, flowing in unending abundance.

They live out their vows in true fear of the Day whose reputation is known far and wide.

And they feed, for the love of Allah, the poor, the orphan and the captive, saying: 'We feed you for the sake of Allah alone: no reward do we wish from you, nor thanks. We only fear the Day of terrible Wrath which comes from our Lord.'

In the life Hereafter, those who in this life have lived in accord with the Will of Allah shall be rewarded. Those who in this life lived as Muslims in fulfilment of their vows, those who have lived a proper life and prepared for the Day of Judgement and those who have cared for the less fortunate, who have shown true charity, will live in peace and contentment in the Hereafter. This is their reward for following the teachings of the Prophets and the Revelations of the Scriptures.

96: THE FAMILY OF IMRAN (AL-I-IMRAN) 3:91

As to those who reject Faith, and die rejecting it, it does not matter how much money they were to offer, even if it were all the gold in the world, they will not be ransomed from what is to come. For there is in store for them a punishment terrible to contemplate, and there is no one who can help them.

There is no help for those who in this life reject the Message of the Holy Prophet and the Revelation of the Holy Qur'an. If they die still rejecting and go to the grave rejecting, then they are lost. It would not help them if they were to be able to offer all the wealth of the world. Once they die rejecting the Message, they are lost and nothing can save them then. In the very grave they will suffer. But this will be as nothing to the Day of Judgement and eternity spent in hell. So do not reject the Message, but accept it. For if you do reject and die rejecting, then nothing and no one can ever help, no matter what you do.

97: THE BELIEVERS (MU-MINUN) 23:99–101

To one of them he says, 'O my Lord! Send me back to life.

'Then I can live righteously in a way which I did not beforehand.' By no means! It is but a word he says; before them is a barrier till the day they are raised up.

Then, when the trumpet is blown, there will be no more relationships between them that day, nor will the one ask after the other!

Again we see the terrible state the damned are in once they have died and realize their dreadful mistake. They long to return to this life, to be allowed another chance. But there is but the one life and but one chance. There is a barrier raised between the living and the dead as well as between those who are virtuous and those who are damned and lost. After death, there is and will be for many a period between their own death and the End of the World on the Day of Judgement. During this time the dead are already under judgement. Those who have chosen the Right Path will feel as though they are lying in a spacious grave, sweet smelling like the Gardens of Bliss. Those who have rejected the Revelation will be crushed by the very walls of their tombs. Such is the barrier between them even before the Day of Judgement, when all the world will be judged, and all that has lived is called forth from the tomb by the trumpet blast.

98: THE CHILDREN OF ISRAEL (*BANI ISRA-IL*) 17:98–99

That is their reward, because they rejected Our Signs, and said: 'When we are reduced to bones and broken dust, can we really be raised up and be a new creation?'

Do they not see that Allah, Who created the Heavens and the Earth, has Power to create them again? He has decreed a fixed time, of this there is no doubt. But the unjust refuse to understand and are ungrateful.

The unbelievers cannot believe that Allah can and will re-create all from the dust on the Day of Judgement. For this lack of Faith they are doomed themselves. Can they not see that Allah, Who created all that has been, can also create all that will be? They mistake the long life of this physical world for permanence. Yet Allah has given it a fixed time to run its course, just as He gives to each person an allotted time for his life. So it is with the world and the stars and all creation. They have their fixed time, at the end of which all will be destroyed. Then from the destruction Allah will resurrect on the Day of Judgement. This the Holy Qur'an reveals. All those who do not believe are truly lost.

99: THE COW *(BAQARA)* 2: 259

> *Take the example of someone who passed by a hamlet which was completely ruined. He said: 'Oh! how can Allah ever restore it to life after such destruction or death?' However, Allah caused him to die for a hundred years, then raised him up again. He said: 'How long were you in that state?' He said: '(Perhaps) a day or part of a day.' He said: 'No, you were thus a hundred years; but look at your food and your drink; they show no signs of age; and look at your donkey; and that We may make you a Sign to people, look closely at the donkey's bones and see how We bring them together and cover them with flesh!' When this was shown clearly to him, he said: 'I now know that Allah has power over all things.'*

In this text and its companion text (see below), Allah shows to one who doubts, and one who knows but wants to understand, how He will resurrect life on the Day of Resurrection. In this verse, the questioner asks how Allah could restore a ruined village. In answer Allah caused the man to fall dead for a hundred years. Yet when Allah raises him up to life again, the man cannot believe that he has been doing anything except sleeping heavily for a few hours. For Allah has retained his food and drink as it was. It is only when Allah points out that the bones of the man's donkey lie beside him, the donkey that was alive before, that the man realizes what has happened. Then Allah brings even the donkey to life, and the doubter is silenced except to praise Allah who is Lord of All. This is how it will be on the Day of Resurrection.

100: THE COW *(BAQARA)* 2:260

> *Behold! Abraham said: 'My Lord! Show me how you give life to the dead.' He said: 'Do you not believe?' He said: 'Yes, but I wish to have a fuller understanding.' He said: 'Take four birds; tame them to fly back to you; put a portion of them on every hill, and call to them: They will come flying to you with great speed. Then you will know that Allah is Highest in both Power and Wisdom.'*

In this companion verse to the former one (see above), a second proof is given of how Allah will resurrect the dead as they were, on the Day of Judgement. Abraham wished to understand how Allah would perform this mighty act. So Allah told him to take four birds, kill them, cut them into pieces, mix up the pieces and place them on the hills around. Then Allah commanded Abraham to call the birds to him and, mixed as they were, dead as they were, scattered as they were, they returned to the Prophet Abraham, whole and in their original forms. Thus will Allah call to life all who have lived, no matter if through the passage of time their bones have turned to dust and been accidentally scattered. However, no person should seek to scatter or break up their bodies. This is why Muslims do not cremate bodies: we only bury them.

101: THE BELIEVERS *(MU-MINUN)* 23:112–118

He will say: 'How long did you stay in the earth?' They will say: 'We stayed a day or part of a day: ask those who kept count.' He will say: 'You stayed for a short span of time, if you only knew. Did you think that we created you in jest, and that you would not be brought back to us (for account)?'

Therefore exalted be Allah, the King, the True; there is no god but he, the Lord of the Throne of Honour. If anyone invokes any other god than Allah he has no authority for this, and he will have to account for this with his Lord! And be sure, the unbelievers will not win!

So say: 'O my Lord! grant forgiveness and mercy, for You are the best of those who show mercy!'

The time after death and before the Day of Resurrection will seem like hardly any time at all. People will believe that they have spent but a few hours, or perhaps, as Surah 20 (verse 103) says, ten days. Yet they may have been dead for hundreds or even thousands of years. But time is timeless when Allah rules. This will be like the time after the Day of Doom, when all is wiped away until the time of the Day of Resurrection. For when the sun and the moon have gone, what will mark the days and nights, weeks and months, years and centuries? Truly, only Allah is Lord of Time.

102: THE WAYS OF ASCENT *(MA'ARIJ)* 70:4–21

The Angels and the Spirit ascend to Him in a day which is (as) long as fifty thousand years: Therefore you should have patience – a patience of beautiful (contentment).

They see the Day as a far-off event, but we see it (quite) near. The Day that the sky will be like molten brass, and the mountains will be like wool. And no friends will ask after a friend.

Though they will be put within sight of each other, the sinner's desire will be: that he could redeem himself from the penalty of that day by sacrificing his children, his wife and his brother, his kindred who sheltered him, and all that is on Earth, so it could deliver him:

By no means! For it would be the fire of hell! – Plucking him out right down to the bone – inviting all those who turn their backs on the Right, who turn their faces away from the Right, who hid their wealth away.

In truth, man was created very impatient; fretful when evil touches him; and niggardly when good reaches him.

Here is presented the panorama of the Last Days. There is the Day which Allah sees as quite near when all that exists will be destroyed, the Day of Doom. Nothing will be left alive or standing; neither man nor beast; hill nor valley; earth nor moon, sun nor stars. Then there will be the unknowably long period when nothing will exist. This is the day which is fifty thousand years – for how can you tell how long a day is if there is no sun or moon? This is a wonder of Allah. Finally there comes the Day of Resurrection and the Day of Judgement, where the pettiness and meanness by which the unfaithful have lived their brief existence on earth will consign them for ever to hell fire.

103: THE CLEAVING ASUNDER *(INFITAR)* 82:1-9

When the sky is split asunder; when the stars are scattered; when the oceans are allowed to burst forth, and when the graves are turned upside down; every soul will know what has been sent forth and what has been left behind.

O man! What has seduced you away from your Lord, the most beneficent? He who created you, made you complete in a right, good shape. He will assemble you in whatever shape He wishes. Nay, but you give lie to the Judgement.

The sheer scale of the physical destruction on the Day of Doom is beyond our imagination. Not only will this Earth be destroyed, but the entire Cosmos. So terrible and utter will be the destruction on that Day that even the dead in their tombs will know that the dread Day has come. Yet out of this utter destruction, as these verses remind us, Allah is able to reconstruct all that has lived, ready to face Judgement on the Judgement Day.

104: THE DAY OF NOISE AND CLAMOUR *(AL-QARI'A)* 101:1-11

The Day of Noise and Clamour: what is the Day of Noise and Clamour? And what will help you understand what the Day of Noise and Clamour is? It is a day when men will be scattered about like moths, and the mountains will be like carded wool. Then he whose weight of good deeds is great will be given a life of good pleasure and satisfaction. But he whose weight of good deeds is but light will end up in the Pit where the Fire burns fiercely.

The Holy Qur'an here describes the Day of Judgement in vivid terms as the Day of Noise and Clamour. On that day, even the mountains are but bits of fluff to be cast to one side. This is the end which awaits all that is material, all that we sometimes foolishly see as permanent. Only Allah is permanent and all that is is only because He Wills it. When this world has been destroyed, we will all be allocated to the place where we shall dwell for eternity. For the righteous, the Gardens of Bliss. For the unbelievers and those who have shown little or no compassion and charity, the darkness and fire of hell.

105: THE FOLDING UP *(TAKWIR)* 81:1-14

When the sun is folded up;
When the stars fall, losing their lustre;
When the mountains vanish;
When the she-camels, ten months with young, are left untended;
When the wild beasts are gathered together in the cities;
When the oceans boil over with a swell;
When the souls are sorted out;
When the baby girl, burried alive, is questioned
For what crime she was killed;
When the scrolls are laid open;
When the World on High is unveiled;
When the blazing fire is kindled to fierce heat;
And when the Garden is brought near;
Then shall each soul know what it has done.

When the Lord ends this world, this universe, what will be revealed is all that man has tried to hide from Allah. All the evil, crimes, murders and other abominations, such as child sacrifice. It will be on that Day that the deeds of everyone will become known and the scrolls of our actions will be brought forth. On that Day, the Day of Reckoning, the Day of Judgement, of reward or punishment, will be at hand.

106: THE SURE REALITY *(HAQQA)* 69:13-18

Then, when one blast is sounded on the Trumpet, and the Earth and its mountains are crushed to dust in one blow, on that Day shall the (great) event come to pass, and the sky will be torn apart, for it will that Day be flimsy, and the Angels will be on its sides, and eight will, that Day, bear the Throne of the Lord above them. That Day you will be brought to Judgement: not an act of yours that you hide will be hidden.

The Trumpet sound heralds the End. Then will everything be torn apart and utterly destroyed. In the midst of this comes the Glory of Allah. The Angels bearing His Throne manifest different aspects of His Divine Glory – just as in ancient courts the number of bearers showed how great a king was. But here is a King of all Kings, who not only rules over the world and the Universe, but also determines its beginning and its end.

107: THE RESURRECTION *(QIYAMAT)* 75:1-15

I call to witness the Resurrection Day; and I call to witness the self-reproaching spirit. Does man think that We cannot assemble his bones? We are able to put together in perfect order the very tips of his fingers. But man wishes to do wrong (even) in the time in front of him. He asks, 'When is the Day of Resurrection?'

At length, when the sight is dazed, and the moon is buried in darkness, and the sun and moon are joined together, that day will man say: 'Where is there refuge?' But there is no place of safety. The only place of rest will be before your Lord. That day will man be told of everything which he has done and failed to do. Man will condemn himself from his own mouth, even though he will try to make excuses.

When all has been destroyed comes the Day of Resurrection. On that Day, the Lord, the Creator, will re-create, down to the very last detail. All those who have died before the Day of Judgement will be brought to life exactly as they were on the day of their death. All those who perished in the Day of Judgement will likewise be raised completely as they were at that time. It will be in this state, the state we were in at the end of our days, that we shall stand forth for Judgement. But in the Gardens of Bliss, all will be ageless; young in body and mind and all equal in age.

108: THE PILGRIMAGE *(HAJJ)* 22: 5-6

O mankind! if you have any doubts about the Resurrection, remember that We created you out of dust, then out of sperm, then

*out of a leech-like clot, then out of a morsel of flesh, partly formed
and partly unformed, in order that we might show Our Power to
you; and We cause whom We will to rest in the womb for an
appointed term, then We bring you out as babes, then foster you
that you may reach your age of full strength; and some of you are
called to die, and some are sent back to suffer feeble old age, so that
they know nothing after having known (much). And (further),
you see the earth barren and lifeless, but when We pour down rain
on it, it is stirred (to life), it swells, and from it comes forth all
manner of beautiful things.*

*This is so, because Allah is the Reality: it is He who gives life to the
dead, and it is He who has Power over all things.*

*And the Hour will come: there can be no doubt about it, or about
(the fact) that Allah will raise up all who are in the graves.*

Here the full majesty of Allah the Creator is spelt out for all to
read, understand and believe. In our narrow understanding of
life, we see ourselves being formed in the womb; being born;
growing up; maturing; growing old and then dying. All this we
can see and so we accept. From this the foolish conclude that this
is all that life is about: that there is no Allah and no Afterlife. But
here the Holy Qur'an shows the full spectrum of life. We are
created out of nothing, from dust in our father Adam. From him
we all descend.

109: WINNOWING WINDS (*ZARIYAT*) 51:1-6

*By the winds that scatter the dust, by those that carry the heavy
clouds, by those that flow with ease and gentleness, and those that
distribute and apportion by Command – Truly, that which you
are promised is true and Judgement and justice must come to pass.*

The role of each type of wind or cloud stands as a Sign of the
purpose God has given to all His Creation. The harmonious
workings of Creation speak of the Truth. So, on the Judgement
Day, all will be judged according to that role which they had in
fulfilling God's purpose. We will be answerable for the doing of

His Will. On that Final Day, justice will be metred out according to the Truth.

110: THE CRITERION *(FURQAN)* 25:22–29

There will be no joy for the sinners on the Day when they see the Angels. The Angels will say: 'There is a barrier beyond which you may not pass.' And we shall turn to whatever deeds they did (in this life), and We shall treat these deeds as worthless dust.

The Companions of the Garden will do well on that Day, and they will rest in the fairest of places.

On that Day the Heavens will be torn apart and Angels will be sent down; that Day the rule of Right and Truth will be in the hands of Allah the Merciful alone. It will be a terrible Day for the unbelievers. That Day the wrongdoer will bite at his hands, saying: 'O how I wish I had followed the Straight Path with the Apostle! Ah! woe is me! Would that I had never taken such a one for a friend! He led me away from the Message (of Allah) after it had come to me! Ah! the evil one is but a traitor to man!'

Once the Day of Resurrection has come, the dead will be arraigned for trial on the Day of Judgement. Then will they see how Satan has led them astray. Then will they regret ignoring or scorning the Message of the Prophets. For no one who has heard the message and rejected it will be saved. But for those who have been faithful to Allah, all will be well for them.

111: THE SHAKING *(ZILZAL)* 99:1–8

When the Earth is shaken to her (utmost) convulsion,
And the Earth throws up her burdens (from within),
And man cries (distressed): 'What is the matter with her?'
On that day will she declare her tidings:
For your Lord will have given her inspiration.
On that day will men proceed in companies sorted out to be shown
*   the deeds that they (have done).*

Then shall anyone, who has done an atom's weight of good, see it!
And anyone who has done an atom's weight of evil, shall see it.

On the Day of Judgement, the very Earth will bear testimony to
the evils and crimes committed upon her. The convulsions of the
Earth will bring home to the unbeliever that the End is upon
him. Then on the Day of Resurrection the resurrected Earth will
lay bear all the wickedness which she has had to bear, and will
cast up the dead from her soil to stand before the Judge.

112: THE INEVITABLE EVENT *(WAQI'A)* 56:8–10

Then there will be the Companions of the Right Hand – what will
be the Companions of the Right Hand?

And the Companions of the Left Hand – what will be the
Companions of the Left Hand?

And the Foremost in Faith will be foremost in the Hereafter.

In the following four quotations, the Holy Qur'an tells us how
the Day of Judgement will proceed, and what is to be expected by
those who have lived on this earth. Remember, the Day of
Judgement has come and all life has ended. Then came the Day
of Resurrection, when all was restored to its former state to stand
before Allah for Judgement. Now comes the Final Day, the Day
of Judgement, from whose justice there can be no escape. Those
who formerly doubted will be unable to do so when the dreadful
reality of its coming is upon them. The resurrected will be
ordered into three groups. The Companions of the Right Hand;
the Companions of the Left Hand, and, most blessed of all, the
Foremost in Faith.

113: THE INEVITABLE EVENT *(WAQI'A)* 56:10–26

And the Foremost in Faith will be Foremost in the Hereafter.
These will be those nearest to Allah, in Gardens of Bliss: a number
of people from those of old, and a few from those of later times.

They will be on thrones encrusted with gold and precious stones, reclining on them, facing each other. Around about them will be young servants, perpetually young, with goblets, beakers and cups filled from clear-flowing fountains: there will be no problems with this, nor will they suffer intoxication: and they will have their pick of fruits, and meat from any birds they wish. And (there will be) Companions with beautiful, big and lustrous eyes, like pearls well guarded. A reward for the deeds of their past (life). No frivolity will they hear there nor any hint of evil, only the saying: 'Peace! Peace!'

The Foremost in Faith are the Prophets and Caliphs beloved of Allah. Those whose lives have been totally dedicated to the Will of Allah will find their rest with Him for ever. Those who in their earthly life have practised restraint, abstinence and self-discipline will find in the Gardens of Bliss enjoyment and fulfilment such as those who took all earthly pleasures never found. This is their reward for their Faith.

114: THE INEVITABLE EVENT *(WAQI'A)* 56:27–40

The Companions of the Right Hand – what will become of the Companions of the Right Hand? They will dwell amongst the thornless Lote tree; amongst Talh trees whose fruits and flowers are piled high. They will dwell in shade and by ever-flowing waters with abundant fruit which never runs out. They will sit on thrones raised high. Their companions which We have created will be pure and virginal, all of the same age – for the Companions of the Right Hand. Many of these will be people of the old times, and many will be people from later times.

The Companions of the Right Hand are those, from all ages of history, who have lived in submission to the Will of Allah. In the Gardens of Bliss, they will all be young, and will thus be able to enjoy the pleasures and beauties of the Gardens as reward for their faithfulness. Here they will dwell for eternity, never growing old, nor suffering from any distress, but only living in tranquillity and pleasure.

115: THE INEVITABLE EVENT *(WAQI'A)* 56:41-56

The Companions of the Left Hand – what will happen to the Companions of the Left Hand? They will be in the midst of the Great Fire and in boiling water, surrounded by black smoke. There will be nothing around them which will refresh them or please them, for they had their fill of living in luxury in this life and persisted in great wickedness. They said: 'What, when we die and have become dust and bones, will we be raised up again – we and our fathers before us?' To which answer: 'Yes, those who came before you and after you, all will be gathered together for the Day you know is coming. Then will you who have chosen wrong and treated the Truth as if it were falsehood taste of the tree of Zaqqum. Your stomachs will be filled with it, and you will drink boiling water as well. Indeed, you will drink like sick camels raging with thirst. Such will be their entertainment on the Day of Requital!

The Companions of the Left Hand, the sinister hand, are those who rejected Allah, His Prophets and His Word. For those who sought pleasure in the wickedness of this earthly life, who in this life went to the side of evil, there is no reward save eternal punishment. For those who cast doubt on the physical resurrection, there are only the torments. Those consigned to hell are from all times in history, for wherever wrong was done, the just punishment will be given out.

116: THE PROPHETS *(ANBIYAA)* 21:35;47;97

Every soul shall have a taste of death: and We test you with evil and with good by way of trial: to Us you must return.

We shall set up scales of justice on the Day of Judgement, so that not a soul will be dealt with unjustly. And if there be (no more than) the weight of a mustard seed, We will bring it (to account): and enough are We to take account.

Then will the true promise draw nigh (of fulfilment): then behold! the eyes of the unbelievers will fixedly stare in horror: 'Ah! woe to us! we were indeed heedless of this: nay, we truly did wrong.'

The first verse is a reassurance given to the Prophet Muhammad 🌸 that the trials and tribulations through which he passed, because of the unbelief of those around him, are for a purpose. No one is immortal. All men must die, and on the basis of how they have lived they will be judged on their resurrection. Evil and temptation are set before us to see how faithful we are to the Will of Allah. Those who are good and decent, and who continue to be true to the Will of Allah despite all manner of setbacks and trials, will be rewarded in the life Hereafter. Those who fall to evil, who give up and reject the Truth, will suffer in the life Hereafter. So when temptation comes, when evil besets you, hold fast and do not give in.

117: THE OVERWHELMING EVENT
(GASHIYA) 88:1-7

> *Has the story reached you of the Overwhelming (Event)? Some faces will be humiliated that Day, labouring (hard), weary, when they enter the blazing fire, and when they are given, to drink, from a boiling hot spring. No food will there be for them but a bitter* dhari, *which will neither nourish nor satisfy hunger.*

The Holy Qur'an, Word of Allah, seeks to reach out and touch the unbeliever, that he may see his mistake and submit to the Will of Allah. The Prophets have all spoken to humanity about the Day of Judgement and the Wrath that will fall on the unjust and the disbelievers. The story has been told so often, yet some people still turn away. Their repentance will come when it is too late to respond to the truth.

118: THE OVERWHELMING EVENT
(GASHIYA) 88:8-6

> *Other faces that day will be joyful, pleased with their efforts – they will be in a Garden on high, where they shall hear no (word) of vanity: there will be a bubbling spring; there will be thrones,*

raised on high, goblets placed (ready), and cushions set in rows, and rich carpets spread out.

For those who have heard the message of the prophets and have believed, there will be rewards undreamt of on this earth. This is the reward for those who follow the Will of Him Who will come as Judge.

119: THE CHILDREN OF ISRAEL (*BANI ISRA-IL*) 17:97

It is he whom Allah guides, who is guided in Truth; but he whom He leads astray – for him there is no protector except Him. On the Day of Judgement We shall gather them together, prone on their faces, blind, dumb and deaf: Their abode will be hell: every time it seems to be abating, we shall increase for them the fierceness of the fire.

The test of temptation is the test which sorts out those who are faithful to Allah and those who will throw away faithfulness at the first opportunity. Those who remain guided by what they know through the Holy Qur'an to be the Will of Allah will be saved. But for those who are led astray by the temptations there will be the eternal fire as their punishment.

120: THE BELIEVERS (*MU-MINUN*) 23:102–108

Then those whose balance (of good deeds) is heavy, they will attain salvation: but those whose balance is light will be those who have lost their souls; in hell will they abide. The fire will burn their faces, and they will therein grin, with their lips displaced. 'Were not my signs rehearsed to you, and you treated them as falsehoods?'

They will say: 'Our Lord! Our misfortune overwhelmed us and we became a people astray! Our Lord! Bring us out of this: if ever we return to evil, then shall we be wrongdoers indeed!'

He will say: 'Be you driven into it (with ignominy)! And speak you not to Me!'

In the balance of sins Allah will display His Mercy. Those who have commited small sins (for no one can be without sin) will have these sins cancelled out if they have also done works of kindness and charity. Likewise, those who have truly repented of great sins, their smaller sins will also be wiped clean. But those who have not repented, those who have not stopped sinning, even after repenting, they will be punished for their sins.

121: THE PROPHETS *(ANBIYAA)* 21:97–100

Then will the True Promise draw close: then behold! The eyes of the disbelievers will stare in horror: 'Ah! Woe to us! We were indeed heedless of this; nay, we truly did wrong!'

Indeed, you disbelievers and the gods that you worship besides Allah are (but) fuel for hell! To it you will surely come!

If these had been gods, they would not have got there! But each one will end up there. There, sobbing will be their lot, nor will they hear anything else.

On the Day of Judgement the falsehood of the world will be revealed for what it really is. The false gods will turn out to be nothing but lumps of wood fit for heating the fires of hell. On that Day, the disbelievers will see that those things in which they put their trust, which were not of Allah, are but useless fakes, worth nothing and unable to help those who worshipped them.

122: THE SURE REALITY *(HAQQA)* 69:19–24

Then he that is given his record in his right hand will say: 'Ah here! Read my record! I really did understand that my account would (one day) reach me!' And he will be in a life of Bliss, in a Garden on high, the fruits of which will hang low and near. 'Eat

*and drink, with full satisfaction; because of the (good) that you
sent before you, in the days that are gone!'*

Those who go through life aware of the final Day of Reckoning
and living their life accordingly will be able to step forward on the
Day of Judgement. They will be secure in the knowledge that
they have lived as Allah willed and that the scrolls of their lives
will ensure them a place in the Garden of Bliss. These are the
Companions of the Right Hand, for in their right hand will be
placed their sheet of good deeds.

123: THE SURE REALITY *(HAQQA)* 69:25-29

*And he who is given his record in his left hand, will say: 'Ah!
Would that my record had not been given to me! And that I had
never realized how my account (stood)! Ah! Would that (death)
had made an end of me! Of no profit to me has been my wealth!
My power has perished from me!'*

The Companions of the Left Hand are so called because on the
Day of Judgement their records are placed in their left hand.
Those of the Left are those who chose the wealth of this life and
the ease of selfishness in preference to the wealth of the life
Hereafter. They will lament that death was not final, because
their few years of earthly pleasure are as nothing in comparison
to the eternity of hell.

124: MOST GRACIOUS *(RAHMAN)* 55:33-45

*O assembly of jinns and men! If you can pass beyond the Heavens
and the earth, do so because only those who are authorized can so
do.*

Then which of the favours of your Lord will you deny?

*On you will be sent a flame of fire (to burn) and a smoke (to choke):
no defence will you have:*

Then which of the favours of your Lord will you deny?

When the sky is torn apart, and it becomes red like ointment:

Then which of the favours of your Lord will you deny?

On that Day no question will be asked of either man or jinn regarding the sins they have committed.

Then which of the favours of your Lord will you deny?

(For) the sinners will be known by their marks: and they will be seized by their forelocks and their feet.

Then which of the favours of your Lord will you deny?

This is the hell which the sinners deny. In its midst and in the midst of boiling-hot water will they wander around.

Then which of the favours of your Lord will you deny?

In all Creation only two creatures have the power to decide whether to obey Allah of their own free will or not. All creation excepting jinns and humanity follow the course set for them by Allah. They live out their lives in submission and will be judged on the quality of their lives as belief does not apply to them. But for jinns and humanity the burden and the glory is great. Because of choice, those who choose submission to Allah will dwell in eternal bliss. For those who choose to reject the proofs of Allah and turn from His Will, the burden will be eternal hell with its terrors. This is the burden and the glory which only jinns and humanity have to face.

125: THE INEVITABLE EVENT *(WAQI'A)* 56:92–96

If he is one of those who has rejected the Truth as being false, who has gone wrong, his fate will be in boiling water and burning in hell-fire. This is the Truth and will come to pass. So praise the Name of the Lord, the Supreme One.

Be not mistaken. The torments of Hell are beyond imagination. They will last for eternity and will never cease. If wrongdoers, those who reject Allah's Message, could only understand one tiny part of what lies in wait for them, they would repent and turn to His Mercy. There is hope for all people. If anyone calls upon Allah and acknowledges His greatness and His Prophets; if anyone will celebrate His Creation and recognize the Creator for Who He is; if anyone will confess their sins and not sin again because of the Message, then they will be saved and will not pass into the flames and the boiling water. Allah is Merciful to those who will hear His Voice and turn to Him.

126: THE HEIGHTS *(A'RAF)* 7:46–47

Between them shall be a veil, and on the Heights will be men who can tell people by their marks. They will call out to the Companions of the Garden: 'Peace be upon you.' They have not entered the Garden, but they do have the assurance of the Garden.

When their eyes turn towards the Companions of the Fire, they will say: 'Our Lord! Send us not to the company of the wrongdoers.'

The people on the Heights are these whose lives have not been good enough to warrant entry into Paradise and access to the Gardens of Bliss, but neither have they been bad enough to warrant sending to hell. They will all be people who have sought to live their lives under the Guidance of the Holy Qur'an but who have fallen just short of the mark. Some say that they are like pending cases in law, awaiting a final decision from Allah as to whether they enter the Gardens or plunge to the Pit. Others say they will abide in this limbo between the two places for eternity.

127: THE HEIGHTS *(A'RAF)* 7: 48–51

The men on the Heights will call to certain men whom they know from their marks, saying: 'Of what use to you now are your hoards of wealth or your arrogant ways?

'Behold! are these not the men whom you swore that Allah with His Mercy would never bless? Enter the Garden you ones, for there is nothing for you to fear or worry about.'

The Companions of the Fire will call to the Companions of the Garden: 'Pour down on us some water or anything else which Allah gives to you.' They will say: 'Both of these things has Allah forbidden to those who rejected him: those who took their religion to be mere amusement and play, and were deceived by the life of the world.' That day shall We forget them as they forget the coming of this Day of theirs, and as they were wont to reject Our Signs.

The people of the Heights can see only too clearly the results of greed, covertness and rejection of Allah, when they look to the fate of those in the fires of hell. Pity those in hell who, looking up, can see the delights of Paradise and who know that this will be denied to them for ever. No help can come to them, for they will be rejected in the life Hereafter just as they rejected the Will of Allah in this life.

128: THE COW (*BAQARA*) 2:25

But give glad tidings to those who believe and who do what is right. Their reward is Gardens, beneath which rivers flow. Every time they are fed with fruits from the Gardens they say: 'Why, this is what we were fed with before,' for they never lack for what they want and enjoy. And they have there companions pure (and holy); and they dwell there for ever.

Glad tiding indeed for those who live faithfully before Allah. For they will dwell in such pleasure and comfort that it is impossible for us to imagine. All pleasures which are available on earth are but faint impressions of the true pleasures of the Gardens.

129: THE COW (*BAQARA*) 2:82

But the faithful and those who do what is right, they are the

Companions of the Garden, where they will dwell for ever.

It is the combination of faith and good works which will ensure eternity in the Gardens. Works of charity alone, whilst pleasing to Allah, are not sufficient. There must also be faith in the grace of Allah. A tradition of the Holy Prophet 🕌 shows this. Once he warned his companions: 'You should know that you will not enter into Paradise merely by virtue of your works.' They asked: 'Is this true of you also?' He replied: 'Yes, I too shall enter Paradise merely by Allah's Grace and Mercy.'

130: THE FAMILY OF IMRAN *(AL-I-IMRAN)* 3:15

Say: 'Shall I give you glad tidings of things far better than those? For the righteous will have Gardens close to their Lord, with rivers flowing beneath; there will be their eternal home; with companions pure (and holy); and the good pleasure of Allah, for in Allah's sight are (all) his servants.'

The glad tidings mentioned in the preceding verses concern the victorious Battle of Badr, when the Muslim forces won an overwhelming victory against superior odds. Yet the glad tidings of this vindication of the Believers is as nothing compared with the glad tidings of what awaits the believer when he or she enters Paradise. But no one should assume their place in Paradise. Allah watches over all his servants to see if they are truly worthy of entry into Paradise. Therefore even believers should see that they live their lives as Allah intends, aware that He is watching at all times.

131: THE INEVITABLE EVENT *(WAQI'A)* 56:88–91

For the one who is Nearest to Allah there is rest and satisfaction in the Garden of Delights. If he is a Companion of the Right Hand there comes the greeting, 'Peace be on you,' from the Companions of the Right Hand.

We end this consideration of the Hereafter with these wonderful, peaceful verses. Here is the reward of the life lived in submission to Allah. Here is the refutation of the disbeliever. Here is the reward for the life well lived. To be near to Allah. To dwell in such a place of rest and pleasure. To have such companions as the other virtuous ones. But, most of all, to have Peace. This life may seem an endless battle against all that is evil and wrong. But the promise which the Holy Qur'an holds out is of a peace and tranquillity which will vindicate all that has been suffered or contested in this life.

7 The Five Pillars of Islam

Declaration of Faith

132: HADITH
BUKHARI AND MUSLIM (Agreed)

The Messenger of Allah ﷺ *said: 'Islam has been built on five (Pillars): testifying that there is no God but Allah and that Muhammad is the Messenger of Allah; performing the prayers; paying regular charity; making the Pilgrimage to the (Sacred) House; fasting in Ramadan.'*

Islam is not a religion in the narrow sense of a spiritual doctrine. It is a way of life, thought, word and deed. For us, Faith without action is meaningless. Faith motivates action and action brings Faith out into the world where it can grow and strengthen. So in Islam, we have have the five Pillars of Islam which are the actions that develop naturally out of the five Pillars of Faith *(Iman)*.

The first is the declaration of the belief in Allah and His Prophet Muhammad ﷺ . A Muslim performs every act in the name of Allah and declares his belief to whomever he can. It is an utterance *(takbeer)* for the love for Allah, for his own soul and for the souls of fellow men who may hear through him the voice of Allah.

Love of our fellow man, self-control, detachment from material desires and sacrifice are essential to spiritual growth, and to this end moderate forms of asceticism are established. Regular prayer requires a sacrifice of time and the ability to detach oneself from worldly concerns, but this does not prevent us participating fully in daily life. Obligatory charity requires the sacrifice of a small portion of our wealth, but does not deny the rights of property. Fasting in Ramadan requires the sacrifice of food and drink, but not to the extent of damaging our ability to continue regular business. The Pilgrimage requires us to give up our work and the comforts of life for a number of days or weeks and to bear the financial cost involved, but only if we can afford it. All these activities involve body and soul, individual and community, and provide each of these with tangible benefits.

133: HADITH
MUSLIM: Book of Faith *(Kitab Al-Iman)*

Mu'adh said: 'The Messenger of Allah ﷺ sent me (as Governor of Yemen) and (as I was leaving) told me: "You will soon find yourself among a community of the People of the Book, so first call them to testify that there is no god but Allah, that I (Muhammad) am the Messenger of Allah, and if they accept this, then tell them that Allah enjoined upon them five prayers during the day and the night, and if they accept it, then tell them that Allah has made zakat obligatory for them that it should be collected from the rich and distributed among the poor, and if they agree to it, do not pick up the best of their wealth (for the Zakat) . . ."'

This hadith establishes the correct manner of teaching Islam to ourselves and others. It begins with the Declaration of Faith – *La ilaha illal Lahu Muhammadur rasulullah* (There is no god but Allah, Muhammad is Allah's Messenger). Until this is established in the mind, there is no point in proceeding to the other Pillars. Whether the individual accepts them or not, observance of them would be meaningless without the Declaration of Faith as the motivating force.

134: HADITH
MUSLIM: *(An-Nawawi's Forty Hadith)*

Sufyan ibn' Abdullah said: 'I asked the Messenger of Allah: "Tell me something about Islam which I can ask of no one but you."'

He said: 'Say I believe in Allah – and thereafter be upright.'

There are many different *takbeers* (utterances of belief) for different occasions, but the theme is of course the same whether we are sitting down to a meal, transacting business, marrying or attending a funeral. We begin an action in His Name and so we sanctify it, protecting ourselves from evil thoughts and deeds.

Prayer

135: THE SPIDER *(ANKABUT)* 29:45

Recite what is sent of the Book by inspiration to you and establish regular prayer: for prayer restrains from shameful and unjust deeds; and remembrance of Allah is, undoubtedly, the greatest (thing in life). And Allah knows what you do.

Regular prayer is the first and foremost duty of a Muslim. It is an expression of nearness and submission to Allah and a reminder that we are his humble servants. Of the five Pillars of Islam, it is the one the Qur'an most frequently and emphatically commands us to observe. However, observation of the other four Pillars is secondary only in the sense that without prayer they have no meaning, for prayer is the remembrance of Allah. Thus it is the first and last step on the path of spiritual growth. By keeping Allah in our thoughts we act for Him in our daily lives, safeguarding ourselves against shameful and unjust acts. There is no higher activity than prayer nor any greater protection against the forces of Satan.

136: HADITH
MUSLIM: Book of Prayer *(Kitab Al-Salat)*

Allah's Messenger said: 'Prayer said in a congregation is twenty-five times more excellent than prayer said by a single person.'

Muslims should always endeavour to pray together, answering the calls to prayer at the mosque, or otherwise praying with those they are with at the time. Communal prayer is essential, for conquering evil not only at an individual level, but at a local and international level. By bringing us together in the name of Allah, our community is reminded of the equality of all human beings in the eyes of Allah. Differences of rank, colour and nationality are levelled, as king and begger, black man and white man, prostrate themselves side by side before Allah. This simple act gives the lie to the false benefits of prejudice, greed and power-seeking. Humbled before Allah with their fellow men, none can doubt that worldly power and wealth, granted by Allah, will count for nothing when they are called to account on the Day of Judgement.

137: THE ROMANS *(RUM)* 30:17–18

So give glory to Allah when you reach evening and when you rise in the morning.

Yes, to Him is praise in the heavens and on earth and in the afternoon and when the day begins to decline.

MYSTIC LETTERS TH *(TA HA)* 20:130

Therefore be patient with what they say and celebrate (constantly) the praises of your Lord before the rising of the sun, and before its setting. Yes, celebrate them for part of the hours of the night and at the sides of the day, so that you may have spiritual joy.

Between them, these two readings enumerate the five daily prayer periods: early morning, early afternoon, late afternoon, sunset and night. The Hadith give further details.

Fajr, or the morning prayer, is said after dawn and before sunrise. A Muslim should therefore begin the day before sunrise, but if he is up late, morning prayer should still be said.

Zuhr, or the early afternoon prayer, can be said any time between the beginning of the sun's descent from its zenith until the beginning of the late-afternoon prayer time.

Asr, or the late afternoon prayer, is said any time between the point when the sun is halfway on its descent until just before sunset. But it is best said when the sun is relatively high.

Maghrib, or the sunset prayer, can be said from when the sun has just set until the last red glow in the sky has faded.

Isha, or the night prayer, is said between the times when the red glow has disappeared and midnight. It is the last act of the day, as the morning prayer is the first.

138: MYSTIC LETTERS TH *(TA HA)* 20:131-2

And do not cast looks of envy on the worldly splendour We have given other people to enjoy, for through this We test them. But the provision of your Lord is better and more enduring.

Enjoin prayer on your people and be constant in it. We do not ask you to provide sustenance. We provide it for you. But the fruit of the Hereafter is for Righteousness.

The luxuries of this world are fragile and temporary and easily lead down the road to hell. Allah warns the Prophet Muhammad 🌸 to teach the people to practise regular prayer *(salat)* because this will instil lawful values into their hearts and minds. Through prayer, they will be content with what Allah provides, both spiritually and materially, and will not miss the tempting pleasures which are sinful.

It is not for Allah's benefit that he enjoins us to pray – clearly, an All-Powerful Creator is not going to be in need of anything. It is for our own good that we must keep regular prayer, as this will lead us on the Straight Road to inner peace in this life and eternal paradise in the next. Furthermore, the collective nature of Islamic prayer ensures the health and cohesion of the community. By praying together five times a day the community never loses sight of its shared purpose and brotherhood.

139: HADITH
BUKHARI 9:6

Abu Huraira reports that he heard the Prophet say: 'If one of you

*has a river at his door in which he washes himself five times a day,
what do you think? Would it leave any dirt on him?' The
Companions said: 'It would not leave any dirt on him, (he would
be perfectly clean).' The Prophet said: 'This is an example of the
five prayers with which Allah blots out all the evils of a man.'*

In the same way that physical cleanliness protects us from
physical ill-health, so does spiritual cleanliness protect us from
spiritual ill-health. The purpose of Allah appointing Prophets on
earth is to purify the people when they have gone drastically
astray and are full of evil thoughts and actions. But no man,
Prophet or otherwise, can be responsible, beyond exhortation
and example, for another individual's purification. Each soul
must be ultimately responsible for itself through prayer, the
foremost act of purification. As long as we are in this world, we
need to cleanse ourselves regularly of the sins that we inevitably
commit, just as we cleanse ourselves of the dirt and germs we
gather.

140: HADITH
BUKHARI: Book of Prayer (*Kitab Al-Salat*)

*'Umar proposed that a man should be appointed who should call
out for prayer, at which the Prophet ✺ ordered Bilal to call out
for prayer in these words:*

*Allah is the Greatest (repeated four times).
I bear witness that nothing deserves to be worshipped except Allah
(repeated twice).
I bear witness that Muhammad is the Apostle of Allah
(repeated twice).
Come to prayer (repeated twice, turning to the right).
Come to success (repeated twice, turning to the left).
Allah is the Greatest (repeated twice).
Nothing deserves to be worshipped except Allah.*

These are the words heard in Arabic from hundreds of thousands
of mosques and Muslim prayer gatherings, all around the world,
five times a day. From before dawn to after nightfall, the

principles of Islam are taught to the world in the simplest terms: that the Unity of Allah and the Prophethood of Muhammad ﷺ are the cornerstones of Faith; that Allah alone must be worshipped; and that success in life, that is full self-development, can be achieved through prayer.

Falah (success or prosperity) does not refer to an accumulation of wealth or prestige but to full development of the self, and the realization of the Divine that is in us all as creations of Allah. This may well lead to greater worldly success, if Allah so chooses, but such prosperity is secondary to the far greater reward of spiritual growth.

141: HADITH
MUSLIM: Book of Prayer (*Kitab Al-Salat*)

> *The Messenger of Allah* ﷺ *said: 'The most virtuous among you shall deliver the* Adhan *(call to prayer) and those having most knowledge of the Qur'an shall act as* imams *(leaders in prayer).'*

Virtue and knowledge are the two most valued attributes of a Muslim. Thus, they are the criteria for selecting the leader of prayer and the one who calls us to prayer.

The *mu'adhdhin* (caller) stands facing towards the *Qibla* wall which points to the Ka'ba in Makkah. He stands either in a minaret or on a raised platform with both hands behind his ears, and delivers the call to prayer in a loud voice so that as many people as possible may hear the invitation to Eternal Peace and Prosperity.

During the prayers the *Imam* stands in front of the congregation, with the worshippers standing behind him in straight lines, facing the Ka'ba. The worshippers follow the *Imam's* actions and recitation from the Qur'an, neither anticipating them nor speaking louder than he. Their submission is to Allah, but the *Imam* is respected and followed as the one whom Allah has chosen to be most knowledgeable of His Word.

142: HADITH
MUSLIM: Book of Prayer (*Kitab Al-Salat*)

> *Allah's Messenger* ﷺ *said: 'Make frequent prostrations before*

Allah, for you will not make one prostration without raising you a degree because of it, and removing a sin from you because of it.'

Islam is total devotion of the spirit, mind and body. Just as we do not set aside only some times or places for Allah, so we do not put aside only a part of ourselves. It is for this reason that submission through prayer involves thought, word and deed. We think of Allah, we recite His Holy Word and we prostrate ourselves before him.

The postures of bowing, kneeling and prostration during prayers are specifically designed to evoke humility and reverence in the worshipper. They give dimension to the religious experience inspired by the words of the Holy Qur'an. The ultimate position of submission to Allah is prostration with the toes, knees, hands and forehead touching the ground.

143: THE COW *(BAQARA)* 2:186

When My servants ask you concerning Me, I am indeed close (to them): I listen to the prayer of every suppliant when he calls on Me. Let them also, with a will, listen to My call and believe in Me so that they may follow the Right Path.

Allah is so close to each one of us that we may speak to Him wherever we are whenever we like. There is no need for temples or special days or priests to make supplication to Allah on our behalf. He is Timeless, Everywhere, All-Hearing, All-Seeing. Indeed, our innermost thoughts and desires reach Allah, even if we do not put them into words. The five prayer periods are the minimum time we should spend communing with Allah, for He is always available to us. The more we pray the more we feel the Divine Presence, and the more we feel His Presence the greater is our ability to live by His Laws.

144: THE CHILDREN OF ISRAEL
(BANI ISRA-IL) 17:79–81

And pray in the small watches of the morning an additional prayer: soon your Lord will raise you to a Station of praise and glory.

Say: 'O my Lord, let my entry be by the Gate of Truth and Honour, and likewise my exit by the Gate of Truth and Honour, and grant me from Your presence an authority to aid me.'

And say: 'Truth has arrived and falsehood perished, for falsehood is bound to perish.'

The name given for this additional prayer is *Tahajjud*, which literally means 'to rise up by breaking sleep'. This is an optional prayer that any Muslim may keep, although Allah is specifically addressing the Prophet Muhammad 🌸 . This surah was delivered about one year before the *Hijrah* (migration) from Makkah to Madinah, when there was a storm of accusations against the Prophet 🌸 in a desperate bid to stem the rapidly spreading Message. Allah's instructions to the Prophet 🌸 to pray in the face of both public abuse and military force show that prayer is not merely an act of individual purification, but a powerful act for the mission of Islam and the Muslim community.

145: FOLDED IN GARMENTS *(MUZZAMMI)* 73:6

Truly, rising by night is the most powerful for governing (the soul) and most suitable for the Word (of Prayer and Praise).

The night is indeed a gift from Allah, so that we may be refreshed not only in sleep, but also in prayer. How easy it is made for us, in the silent and tranquil night, to turn away from worldly distractions toward pure thoughts of our Guardian-Lord. The heavenly lights remind us of His Messengers of Light, the Angels, who watch over us and deliver His eternal Words to the Prophets so that all mankind may benefit.

146: THE WOMEN *(NISAA)* 4:101

When you travel through the earth there is no blame on you if you

shorten your prayers, (especially) when you fear the disbelievers
may attack you. For the disbelievers are your open enemies.

The advice regarding prayer while travelling was relevant to the
particular situation of Muhammad ﷺ and his followers. In his
lifetime and since, the persecution of Muslims has meant that
wartime expeditions and emigration were often necessary and, in
fact, were advocated by the Qur'an in preference to being forced
to forsake Islam. The shortening of the obligatory part of the
salat (prayer) for travel during peacetime is to reduce four *rak'ats*
to two *rak'ats*. During war there is no prescribed limit.

However, Muslim scholars do not all agree as to when the
concessions given for travelling apply. Some maintain that they
are exclusively intended for journeys in the Cause of Allah such
as *Jihad, Hajj,* (see 246–255 and 184–201) or in quest of
knowledge, etc. Others argue that it is applicable to any journey
for lawful purposes; and a third school argue that any journey
elicits these concessions. The lawful or unlawful nature of the
journey is separate from the right to avail oneself of the travel
concessions.

147: THE WOMEN (*NISAA*) 4:102

When you (Muhammad) are with them and stand to lead them in
prayer, let one part of them stand up (in prayer) with you, taking
their arms with them. When they finish their prostrations, let
them take their positions in the rear and let the other party which
has not yet prayed come up and let them pray with you, taking all
precautions and bearing arms. The disbelievers hope if you are
negligent of your arms and baggage to assault you in a single rush.
But there is no blame on you if you put away your arms because of
the inconvenience or rain or because you are ill, but take
precaution for yourselves. For the disbelievers, Allah has
prepared a humiliating punishment.

These verses refer to wartime, and therefore give instructions for
what is known as the Salat of Fear. The essential point is that
salat should be maintained but in a manner and time that are
suitable in the face of external pressures. Allah will deal with the

disbelievers if we concern ourselves with living as piously as possible within the worldly framework.

Muslim armies, now as in the past, come together in regular prayer as this is the true source of their strength. The two benefits of prayer are particularly obvious during war: first, that of reaching the Divine Presence, which is always with us and will protect us if we but ask; and, second, that of unifying all believers for the one great purpose – Islam. This is how Muhammad ﷺ and his followers conquered two of the most powerful empires in the world, how they triumphed against armies which were two, three and even ten times their size.

148: THE WOMEN (*NISAA*) 4:103

When you pass (congregational) prayers, celebrate Allah's praises standing, sitting down, or lying down on your side; but when you are free of danger, set up regular prayers, for such prayers are enjoined on Believers at stated times.

If it is not possible to bow and prostrate before Allah as this would give advantage to attackers, then the positions of worship may be performed symbolically. In the same context of war, 'The Cow' (*Baqara*) 2:239 says: 'If you fear an enemy, pray on foot, or riding as may be most convenient...' Further details for the performance of the Salat of Fear are given in the many books of Islamic Law and Regulations.

149: THE TABLE SPREAD (*MA'IDA*) 5:6

O you who believe, when you prepare for prayer, wash your faces and your hands to the elbows; rub your heads with water and your feet to the ankles. If you are in a state of ceremonial impurity bathe your whole body ... Allah does not wish to place you in a difficulty but to make you clean and to complete His favour to you so that you may be grateful.

These are the cleansing instructions for partial ablution called *wudu* to be performed before going to prayer. It may be performed before every prayer but it is compulsory only after passing urine, stools or wind. Allah's wisdom is easily seen here for not only do these ablutions act as a Sign of the spiritually purifying effects of prayer, but they are beneficial to physical health. The habit of regular washing within the community maximizes the appreciation of cleanliness in both senses of the word and minimizes the spread of disease.

The Hadith provide extremely detailed information about washing. They state that face-washing automatically presumes that the hands are first washed. The mouth and nostrils should be cleaned and the whole face wiped over. Both hands and feet are washed, beginning with the right side.

150: THE WOMEN *(NISAA)* 4:43

> *O you who believe, do not approach prayers with a mind befogged until you can understand all that you say – nor in a state of ceremonial impurity (except when travelling on the road), until after washing your whole body; and if you are ill or on a journey or one of you comes from relieving yourself, or you have been in contact with women and you find no water, then take for yourselves clean sand or earth and rub it on your faces and hands, for Allah blots out sins and forgives again and again.*

The verse refers first to intoxicants as, at the time of Revelation, there were Muslims who drank to excess and had gone so far as to pray while drunk. This is the second occasion for a commandment against drinking (see 343) and is followed by a total prohibition on it (see 332). But the admonition is broader than simply against intoxicating liquor; it refers to anything that leaves the mind muddied, whether another type of drug or a heavy sleep. If prayer is to purify our souls and bring us closer to Allah, it must come from the heart and mind, not simply the lips.

The instruction to cleanse ourselves with earth if no water is available highlights the symbolic importance of purification. Rubbing earth would not appear to clean us in the strictly physical sense of the word, but it keeps alive in us the awareness of purification through prayer.

151: THE HEIGHTS (*A'RAF*) 7:31

> *O Children of Adam, wear your beautiful clothes at every time and place of prayer. Eat and drink but do not waste by excess, for Allah does not love wasters.*

It befits the sanctity of prayer, the time when we focus our thoughts purely on the Presence of the Almighty, that we should dress with grace and cleanliness, taking great care over the details of our dress. This is not a licence for personal vanity but for the utmost respect in His Presence. Modesty of dress is also implicit in the word *zinat*, here translated as 'beautiful'. The admonition specifically forbids worshipping in the nude or half-dressed, a practice which was common amongst some tribes at the time. Likewise, indulging in self-imposed starvation or overeating transgresses Allah's laws. We should eat and drink what Allah provides, in moderation.

152: HADITH
BUKHARI 10:46

> *Those who are well grounded in knowledge and possess the greatest excellence are most entitled to* imama *or the leadership of prayer.*

Each of the five prayer periods include a number of obligatory *rak'ats* in which an *Imam* reads from the Qur'an for all those gathered together. The leader is chosen from the community on the basis of learning and piety. There is no religious career ladder in Islam for men to climb or be born into in the name of Allah. The *Iman* is chosen from the community. Women are only ever selected when the prayer gathering is of women only.

153: THE ASSEMBLY OR FRIDAY PRAYER (*JUMU'A*) 62:9–10

> *O you who believe, when the call is proclaimed to* Jumu'a *(Friday prayer) hasten earnestly to the remembrance of Allah and leave off business – that is best for you if you but knew.*

And when the Prayer is finished, then you may disperse through the land and seek of the bounty of Allah and celebrate the praises of Allah often (and without stint) that you may prosper.

Friday prayer is the weekly meeting of the full congregation when we gather at the mosque in as large a number as possible. Although it is always best to pray with others in a spirit of unity, the daily prayers may be said alone if circumstances necessitate. Every effort must be made to attend the weekly Friday service at the mosque. This is the second of the four levels of worship in Islam that knit the neighbourhood, village, town and international community together in a spirit of collective purpose and brotherhood. The first level is the five daily prayers when each Muslim remembers Allah with those near at hand in the home, workplace, open air or mosque. The third level of worship is at the two *Eids* every year (see 182) when there is an even larger local meeting than the Friday assembly, at a central mosque. The fourth level happens once in a lifetime, if possible, when each Muslim makes the pilgrimage to Makkah to join the international community assembled there as one family of Islam.

The Day of Assembly includes a *khutba* (sermon), in which the *Imam* speaks on spiritual and material matters currently concerning the community. The day differs from the Jewish Sabbath or Christian Sunday as these are official days of rest in commemoration of Allah's day of rest as reported in the Old Testament. In Islam, Allah has no day of rest (see 202) and we do not segregate worship from daily life. On the contrary, we believe it is essential that all activities are performed as worship to Allah and therefore in remembrance of His Presence.

154: NEIGHBOURLY NEEDS *(MA'UN)* 107:4–7

So woe to the worshippers who are neglectful in their prayers, those who (want but) to be seen (by men) but refuse the needs of their neighbours.

This is a warning to those hypocrites who are seen praying but who are, in fact, only sincere in their wish to be considered pious rather than in a genuine wish to be guided by Allah and praise

His Name. It is easy to spot people like this. Their step from
Belief in the Supreme Creator to seeking His Divine Guidance in
prayer is revealed as false by their failure to take the next
inevitable step of giving to others in His Creation. This is most
obvious in the little acts of neighbourly kindness and
consideration that are overlooked by those whose hearts are not
genuinely virtuous and who look only for ostentatious acts of
piety. If this principle of *zakat* (regular chairty) is not practised,
then prayer becomes useless. It is seen to be form without
content.

155: FOLDED IN GARMENTS (*MUZZAMMIL*) 73:20

*The Lord knows that you stand to (pray) nearly two-thirds of the
night, or half the night or a third of the night, and so do a party of
those with you, but Allah appoints night and day in due measure.
He knows that you are unable to keep count like this, so He has
turned to you (in mercy). Therefore, read the Qur'an as much as is
easy for you. He knows that there may be among you some in ill-
health, others travelling through the land seeking Allah's bounty,
yet other fighting in Allah's Cause. Read, therefore, as much of
the Qur'an as may be easy, and establish regular Prayer and give
regular alms and loan to Allah a beautiful Loan, and whatever
good you send before your souls, you shall find it in Allah's
Presence – truly better and greater in Reward and seek the Grace
of Allah for Allah is ready to forgive and be merciful.*

The Prophet and some of his most devoted companions were
given to long watches of praying and reciting the Qur'an. At the
same time, they would walk about until their legs and feet
swelled. But Allah knew of the long years that lay ahead in which
Muhammad ﷺ would continue receiving the Qur'an from the
Angel Gabriel and would establish Islam in order to change the
course of human history. He did not wish the Prophet ﷺ to
exhaust himself for the great task ahead, nor indeed does he
desire any of us to overtax ourselves in carrying out our duties to
Him. To help us, He has not fixed immutable times for worship,
as with the days and nights of the year, but simply required that
we pray regularly five times a day or as often as is possible given
the pressures of daily life.

Regular charity *(zakat)* is the natural extension of this, and the 'Beautiful Loan' refers to spending in the cause of Allah. By spending for Allah we may have many blessings, whereas by hording for ourselves we may even lose what we have because, in reality, everything belongs to Allah. The loan is not really the money we spend, but our own souls which we lend to the cause until the time of Judgement. We should expect no worldly returns, for the reward we shall find with Allah will be infinitely greater.

156: HADITH (BUKHARI) 7:1

The whole of the earth has been made a mosque for me.

These words of the Prophet Muhammad ﷺ remind us that Muslims may say prayers wherever they like, for there is nowhere that is not in His sight. Nature worships Allah everywhere in the universe (see 215), so in that sense everywhere is a *masjid* (mosque), meaning a place to prostrate oneself. A home, workplace or simply a clearing in the trees needs no other consecration than the pure thoughts of those who wish to pause in their daily life and remember the Creator.

157: REPENTANCE OR IMMUNITY
(TAUBA OR BARAAT) 9:17-18

It is not for those who join gods with Allah to visit or maintain the mosques of Allah while they witness against their own souls by disbelief. The works of such bear no fruit. They shall dwell in the fire.

The mosques of Allah shall be visited and maintained by those that believe in Allah and the Last Day, establish regular prayers and practise regular charity and fear none except Allah. It is they who are expected to be on true guidance.

Before the Prophet ﷺ began to preach Islam, the Quraish who controlled Makkah maintained the Masjid-i-Haram (Sacred

Mosque) and organized vulgar rites around the *Ka'ba* (see 184) for their own financial benefit. When the Muslims reclaimed Makkah eight years after migrating to Madinah, they purified it and re-established true worship of Allah. These verses relate to the question of whether those who once worshipped there as idolators should be allowed to re-enter. The answer is clear, that only those who are true believers should be allowed access for worship. The practice of *shirk* (idolatry) disqualifies even those who, as descendants of Abraham, claim to be the owners of the mosque. Every mosque belongs to Allah and only those who practise *Tawhid* (worship of Him alone) are suitable caretakers and worshippers. These verses are taken as a general rule for all mosques. Non-Muslims may be allowed into the mosque provided they observe the rules.

158: HADITH
ABU DAWUD 2:11

> *I have not been commanded to raise the mosques high . . . the hour of doom will not come until people vie with one another in (the building of) mosques.*

We must never lose sight of the purpose of a mosque as a place to prostrate ourselves before Allah, not a place to express our own vanities and superiorities. The Prophet's mosque at Madinah was a simple structure in a large courtyard where tents could be pitched. The mosque was constructed from baked bricks, with palm-tree trunks for its pillars and a roof of clay and palm leaves. This simplicity became an established tradition. Mosques were, and still are, unfurnished except for mats or carpet and a pulpit for the Friday sermon (see 133). The domes and minarets were a later development, but nevertheless their beauty is still based on their simplicity of form. The chief decoration of mosques are the verses of the Qur'an painted or inlaid on the walls.

159: THE COW *(BAQARA)* 2:142–143

> *The Fools among the people will say: 'What has turned them from*

the Qibla which they once used?' Say: 'Allah owns both east and west. He guides whom He wills onto the straight way.'

Thus We have made you a justly balanced nation (ummat), so that you might be witnesses over the nations, and the Apostle a witness over yourselves: and we appointed the Qibla to which you formerly turned only to test those who followed the Apostle from those who would turn on their heels (from the Faith). Indeed, it was a momentous (change) except to those guided by Allah, and Allah would never let your faith go to waste, for Allah is full of kindness and mercy for all people.

The *Qibla* is the direction in which all Muslims turn in prayer as a symbol of unity. Allah is everywhere and all belongs to Him, so the gesture should not be misunderstood as literally facing Allah. Its significance is as a symbolic gesture of unity for the new community in which Allah had chosen to spread His Message.

In the past, the people had used as their *Qibla* the Holy City of Jerusalem which was sacred to both the Jews and the Christians. This was a gesture of commitment to Allah's Revelations as given to the prophets of the People of the Book (see 19–56). However, as those who feigned allegiance themselves forced Muhammad 器 and his followers to emigrate from Makkah to Madinah, it was apparent that a fresh uncorrupted symbol was needed. In these verses, revealed about a year and a half after the migration, Allah told the Prophet 器 that the *Ka'ba* would henceforth be the *Qibla*. In this way, a far older centre than Jerusalem became the focus of worship, for not only was the *Ka'ba* the House of Worship built by Abraham, but it is on this site that Adam is said to have first set foot on earth. It may seem strange that the very city from which they were exiled should become the new *Qibla* but, as Allah would have it, the city was to be reclaimed by the exiles for Him.

160: THE COW (*BAQARA*) 2:148–149

To each is a goal to which Allah turns him. Then strive together (as in a race) towards all that is good. Wherever you are, Allah will bring you together. For Allah has power over all things.

From wherever you start, turn your face in the direction of the Sacred Mosque; that is indeed the truth from your Lord. And Allah is not unmindful of what you do.

All human beings start from their individual point in life, the nationality, class, gender, personal talents, failings and circumstances that Allah has given them, but all should be united in the one goal of Truth and Goodness. The brotherhood of Islam is united in this goal every time its members all over the world pray facing the same point, like runners all poised to reach the same finishing line. For this reason, the *Qibla* is integral to prayer as both a submission to One God and an expression of shared purpose and mutual co-operation. The single direction symbolizes the unity of Allah and of the Islamic community.

Zakat

161: THE CLEAR EVIDENCE (*BAIYINA*) 98:5

And they have been commanded no more than this: to worship Allah, offering him sincere devotion, being True; to establish regular prayer and practise zakat *(regular charity). And that is the religion right and straight.*

The three principles from which all other aspects of religion spring are Faith and its complements, *salat* (regular prayer) and *zakat* (obligatory charity). By its nature, Faith inspires prayer as the means of drawing nearer to the Allah, and it inspires charity as an expression of love for His Creation and gratitude for His gifts to us.

There is no equivalent word for *zakat* in the English language. It is variously described as regular charity, alms-giving, a tax or a tithe. But it is more than any of these things. It is a spiritual act and the most important duty next to prayer. It is a legal obligation set by Allah and as such is distinct from voluntary charity.

At the end of each year, all Muslims, women and men, must pay 2.5 per cent of their savings as *zakat*. The Hadith deal in some detail with the permutations of incomes and assets which can complicate the assessment of a person's surplus wealth, but the spirit of *zakat* should be to give generously, not to try to evade through financial juggling. The 2.5 per cent set is the minimum rate; there is no maximum other than that we do not endanger our capacity to provide for ourselves and our family.

162: REPENTENCE (*TAUBA*) 9:60

Alms are for the poor and the needy and those employed to administer the funds; for those whose hearts have recently turned to Islam; for those in bondage and in debt; in the Cause of Allah; and for the traveller. . . .

THE COW (*BAQARA*) 2:273

Charity is for those in need, who because they work in Allah's cause are not free to seek paid work or trade. The ignorant man thinks that, because of their modesty, they are free from want. You should know them by their mark: they do not beg indiscriminately from all and sundry. And whatever good you do, be assured Allah knows it well.

From these two verses we know those who are to have the *zakat* distributed among them. They are: poor Muslims unable to look after themselves such as young orphans, widows or disabled people; needy Muslims who do not have the money to establish or re-establish themselves in work; converts to Islam trying to settle into their new community and way of life; Muslim prisoners of war and slaves wishing to buy their freedom; Muslims in debt; Muslims working in the service of Allah who are therefore unable to earn a living; Muslim travellers without enough money to return home. When the economy of the community is so well balanced that there is more *zakat* than individuals in need of it, the money is used directly in propagating the cause of Allah. In addition the *zakat* is used to pay the wages of those appointed to collect it. In an Islamic nation the responsibility for collecting and distributing the *zakat* lies with the government. In a non-Muslim nation, this devolves on organizations at the local community or national level set up by the Muslim population.

163: FAMILY OF IMRAN (*AL-I-IMRAN*) 3:133–134

Be quick in the race for forgiveness from your Lord and for a Garden whose width is that of the Heavens and of the earth, prepared for the righteous.

Those who spend freely whether in prosperity or in adversity, who restrain anger and pardon all men, for Allah loves those who do good.

The way to forgiveness and Paradise begins, but does not end, with the *zakat* of 2.5 per cent. As a religious act it is founded on a generosity of spirit that gives both spiritually as well as materially, offering patience and encouragement instead of harsh words and cynicism. Such a person remembers with humility his own mistakes and is quick to give others the benefit of the doubt.

164: HADITH
An-Nawawi's Forty Hadith 26 (Agreed)

The Messenger of Allah ﷺ said: 'Each person's every limb must perform a charity every day the sun comes up: to act justly between two people is a charity; to help a man with his mount, lifting him on to it or hoisting up his belongings onto it is a charity; a good word is a charity; every step you take to prayers is a charity; and removing a harmful thing from the road is a charity.'

Charity is a good thought turned into action, so it can be anything that brings benefit to ourself or others. It is the natural and lawful state of being for all people. There are many hadith enumerating charitable acts from a smiling face to giving food to ourself and our families.

Charity links us as individuals to our families, our neighbours and the community at large, in the spirit of love and concern which is fundamental to the social order designed by Allah. It is powerful example of Islam's moderate way, giving personal and social responsibility to all according to each person's ability to bear it. It eschews both the extreme self-seeking of capitalism and socialism's oppressive denial of individual responsibility and justly earned rewards. Individual and society, citizen and state, material and spiritual concerns are kept in balance through charity. The moderate way is the balanced way, the just way, the Way of Allah.

165: INNER APARTMENTS (*HUJURAT*) 49:15

Only those who have believed in Allah and His Apostle and have never since doubted but have striven with their belongings and their person in the cause of Allah. Such are the sincere ones.

All acts of charity performed for the love of Allah are in His Cause, whether it be lending a sympathetic ear to someone in distress or contributing a portion of our income to the teaching of His Message. And there can be no sincere Faith without constant charity, for charity is both a product of and sustenance for our Faith. Submission and love of Allah inspire love and compassion towards His Creation and the desire to work for His cause. In turn, these charitable acts release our soul from the bondage of greed and material acquisitiveness so it can reach into the spiritual realm.

166: REPENTENCE (*TAUBA*) 9:103

Of their goods take alms, so that you might purify them. . . .

The Prophet 🕌 was appointed by Allah to cleanse evil from the souls of men. Throughout the Qur'an *zakat* is spoken of as a form of purification and, in fact, the word is used at times as a synonym for purity. Our *zakat* purifies the material wealth we keep. If we do not observe this obligation, we are keeping what is not ours to keep. All we own becomes tainted like a thief's loot. If we do observe *zakat*, the purifying effects are far-reaching. The heart of the one who gives is cleansed of selfishness and avarice. The heart of the one who receives is cleansed of envy and hatred. The material relief of the needy creates a society that is happier, healthier and more equal. Distrust, injustice, exploitation and class warfare, to name but a few of the evils that stain the heart of society, are purged by goodwill and compassion.

167: THE COW *(BAQARA)* 2:268

The Evil One threatens you with povery and lures you to unseemly conduct. Allah promises you His forgiveness and bounties. And Allah cares for all and He knows all things.

One of the weapons of Satan to prevent us saving our own souls with charity is to strike fear into our hearts that we may run short ourselves. But we must trust in Allah and the bounties he gives to us. In truth, it is by falling for the whispers of the Evil One that we endanger our possessions.

168: THE COW *(BAQARA)* 2:195

And give generously in the Cause of Allah. And do not make your own hands contribute to your destruction, but do good, for Allah loves those who do good.

The talents and abilities Allah has given us so that we can earn a living may bring about our own destruction, spiritually and materially, if we do not give of our earnings. A tradition of the Prophet 	says that two Angels come to us every morning, one of whom asks Allah to give more to the one who spends in his Cause and the other of whom asks Allah to bring destruction to the one who withholds (Muslim: Book of Charity, 2205).

One of the signs of Allah is the speed and severity with which a rich and verdant landscape may be laid waste by a natural disaster such as fire or drought. It is nothing for Him who has this Power to lay waste to the personal riches of the miserly individual. But the risks to our material wealth are of little consequence compared to the harm we do our own souls through penury. It is eternal damnation in the fires of hell that is the destruction we must truly fear.

169: TIME OR MAN *(DAHR* OR *INSAN)* 76:8–9

And they feed, for the love of Allah, the indigent, the orphan and the captive,

Saying: 'We feed you for the sake of Allah alone. No reward do we desire from you, nor thanks.'

Love of Allah should be the motive behind all acts of charity. In this way they become acts in the Cause of Allah. Such acts should not be sullied with expectations of gratitude or service in return. To give on this basis is to act with selfish motives, a negation of the spirit of charity.

170: THE COW *(BAQARA)* 2:263

Kind words and the covering of faults are better than charity followed by injury. Allah is Free of all wants and He is most patient and tolerant.

He who is Perfect, deficient in nothing, gives us His Bounty when we are in need and gives us His Forgiveness and Forbearance over and over again when we are deficient in our obedience to Him. We should remember this with humility and not seek to expose the weaknesses of others nor harm their self-esteem. An act of charity that results in injury, either because that which we give is harmful or because we use our position as giver to intimidate the recipient, is a harm for which we will be accountable to Allah.

171: THE COW *(BAQARA)* 2:261

The parable of those who spend their substance in the Way of Allah is that of a grain of corn – it grows seven ears and each ear has a hundred grains. Allah gives manifold increases to whom He pleases and Allah cares for all and He knows all things.

The concepts of purification and of growth are inextricably

linked in Islam. Purification leads to growth, just as impurity leads to decay, and there is no better example of this than in the purifying act of *zakat* for which the literal translation is 'to grow'. When we give for a cause greater than ourself we experience ourself as a part of a greater whole – the universal family of humanity. Our personal horizons are expanded, our spirit grows. Furthermore, the return to us in love and care from our fellow human beings and from Allah will multiple far beyond the value of that originally given.

Such acts also help the wealth of the society as a whole to grow. Materially, the redistribution of wealth through *zakat* increases the number of people with a decent standard of living and the ability to earn money – poverty is the first stumbling block in establishing a means of earning a living. Spiritually the society grows, through the greater equality that is created and feelings of love and compassion which spread out from each act of goodness.

172: THE FAMILY OF IMRAN *(AL-I-IMRAN)* 3:92

> *You will never attain righteousness till you give freely of what you love . . .*

There are many things we can give that entail no sacrifice. We may have possessions that we no longer care for, or a lot of money from which we give a tiny proportion, barely noticeable to us. Naturally, such spending is better than none at all, but it is when the element of sacrifice comes in that our soul is truly giving of itself. For some a deep attachment to money may indicate this is the area where they need most to practise charity. For others it may be power or knowledge or pity that they hoard for themselves and need to share. To attain righteousness – that is, to be free from the confines of self-seeking – we should each look to dispel our own secret greed through charity.

After this verse had been revealed a wealthy property owner of Madinah, Abu Talha, offered his garden as his most beloved possession to the Prophet . The Prophet would not take it for himself, but instructed Abu Talha to distribute it among his relatives (Muslim: Book of Charity, 2185).

173: THE COW *(BAQARA)* 2:264

O you who believe, do not cancel your charity by reminders of your generosity or by injury – like those who spend their substance to be seen by men but believe neither in Allah nor in the last Day. They are in parable like a hard barren rock on which is a little soil: on it falls heavy rain which leaves it bare stone. They will be able to do nothing with what they have earned. And Allah does not guide those who reject faith.

A thin veneer of virtue is soon washed away if beneath it lies arrogant or malevolent intent. Charity which falls on the deep, rich soil of true virtue makes it a source of growth and abundance which grows deeper and richer. In this parable we are reminded that practice cannot be divorced from sincere Faith anymore than Faith can be divorced from practice. One without the other is as useless as rain without soil to absorb it or soil without rain to nourish it.

THE COW *(BAQARA)* 2:265

And the likeness of those who spend their substance seeking to please Allah and to strengthen their souls is as a garden, high and fertile. Heavy rain falls on it but makes it yield a double increase of harvest, and if it does not receive heavy rain, dew suffices. Allah sees well whatever you do.

Charity with Faith can only serve to increase Faith and the benefits Faith brings in this world and the next. If charity is given in large quantity then the rewards are great, but even if it is only the regular, unassuming acts of care and consideration which we can give, the garden of virtue will flourish as under the gentle moisture of dew.

175: THE COW *(BAQARA)* 2:271

If you disclose charitable acts, it is nevertheless good, but if you conceal them and make them reach those really in need, that is best for you: it will remove from you some of your stains of evil. And Allah is well acquainted with what you do.

If there is a clear spiritual benefit to be gained by the disclosure of our name in relation to a contribution, such as prompting others to follow our example, it is permissable to do so, but we must beware of self-deceit. Could the same end not be achieved with the deed being made public while the contributor remained anonymous? Are we not in truth being vainglorious? It is Allah alone whom we should seek to please and He knows without a word being spoken.

176: THE COW (*BAQARA*) 2:267

O you who believe, give of the good things which you have earned honestly, and of the fruits of the earth which We have produced for you, and do not even aim at getting anything which is bad, in order that out of it you may give away something when you yourself would not receive it except with closed eyes. And know that Allah is Free of all wants and Worthy of all praise.

If we have earned our money in ways that are unlawful in the eyes of Allah, then no amount of charity will save our souls. There is no more merit in giving away money or possessions gained by corrupt means than in giving diseased fruit. We only compound our crimes with hypocrisy. And if indeed we give what will bring harm to others, such as alcohol or drugs, we condemn our souls yet again.

177: HADITH
MUSLIM: Book of Charity (*Kitab Al-Zakdt*) 2229

The Messenger of Allah 鬠 said the likeness of the miserly man and the one who gives charity is that of two persons who have coats-of-mail over them. When the giver of charity makes up his mind to give charity, his coat-of-mail expands so much that the footprints are also obliterated. And when the miserly man intends to give charity, it contracts over him and his hands are tied up to

his collarbone and every ring is fixed up to another. He would try to expand it, but he would not be able to do so.

When a person sincerely intends to give charity, he gives easily and cheerfully for the love of Allah. He is not restrained by a lust for wealth or fears that he may need what he gives another time. His soul expands with generosity and is safeguarded from Evil by the love of Allah. The allusion to footprints means that there is no trace of his evil deeds left – these are erased by his goodness.

On the other hand the miserly man is so attached to his wealth that even when his mind decides to give his will prevents it. He does not have the strength to override his own selfishness, but becomes imprisoned by it.

178: HADITH
AHMAD: vol. IV

Whoever tills a field, and birds and beasts eat of it, it is a charity.

The sphere of charity is not bounded by humanity – it extends to all Allah's Creation. We are rewarded for kindness to animals as we are for kindness to humans and just as we are punished for cruelty to them. The Prophet 🌼 told his companions of a prostitute who saw a dog almost dead with thirst on top of a well. She tied her scarf to her boot and filled it with water for the animal and for this goodness her sins were forgiven.

179: HADITH
BUKHARI: 24:31

The Prophet 🌼 *said: 'Sadaqa is incumbent on every Muslim.'*

They (his companions) said: 'And what about he who has nothing?'

He said: 'He should work with his hand and profit himself and give in charity.'

They said: 'If he still has nothing?'

'He should help the distressed one in need'

They said: 'If he is unable to do this?'

'He should do good deeds and refrain from doing evil – this is charity on his part.'

We should work in whatever capacity we can to be able to give of our material wealth to others, but if Allah has decreed that we shall be poor, then we should give of the goodness in our hearts. We all have our own soul to give. Kindness can be given in a word or gesture.

Fasting

180: THE COW *(BAQARA)* 2:183

O you who believe, fasting is prescribed to you as it was prescribed to those before you, so that you may learn self-restraint.

The month-long fast from the new moon of the ninth month (Ramadan) of the Muslim calendar to the new moon of the tenth month is the fourth Pillar of Islam. The purifying process of fasting in which the stomach is emptied so spirit may be filled with piety and righteousness has been practised throughout history and was well established amongst the Arabs at the time of the Prophet 鬱. The Christian Lent and the Jewish Passover both recognize the importance of fasting, but it is only in the fast of Ramadan that the practice takes the true form intended by Allah. This is a total abstinence from physical consumption. Eating, drinking, smoking and sex are all forbidden from dawn to sunset. Control of our physical urges is the first step to spiritual growth. Only by controlling the body can we transcend it. The intention is not simply to deprive ourselves but to rise above the desires themselves. To loosen our worldly attachment and move closer to Allah. The Pillars of prayer and *zakat* – that is thoughts of Allah and of others rather than ourselves – are our allies in this endeavour.

181: THE COW *(BAQARA)* 2:184

Fast for a fixed number of days, but if any of you is ill or on a journey the prescribed number should be made up later. For those who can do it (with hardship), the feeding of a poor person is a ransom. He that does good of his own account shall be rewarded, but it is better for you to fast if only you knew it.

In this fourth Pillar, the self-discipline practised daily and weekly in the Pillars of prayer and *zakat* is taken a step further with far-reaching spiritual benefits. Although there are set amounts of charity which can be given as a ransom instead of fasting if a person is old, sick, travelling or pregnant, it is better that charity be an addition to, rather than in place of, fasting.

We are taught the lessons of equality and compassion for all Muslims; rich and poor, upper and lower class are levelled in the moderated hardship. Hunger and thirst are the lot of all. Sympathy for those who have no choice but hunger is given the depth of experience. This is the way of Islam, to show by example.

The fast builds our Faith and our morality. Only Allah and our conscience know truly whether we have honoured our fast. Therefore the strength of our resolve is based on sincere devotion and our own conscience, not the force of social pressure.

Patience and perseverence are developed and we receive a great lesson in being able to adapt to new circumstances. We are thrown into a completely different set of rules and hardship to which we adapt ourselves and our daily life. For many Muslims who have emigrated for one reason or another these attributes of perseverence and adaptability are of great spiritual and physical advantage.

For all these reasons, the successful completion of Ramadan not only brings us closer to Allah but it creates a sense of freedom, self-assurance and compassion. These are the building blocks of peace – peace with ourselves, with Allah and with humanity. As always, our acts of devotion are greatly rewarded by Allah.

182: THE COW *(BAQARA)* 2:185

> *Ramadan is the month in which the Qur'an was sent down as a Guide to mankind, full of clear signs of guidance and judgement between right and wrong. So every one of you who is at home during that month should spend it in fasting, but if anyone is ill or on a journey the prescribed period should be made up later. Allah desires your well-being, not to put you in difficulties. He wants you to complete the prescribed period and to glorify Him and to be grateful for His Guidance.*

Although the Qur'an was delivered piecemeal over twenty-three years, it is believed that the Book as a whole was sent down with Gabriel at this time to the lower heaven or to some place known only to Allah. The Prophet 🕊 also received the first Revelation during Ramadan. To be of value to us the fast must be understood as an act in the tradition of God's Guidance. He sent us the Book in the month of fasting because both are ways in which He provides us with Guidance. Therefore it is particularly beneficial in this month to spend extra time reading and studying the Qur'an.

The breaking of the fast, is the occasion for glorifying Allah at one of the two *Eid* Festivals of the year, the second being after the *Hajj* (see 194). This Festival of Joy is a day when we express our gratitude to Allah for His Guidance in sending the Qur'an and in helping us complete the fast. *Eid* is a day of peace and Remembrance of Allah. It is a time for charity and visiting the sick, for Remembrance of Allah is never far from remembrance of all humanity.

183: NIGHT OF POWER *(QADR)* 97:1-5

> *We have indeed revealed this Message in the night of Power.*
>
> *And what will explain to you what the Night of Power is?*
>
> *The Night of Power is better than a thousand months.*
>
> *It was then that the Angels and the Spirit came down by Allah's permission on every errand.*

Peace until the break of dawn.

The Night of Power is the night during Ramadan when the Qur'an came down. It is not known exactly which night this was, but according to Sayings of the Prophet 🕌 it was one of the last ten nights of Ramadan falling on an odd-numbered day. To be in a state of Worship on this night of power when all the Angels come down is worth more than a thousand Ramadan months of fasting. Many Muslims spend the last ten days of the month solely in the mosque. This was a practice of the Prophet's. Not only is the worshipper well-placed for the Night of Power, but he increases his detachment from worldly affairs — gained by fasting — by physically removing himself for a period.

Pilgrimage

184: THE FAMILY OF IMRAN (AL-I-IMRAN) 3:95–96

The first House (of worship) appointed for men was that at Makkah: full of blessing and of guidance for all people.

In it are manifest signs; (for example) the station of Abraham; whoever enters it attains security; Pilgrimage there is a duty men owe to God – those who can afford the journey – but if any deny Faith, God does not stand in need of any of His creatures.

These verses reveal the fifth Pillar of Islam – the *Hajj* (pilgrimage) to the *Ka'ba* (Sacred House) at Makkah. The *Ka'ba*, built by Adam as the first House of Allah and rebuilt by Abraham and Isma'il, is visited every year by hundreds of thousands of Muslims from all around the world. There is no higher religious experience for the individual Muslim nor any greater expression of brotherhood for the Islamic community than the *Hajj*. It is the largest annual convention of Faith in the world where people of every race, nation and class come together as equals before Allah. It is a short but glorious time during which each individual finds peace with Allah, with himself, with humanity and with all Creation. It is a time of prayer and ritual and a time to share problems, experiences and feelings with one another. The peace, security and new understanding the *Hajj* brings to each participant are a blessing and guidance which remain with them all their life.

The *Hajj* is only required once in each individual's lifetime although if one can afford it, there is, of course, no prohibition on repeating the *Hajj*. If a person is unable to afford it or cannot physically manage the *Hajj*, then they are not obliged to go. In fact, it is unlawful to go on *Hajj* if one cannot provide for oneself and one's family while we are away. Allah does not ask of us what we are not able to give.

185: PILGRIMAGE *(HAJJ)* 22:26–27

Behold, we gave the site of the (Sacred) House to Abraham, saying: 'Do not associate anything with Me and sanctify My House for those who circle it or stand up, or bow or prostrate themselves in it.

'And proclaim the Pilgrimage among men. They will come to you on foot and on every kind of camel, lean from journeying through deep and distant mountain highways.'

The *Ka'ba* stands in the centre of the Sacred Mosque in Makkah. It is a startlingly simple cube-like stone building. But its survival in a land so often torn by war and destruction and its unchallenged religious status since the time of Abraham are witness to the great spiritual force that Allah has invested in it. Of course, the House is not an abode of Allah, for He is everywhere. But it has been given to us by Allah as the worldly focus for our worship of the One Who is Unseen. Pilgrimage to the *Ka'ba* is the symbolic experience in this life of our return to Allah on the Day of Judgement. As the great tide of humanity sweeps toward Makkah without distinction between them in action, dress, status or purpose, we are reminded of the oneness of the human family and the final appointment we all have with our Lord.

186: THE COW *(BAQARA)* 2:189

> *They ask you concerning the New Moons. Say: 'They are but signs to mark fixed periods of time for men, and for Pilgrimage...'*

In the sublime complexity of Creation there is an equally sublime simplicity which unerringly meets the physical and spiritual needs of men. The Islamic calendar runs on a twelve-month lunar cycle, which is nine or ten days shorter than the solar year. The months of *Hajj* are the last three – *Shawwal, Zul-qa'd* and *Zul-hajj* – and pilgrimage season can start at any time up to the tenth or thirteenth day. The preliminary rites may begin in the first two months with an approach to Makkah, but it is in the last month, *Zul-hajj* – on the eighth, ninth and tenth days in particular – that the chief rites are performed.

187: THE COW *(BAQARA)* 2:197

> *The months for* Hajj *are well known. If any one undertakes that duty, let there be no obscenity, nor wickedness, nor wrangling in the* Hajj. *And whatever good you do, be assured that Allah knows it. And take a provision for the journey but the best of provisions is right conduct. So fear Me you who are wise.*

The injunction to observe the *Hajj* had been given to the Prophet Abraham (see 185). In the 2500 years from then until the time of Muhammad ﷺ Arabs from all over the land made pilgrimages to the *Ka'ba* as the House of Worship of their forefather Abraham, despite their pagan beliefs. Even in the darkest days of violence and paganism, peace reigned by Divine Law during the months of *Hajj*. In this we can see how Allah's commands not only benefit us in the Hereafter, but in this life as well. In the four months of pilgrimage (including the month after), the often besieged Arabian trade and traffic could flow safely again along the roads and byways, providing economic relief for all.

Nevertheless, by the time of Muhammad ﷺ, the *Ka'ba* had been polluted by idolatry and the ritual of *Hajj* had become corrupted. After the conquest of Makkah, the Prophet ﷺ cast out 360 idols from the House, sanctified it, as had Abraham, and re-established the Laws and true principles of *Hajj*. Righteous behaviour is paramount during the *Hajj*. To sin at this time is worse than in the normal routine of life. To help us in this, pilgrims enter into the condition or attitude of *ihram*. This means 'to declare forbidden'. By entering this state the pilgrim proceeds to Makkah in a true state of mind, suitable for this great event. However, the injunction to take provisions was in direct response to the practice of going without provisions as a show of asceticism. There is no virtue in burdening others with our needs. Devotion to Allah does not absolve us of social responsibility.

188: HADITH
BUKHARI 3:53

> A man asked the Prophet ﷺ : 'What should a man wear in the state of ihram? He said: 'He shall not wear shirt, nor turban, nor trousers, not head-gear, nor any cloth dyed with wars (plant dye) or saffron, and if he does not find shoes, let him wear leather stockings, and he should cut them off so that they may be lower than the ankles'.

HADITH
ABU DAWUD 11.29

> The Messenger of Allah ﷺ forbade women in a state of ihram to wear gloves or a veil, garments dyed with wars, but said that besides this they could wear what they liked of garments coloured with safflower or made of silk or ornaments or trousers or shirt.

During the period of *ihram* the pilgrim gives up the comforts of life to focus his mind and spirit in pure submission to Allah.

While men are in *ihram*, they wear two white sheets, one from the belly to below the knee and the other covering the upper torso. The women wear ordinary dress but it is understood that it will be simple and modest. *Ihram* dress is put on after washing and declaring the intention to put on *ihram*. The dress is profound in its significance. First, it immediately establishes our position as equal and humble servants before Allah. All signs of rank between individuals have been removed. Gloves and veils were signs of rank in time of the Prophet 襚 , unlike ornaments which women of all classes wore. Whether royalty or working class, rich or poor, black or white – that is all nullified by the *ihram* dress and the single experience everyone is sharing. Secondly, the two sheets reminds the wearer of his death when his body will be wrapped in white sheets as his soul returns to His Lord. Thirdly, the clothes are an expression of simplicity which is the way of Islam.

189: HADITH
BUKHARI 25:6

The uttering of labbaika (proclamation of obedience) *by the Messenger of Allah was thus: 'I am at Your service, o Allah, I am at Your service. I am at Your service. You have no associate, I am at Your service. Yours is the praise and Yours the favour and Yours the kingdom. You have no associate'.*

There are the words proclaimed loudly in Arabic by the thousands of pilgrims as they flow in one direction united by the one language and submission to Allah. Thus we are united in the brotherhood of all men as servants of Allah.

190: HADITH
TIRMITHI 11:3

The Prophet said: 'Circling the House is like prayer, except that you talk in it, and whoever talks in it, let him only talk nothing but good.'

As in prayer, when we process round the *Ka'ba* we draw closer to our Lord and Cherisher. The *Ka'ba* is circled in a clockwise direction seven times beginning from the Black Stone (see below). This is the first act of the pilgrims when they arrive at Makkah and the last before they leave. However, the only compulsory time for circumambulation is when they have completed the rites which Allah has set for us. With the *Ka'ba* we come at last to the symbolic heart of the religious journey that commemorates the establishment of Islam by Abraham and Isma'il and confirms our own commitment to Allah.

191: HADITH
BUKHARI 25:56

> *'Umar Ibn. al-Khatab said one day he came in front of the black stone and kissed it and said: 'I know you are a stone which has no power to do me harm or good. If I had not personally seen the Prophet Muhammad ☙ kiss you, I wouldn't do it.'*

Non-Muslim observers have been quick to cry idolatry when they see pilgrims kissing the Black Stone set in the corner of the *Ka'ba*. But, not knowing the history of the stone, they confuse a token of devotion to Islam and respect for the Peacemaker Muhammad ☙ as worship of it. In the life of Muhammad ☙ before he had become a prophet, the *Ka'ba* was under reconstruction. The Arab chiefs organizing the work had great reverence for the Stone, for which varying reasons are given, including the claim that it was the only stone surviving from the original structure of the Sacred House. Whatever their reasons for honouring the Stone, the chiefs soon began to quarrel over who should restore it to its place in the building. Just when it looked as if war would break out over the issue, Muhammad ☙ appeared and was chosen to arbitrate. His solution was to wrap the Stone in a piece of cloth, then ask the chiefs to take an edge each and lift it into place. In this way, everyone shared in the honour and peace was maintained. It is this story which so exemplifies why Muhammad ☙ was chosen to bring the Message of Peace, and it is for this that we kiss the Black Stone.

192: THE COW (BAQARA) 2:158

> *Behold, Safa and Marwa are among the symbols of Allah. So if those who visit the House in the Season or at other times should circle there is no blame on them . . .*

When a pilgrim first arrives at Makkah, his second act after circling the *Ka'ba* is a fast walk between the hills of Safa and Marwa. They are a symbol of patience in the face of hardship, for it is between these two hills that Hagar, the wife of Abraham, ran back and forth to get water for her baby Isma'il when she was left on her own by Abraham.

193: THE COW *(BAQARA)* 2:198-200

Then when you pour down from 'Arafat, celebrate the praises of Allah at the Sacred Monument, and celebrate His praises as he has directed you, even though, before this, you went astray.

Then pass on quickly from the place whence it is usual for the multitude to do so and ask for Allah's forgiveness, for Allah is Oft-Forgiving, Most Merciful.

The *Hajj* proper begins on the eighth day of the month of Zul Hijah with a sermon in Makkah on the meaning of the *Hajj*. It is a three-day journey that acquaints us with the spiritual and historical environment of the Prophet Muhammad 鑠 and those who came before him. We travel out from the Holy City, glorifying Allah with the *labbaika* and praying at the various sites steeped in religious history. The plain of 'Arafat is the site of the reunion of Adam and Eve after their wanderings. Its name means Knowledge of God and it is from the Mountain of Mercy above it that a sermon is delivered by the *Imam*. This is followed by a full afternoon of praying and calling out the *labbaika*.

The short stay at 'Arafat encompasses essential ceremonies of the *Hajj*. Not long before these verses were revealed, the Quraish of Makkah had started making a short cut to the Sacred Monument without bothering about 'Arafat. They claimed they were above everyone else and need not bother with the true route, and then began dispensing similar exemptions to their allies. Such arrogance undermines the rigorous equality of the *Hajj* which requires the same duty of us all. Although the true route had been resumed by most when these verses were revealed, the people were warned to pray for forgiveness for their transgression.

194: PILGRIMAGE *(HAJJ)* 22:28

Let them witness the benefits given to them, and celebrate the name of Allah through the days appointed, over the sacrificial cattle which He has provided for them; then eat of that and feed the distressed ones in need.

The tenth and last day of the *Hajj* is the Day of Sacrifice. It is one of the two *Eid* festival days in the Islamic year, the other being at the end of Ramadan. *Eid* means 'recurring happiness' and this is indeed a day of rejoicing, for the Cause of Allah is advanced by every pilgrim who has completed the *Hajj*.

On this day, pilgrims and all Muslims (see 199) are recommended to sacrifice an animal to Allah, part of which will be eaten by them and part of which will go to help the poor, needy and distressed. The sacrifice puts into practice the lesson of equality and brotherhood of the *Hajj* by addressing itself to the right of all humanity to be fed.

195: PILGRIMAGE *(HAJJ)* 22:32–33

And whoever honours the symbolic sacrifices made to Allah shows piety of the heart.

You have benefited from them for an allotted time. In the end their place of sacrifice is near the ancient House.

The animals of sacrifice – camels, sheep, cows, oxen, goats – have been given to us by Allah so that they might feed, clothe and transport us. Their slaughter at Mina near Makkah is a relinquishing of worldly wealth and a recognition that, indeed, everything belongs to Allah and will return to Him.

196: PILGRIMAGE *(HAJJ)* 22:36

We have made the sacrificial camels as symbols for you from Allah. There is much benefit in them for you. Pronounce the name of Allah over them as they line up for sacrifice. When they are down on their sides (after slaughter), eat of them and feed the people that live in contentment and those that beg with due humility. Thus we have made animals subject to you so that you may be grateful.

The *Hajj* sacrifice is not an offering made to feed and appease a deity, but a deeply symbolic gesture. It is a commemoration of Abraham's willingness to sacrifice his own son (see 44–45). True piety requires a commitment to give up what we most love in His service if He asks it of us. Abraham was willing even to forfeit his son's life, but when Allah knew Abraham's heart was sincere he allowed an animal to be sacrificed in Isma'il's place. Our act of sacrifice is likewise a symbol of our commitment to sacrifice ourselves in whatever form Allah asks, even our own lives.

197: PILGRIMAGE *(HAJJ)* 22:37

It is not their meat nor their blood that reaches Allah, it is your piety that reaches Him. He has thus made them subject to you so that you may glorify Allah for His Guidance to you. And proclaim the Good News to all who do right.

The animal sacrifice is not made in the spirit of bloodshed but of deep piety. It is not forgotten that an animal dies. Indeed, our power over that animal, given to us by Allah, is a reminder to us all of the One who has power over our lives. We slaughter with humility and compassion in the name of Allah.

198: PILGRIMAGE *(HAJJ)* 22:29

'Then let them complete the prescribed rites, perform their vows, and circle the Ancient House.'

The completion of the prescribed rites entails shaving or cutting the hair, washing, etc., to mark the emergence from *ihram*. The period of outward ritual is almost finished, but the spiritual intensity is carried over in a personal vow to perform a service in Allah's Cause, which may involve self-improvement or active service in the community. Then the *Ka'ba* is circled for the last time.

199: THE COW *(BAQARA)* 2:196

And complete the Hajj *or* 'Umra *in the service of Allah. But if you are prevented send an offering for sacrifice, such as you may find . . .*

The Day of Sacrifice is celebrated by Muslims all around the world, so that they too may share in the brotherhood of Islam before Allah. Great efforts have been made in the last few years to ensure that the vast quantities of meat sacrificed on this day are frozen, dried, or canned and transported if they cannot be consumed by those in need in the vicinity. For although sacrifice is a key aspect of devotion to Allah, to waste his bounties while people in the world go without is an offence against His Creation.

200: THE COW *(BAQARA)* 2:203

Celebrate the praises of Allah during the appointed days, but if anyone hastens to leave in two days he is not at fault, and if any-one stays on he is not at fault, if his aim is to do right. Then fear Allah and know without doubt that you will be gathered unto him.

Once the Day of Sacrifice is over, the pilgrims are asked to stay for at least two days. Although there is very little in the way of ritual left, these days are of great importance for they allow the deep spiritual experiences of the last few days to settle and be consolidated within the soul. The atmosphere of devotion and enlightenment is ideal for warm, open communion between the many many people who have never met before but have shared the greatest experience of their lives.

201: HADITH
MUSLIM: Book of Pilgrimage *(Kitab Al-Hajj)* 2976

Jabir reported: 'I saw Allah's Apostle ﷺ *flinging pebbles while riding his camel on the tenth day and he was saying: "learn your rituals (by observing me) for I do not know whether I will be performing Hajj after this Hajj of mine."'*

On the last day of *Hajj*, the tenth day, and the three days following, pilgrims are required to throw seven stones at specified places in the name of Allah. The casting of stones is a metaphorical casting out of evil. It teaches through ritual action that a person must keep the Evil One at bay – at least a stone's throw away.

8   The Creation and Destiny

202: *QAF* 50:38

> *We created the heavens and the earth and all between them in six days, nor did any sense of weariness touch Us.*

All Creation was made by the Will of Allah. To those who say 'Six days?' the Qur'an answers that a day is as long as Allah makes it. In Surah 70:4: 'Angels and Gabriel ascend to Him in a day which is equal to 50,000 years.' Unlike the texts of the Torah or Genesis, the Qur'an makes no reference to a seventh day of rest. How can the Infinite need rest? He is inexhaustible in His Creation and His Wisdom.

203: REVELATIONS WELL EXPOUNDED (*FUSSILAT*) 41:9–10

> *Say: 'Would you deny Him who created the earth in two days? And do you set up equals with Him? He is Lord of all the worlds.'*
>
> *He set on the earth, firmly rooted mountains rising above it, and blessed the earth and provided sustenance for all, according to their needs, in four days.*

In the first two days Allah laid out the earth and within the first four had filled the earth with all that is necessary for life. This coherence of design is clear proof of a single God and Creator. But, like the people of Makkah at the time of the Prophet ﷺ, many people today see but do not understand, are told but do not believe. There is hunger, environmental destruction and civil strife because humanity has broken the laws of Allah, not because it is His Will. Allah has provided enough for the honest needs of all His Creation. Thus Muslims are forbidden to hoard beyond their genuine needs. To do so is to abuse Allah's Creation.

204: REVELATIONS WELL EXPOUNDED (*FUSSILAT*) 41:11–12

Furthermore He included in His design, the sky. And it had been smoke, and he said to it and to the earth: 'Come together willingly or unwillingly.' They said 'We come together willingly.'

So He completed them as seven firmaments in two days and He assigned to each heaven its duty and command. And We adorned the lower heaven with lights and provided it with a guard of Angels. Such is the decree of the Mighty and Wise Allah.

Allah commanded that the sky and the earth come together whether they wished to or not and, in obedience to His Will, these elements of His Creation did so without question. This is the way of nature. The natural laws which we observe all around us, from a bee collecting pollen to the movement of the heavenly bodies, are the decrees of Allah. To act according to natural laws is to do the Will of Allah, for He alone is the creator of these laws. Unlike nature, humanity and the *jinn* (spirits) have the choice to obey or break these laws. To disobey is to fall below obedient nature. To obey by choice is to be raised above the rest of nature.

Here on earth we can only see the heaven immediately above us. The lights which adorn this lower heaven are, of course, the stars, sun and moon. In addition, there are the Angels, made of light. They are part of Allah's purpose for the lower heaven, which is to light and guide the earth and its inhabitants. It is not only physical guidance that is given but also spiritual as is explained in Surah 67:5: 'And We have adorned the lowest heaven with Lamps, and We have made such lamps as missiles to drive away the Evil Ones, and have prepared for the penalty of the blazing fire.'

205: LIGHT (NUR) 24:45–46

*And Allah has created every animal from water: some that creep
on their bellies, some that walk on two legs, some that walk on
four. Allah creates what He Wills, for truly Allah has power over
all things.*

*We have indeed sent down Signs that make things manifest. And
Allah guides whom He wills to the way that is straight.*

Allah brought forth all life from the waters of Creation and with
these waters He sustains all life. In the arid lands of the Prophet
☆ , it was deeply appreciated that water was essential to life.
How easily we, who have piped water, forget our dependence on
it even though science now tells us life began in primeval waters,
and that most of our body is constituted of water. The Holy
Qur'an tells of these things and, more importantly, tells us that
all existence is due to Allah's Will. Everything in Creation is a
Sign of Him for those who wish to know. It is only by sincerely
wishing to know Him that we will be guided, for whoever turns
to Allah, Allah turns to him.

THE CATTLE (AN'AM) 6:37–39

*They say: 'Why isn't a Sign sent down to him from his Lord?'
Say: 'God certainly has the Power to send down a Sign but most of
them do not understand.'*

*There is not an animal that lives on the earth, nor a being that flies
on its wings, but forms part of communities like you. Nothing have
We omitted from the Book, and they all shall be gathered to their
Lord in the end.*

The disbelievers challenged the Prophet's words of God by
claiming that if he really was a divine messenger, then His Lord
would send Angels or some other miracle to protect Muhammad
against their stones and as a Sign to convince mankind.
    In these verses God tells the Prophet to reply to the
unbelievers that his Lord has the Power to send down Signs, and

does so according to His Will, not the will of mankind. We are surrounded by these Signs. For instance, every creature on earth lives with its own species as part of God's Design. But we have the choice as to whether we see these Signs or not. That is our test on earth – to use our power of reason correctly and to control the lusts of our body which delude us into seeing the earth merely as a place of sensual pleasures. If the Signs of the Unseen were so naked as to offer no alternative except believing, there would be no test and so God's Purpose would be defeated.

The testing period continues as long as the Unseen remains veiled. When the Unseen becomes self-evident, the test will be finished and it will be the time of the results, the Judgement Day. All creatures will be held to account on the Final Day, for even the actions of the tiniest creature are recorded by God in His Book. Since animals are not capable of disobeying the Laws of God, they will without exception be gathered to Him. On the other hand, mankind have had the choice and may enjoy the greatest rewards or the greatest punishments.

207: THE COW *(BAQARA)* 2:30–33

Behold, your Lord said to the Angels: 'I will create a viceregent on earth.' They said: 'Will You place there one who will make mischief there and shed blood, while we celebrate Your praises and glorify Your Holy Name?' He said: 'I know what you do not know.'

And He taught Adam the nature of all things: then he placed them before the Angels and said: 'Tell Me the nature of these if you are right.'

They said: 'Glory to You of Knowledge. We have none, except what You have taught us: in truth it is You who are perfect in Knowledge and Wisdom.'

He said: 'Adam, tell them their natures.' When he had told them Allah said: 'Did I not tell you that I know the secrets of the heavens and earth and I know what you reveal and what you conceal?'

Human beings' role on Earth as Allah's viceregents, His *Khalifahs*, is to be a cornerstone of Islam. We have been put in charge of the earth to implement Allah's Law. In our every action and use of the world's resources we must follow our Sovereign Lord's instructions. It is treason to assume sovereign power ourselves or to obey someone other than our Lord. This is what the Angels feared and we can see for ourselves how right they were to do so. Yet Allah knew from the time of Creation that, through the words of the Prophets and through the Qur'an, humanity will come at last to know its true role as His viceregents on earth. In His infinite wisdom, Allah rejected the Angels' fears. In this we take heart for we know that Divine Justice and Good will finally be done.

One sign of humanity's special role as viceregents is that Adam was taught the true nature of all things. This knowledge is not known even to the Angels. Although the Angels are given their own particular areas of knowledge such as the clouds, water, air, and so on, they do not have the depth of knowledge given to humanity by Allah.

208: *SAD* 38:71–76

Behold, the Lord said to the Angels: 'I am about to create man from clay.

'When I have perfected him and breathed My Spirit into him, Fall down in obedience to him.'

So the Angels prostrated themselves, all together. Not so Satan (Iblis). He refused to be among those who bowed down.

Allah said: 'Satan, what is your reason for not bowing down to the one whom I have made with My hands? Are you too proud or do you think you are high and mighty?'

Satan said: 'I am better than he. You created me from fire and You created him from clay.'

Allah's Spirit blows life into man making us worthy viceregents, but we must not confuse this with having any part of godhead ourselves. The Angels bow down to Adam both because of the Spirit of Allah that has touched him, and because of his role as viceregent. As viceregents we have the power of choice, whereas the Angels, like nature, have no choice but to obey instinctively the Will of Allah. On the other hand, our obedience to Allah is the result of self-discipline and continual efforts to seek knowledge and improve our moral quality. Thus, if we succeed we have reached the highest achievement of any in Allah's Creation.

There are only two Creations which are able to choose to obey or disobey Allah. The first is the *jinn*, the spirits made from fire, who usually choose disobedience and evil. The second is humanity, made from wet fermenting clay. As the final creation, humanity is ultimately superior to the *jinn*. Satan was made from fire, so he is a *jinn* and could therefore choose not to bow down as commanded by Allah. But of course he will reap the punishment. The main name of Satan in the Qur'an is Iblis, meaning 'one who has nothing to expect from the Mercy of Allah'. Another title is Al-Aduw, meaning 'enemy of Allah'.

209: ROCKY TRACT *(AL-HIJR)* 15:34–43

Allah said: 'Be gone, for you are rejected and accursed until the Day of Judgement.'

Satan said: 'Lord, give me reprieve until the Day the dead are raised.'

Allah said: 'Reprieve is granted you until the Appointed Day.'

Satan said: 'Then because You have put me in the wrong, I will make wrongdoing attractive to those on earth, and I will put them all in the wrong – except those who are Your sincere servants, purified by Your Grace.'

Allah said: 'This way of My sincere servants is indeed a way that leads straight to Me. For you shall have no authority over My servants except those who put themselves in the wrong and follow you. And truly Hell is the promised abode for them all.'

This is the central message of Islam – salvation through obedience to Allah. The story of Satan's disobedience and threatened revenge is told many times in the Qur'an as a warning to us. We are ultimately reponsible for our own downfall. Satan (Iblis) cannot tempt us if we are sincere in our Faith. One of the teachings of Islam is that temptation is always there, and indeed is part of His Creation, to test our fortitude and our Faith. Disbelievers are already ensnared by Satan and even believers face Satan's daily attempts to trap them. But Satan cannot tempt beyond the limits permitted by his Creator, as he himself admits in the above verses. We have the freedom to seek Allah's Guidance and Protection from Satan, which Allah in His great Mercy will give to those who truly submit to His Will.

210: THE WOMEN (*NISAA*) 4:1

Mankind, revere your Guardian-Lord Who created you from a single person; created, of like nature, your mate, and from these two scattered (like seeds) countless men and women. Revere Allah in Whose Name you plead with one another and revere the wombs that bore you, for Allah is ever watching over you.

The Qur'an tells us that we are all the descendants of Adam and his wife. This verse exhorts us to revere our Lord and then our mother as her lawful right; it is a fitting start to the sura devoted to woman. Of course, women are addressed in all the general teachings of the Qur'an, but much care is taken in both the Revelations and the Traditions over the specific concerns of women. For while Islam has returned to women the equality and rights denied them by other religious and political systems, it also recognizes and reveres their differences from men. Woman is the equal of man, created from the same soul with the same moral nature and with a vital role to play in society. In her role as child-bearer and nurturer, she deserves the greatest reverence from men.

211: MYSTIC LETTERS TH *(TA HA)* 20:115–121

We had already, beforehand, taken the covenant of Adam, But he forgot: and We found on his part no firm resolve.

When we said to the Angels: 'Prostrate yourselves to Adam', they prostrated themselves, but not Iblis: he refused. Then We said: 'O Adam, truly, this is an enemy to you and your wife, so do not let him get you both out of the Garden so that you are landed in misery. There is within enough for you not to go hungry, nor to go naked, nor to suffer from thirst, nor from the sun's heat.'

But Satan whispered Evil to him. He said: 'Adam, shall I lead you to the Tree of Eternity and to a kingdom that never decays?'

As a result, they both ate from the tree and so their nakedness appeared to them. They began to sew together leaves from the garden as covering for themselves. In this way, Adam disobeyed his Lord and allowed himself to be seduced.

It was man's weakness of resolve, forgetfulness and his innate and unnecessary fear of death that allowed Satan to tempt him to break the first covenant of obedience. These are still the failings that each one of us must guard against. It is worth noting here that the Qur'an does not blame woman as she is blamed in the Jewish and Christian traditions for the first gesture of disobedience to Allah. Each individual is reponsible for his or her own failure to repel Satan.

The Garden is a primal image of bliss etched in the collective memory of humanity. It is beyond time and space and full of Allah's bounties, engulfed in Holy Light and Eternal Peace. It was the first abode and it will be the last for those who follow the Will of God. It is the paradise – free from hunger, thirst, nakedness and the scorching sun – which man was given and lost, but to which we may return.

The imagery of the Garden pervades not only the Qur'an, but Islamic art, poetry and architecture, for in fact we are all now gardeners on this Earth. As the Prophet 🌺 said, it is 'the sprouting bed for the Hereafter'. The Garden, literal and metaphorical, is an original memory inspiring us to be worthy of it again.

212: MYSTIC LETTERS TH *(TA HA)* 20:122–123

But his Lord chose him (for his grace). He turned to him and gave him guidance. He said: 'Get down both of you – all together from the Garden, with enmity one to another. But if, as is sure, there comes to you Guidance from Me, whoever follows My Guidance will not lose his way, nor fall into misery.'

The original nature of man as Allah's Creation was not tainted by the first act of disobedience. Adam and his wife both sincerely repented, saying: 'Our Lord, we have wronged our own souls. If you do not forgive us and bestow Your Mercy, we will surely be lost' (The Heights *(A'raf)* 7:23). Allah granted His forgiveness as He always does to those who sincerely repent. He did not banish Adam in disgrace and his descendants from the eternal Garden, nor abandon them. Our sojourn on earth is as Allah's viceregents, with prophets and inspired messengers given by His Infinite Mercy to guide us back to the Path of Righteousness. We must face the trials and tribulations of the body as a challenge, but it need not be a life of misery. This Earth with all its blessings is itself a reminder to us of that far more beautiful Paradise where there is no suffering. If Allah's gifts are accepted with gratitude and His guidance sought in all things, if the path of piety and obedience is followed, then we will be protected against the temptations of our enemy. We will return again to the eternal Garden.

213: THE HEIGHTS *(A'RAF)* 7:172–173

Your Lord drew forth from the loins of Adam's children their descendants, and made them testify concerning themselves. He said: 'Am I not your Lord?' They said: 'Yes, we testify that You are.' This He did lest you should say on the Judgement Day: 'We had no knowledge of that' or 'Our forefathers may have taken false gods but we came after them. Will You destroy us, their descendants, because they followed falsehood?'

This verse makes it clear that each one of us is culpable if we do not follow the repentance of Adam. We were all brought forth by

Allah at the time of Creation and promised then to be faithful to Him. So it is not Adam's promise but our own which we break if we are unfaithful. Our first covenant remains as a tiny spark in our memory – it is the conscience that flares when we think or act immorally.

It is also clear from this verse that Time and its laws are creations of Allah's. It is no more difficult for Him to raise up the unborn than it is to raise up the dead.

214: WINNOWING WINDS (*ZARIYAT*) 51:56–58

I have only created jinns and men so that they may serve Me. I do not require sustenance of them, nor do I require that they should feed me. For Allah is He who gives all sustenance – Lord of Power, invincible for ever.

Allah's purpose in creating us and therefore our own purpose in life is to serve Allah alone as the source of instruction, prayer and glory. There is nothing we can give to Allah except our obedience. If we do not, it is only ourselves whom we harm, for He is Creator of all and needs nothing to sustain Him. It is both arrogant and ignorant to make offerings to Allah – as was done by the people of Makkah at time of the Prophet 鐵. It is not for humanity to offer Allah portions of His own Creation. The gods of those who even today perform offerings are proven to be false, both because they share power with associate gods and because they rely on mankind for food. Such gods need an omnipotent God for they are not masters of the universe, but an omnipotent Allah has no need of them. Their existence is a logical absurdity.

215: THUNDER (*RA'D*) 13:15

All life in the skies and on earth worship Allah, either willingly or in spite of themselves. So too do their shadows bow to Him in the mornings and evenings.

The purpose of Allah's Creation is to worship Him and do His Will. There is no escaping this purpose; to follow the Right Path is to worship Allah as He wills. None can defy these Laws, not even humanity and the *jinn* who have been granted their own will. Neither the believer nor the unbeliever can obstruct Allah's Will. The difference is that while the believer submits with a willing heart, the disbeliever is unwilling in his heart and deludes himself that he can make his own laws, not seeing that his fate will be against his wishes.

216: THE ROMANS (*RUM*) 30:22

And among His Signs is the creation of the heavens and the earth and the variations in your languages and your colours; truly in that are Signs for those who know.

The great variety in race and culture at different times and places on the earth are the Blessings of God, as are all the wonderful variations in nature which enrich our lives and remind us of the great Beneficence and Wisdom of the Creator. Not only does Islam proclaim all humans as equal before Allah, but it rejoices in our differences – between individual and individual, man and woman, race and race. Racial prejudice is a crime against humanity and a sin against Allah's creation. It also throws away the great benefits which can be gained from the sharing, complementary relationships that can be established between different peoples.

217: THE CAVE (*KHAF*) 18:7–8

That which is on Earth We have made as a glittering show in order to test them as to who is best in conduct.

Truly, We shall make what is on Earth dust and dry soil.

The Creation, with all its possibilities, is set before us as both a gift and a test. We have the choice of obedience or disobedience to Allah. Having failed the test in the Garden, Mankind has been granted a second chance on Earth. If we remember from Whom the gifts of this life come, and obey Him, then we can be at peace, knowing that the gifts in the Hereafter will be even greater. If we forget from Whom everything comes and turn towards temptation and pride, then we have failed the test. Our punishment will be inescapable, for this Earth is not eternal. When the test is completed, Allah will end this Universe and all will be called to account on the Judgement Day.

218: THE BELIEVER (*MU-MIN*) 40:67

It is He Who has created you from dust, then from a sperm-drop, then from a leech-like clot. Then He brings you out into the light as a child, then lets you grow to your age of full strength, then lets you grew old – though of you there are some who die before – and lets you reach a term appointed so that you may learn wisdom.

All Creation in the beginning and ever since is the work of Allah. Nothing is created by chance or accident. Allah's Will and Purpose lie behind everything. Every moment of our lives is lived by the Grace of Allah. His design and knowledge are complete and absolute so that even our lifespan has been predetermined. By giving us the freedom to obey or disobey Him, Allah has made us responsible for our own destiny in the Hereafter.

219: HADITH
MUSLIM, Book of Destiny (*Katab ul-Qadr*) 6392

Allah's Messenger 🕊 *said: 'When the drop of (semen) remains in the womb for forty days, the Angel comes and says: "My Lord, will he be good or evil?" And both these things are written down. Then the Angel says: "My Lord will he be male or female?" And both these things would be written. And his deeds and actions, his death, his livelihood; these are also recorded. Then his document of destiny is rolled and there is no addition to and subtraction from it.'*

Destiny does not mean that Allah forces us to do what he has decreed in His Knowledge and Power. It means that He sees all of Time and Space as one picture, so He knows what lies 'ahead' in our terms. Because we operate within the confines of Time we cannot know our future choices as He knows them. Allah's knowledge of His Creation is like a light in a dark room – it is there but it does not interfere with the arrangement of the furniture. It is enlightening if we choose to walk in with our eyes open, but if we close them to block out the light, Allah will not rearrange the furniture to prevent us hurting ourselves.

220: JONAH *(YUNUS)* 10:100

No soul can believe except by the Will of Allah and He will place doubt on those who will not understand.

There is nothing that is not Allah's Will, so even those who do not believe and condemn their souls to hell-fire act in accordance with His Will. Allah has given us the rationality and will to have faith, but if there is insincerity in our soul, He can blind us from the Straight Path. Those who demand proof but make no efforts in their thoughts or deeds will not be given a glimpse of the Hidden.

221: THE CATTLE *(AN-AM)* 6:37–39

They say: 'Why isn't a Sign sent down to him from his Lord?' Say: 'Allah certainly has the Power to send down a Sign but most of them do not understand.'

Those who reject Our Signs are deaf and dumb in the midst of profound darkness. Those whom Allah Wills He leaves to wander and those whom He Wills He places on the Straight Way.

The disbelievers challenged the words of the Prophet's words about Allah, claiming that if he really was a Chosen Messenger, then His Lord would send Angels or some other miracle to protect Muhammad 🕌 against their stones and as a Sign to convince mankind.

In these verses Allah tells the Prophet 🕌 to reply to the

disbelievers that his Lord has the Power to send down Signs, and does so according to His Will, not the will of mankind. We are surrounded by these Signs. But we have the choice whether we see these Signs or not. If the Signs of the Unseen were so naked as to offer no alternative except believing, there would be no test and so Allah's Purpose would be defeated. The testing period continues as long as the Unseen remains veiled. When the Unseen becomes self-evident, the test will be finished and it will be the time of the results, the Judgement Day.

222: THE NARRATION (*QASAS*) 28:56

It is true that you will not be able to guide everyone whom you love, but Allah guides those whom He will and He knows best those who receive guidance.

The immediate circumstances of this verse was the death of Abu Talib, a much beloved uncle of the Prophet, whom the Quraish had persuaded not to abandon the pagan beliefs of his forefathers. Thus the grief of the Prophet 🌸 was twofold – for the loss of his uncle in this life, and more importantly for the loss of his Soul. But Allah tells us we must accept that guidance ultimately lies with Him – all we can do is communicate His Message and then leave it to Him, for only He knows truly what goes on in a person's soul, who will be guided and in what way. Our time on earth is a test and that means there will be those who fail.

223: THE CONFEDERATES (*AHZAB*) 33:35

For Muslim men and women – for believing men and women, for devout men and women, for true men and women, for men and women who are patient and constant, for men and women who humble themselves, for men and women who pay zakat, for men and women who fast, for men and women who guard their chastity, and for men and women who engage greatly in Allah's praise – for them has Allah prepared forgiveness and great reward.

Women bear the same responsibilities as men, are as accountable for their deeds and are subject to the same rewards and punishment from Allah.

224: THE COW *(BAQARA)* 2:126

And remember Abraham said: 'My Lord, make the city of peace and feed its people with fruits – those who believe in Allah and the Last Day.'

He said: '(Yes) and such as reject faith – for a while I will grant them their pleasure, but will soon drive them to the torment of Fire – an evil destination (indeed)'.

In his prayer to Allah for the city of Makkah Abraham pointedly excludes from its benefits the disbelievers because Allah had warned him that only those of his descendants who were *Muslims* would be eligible as *imam* (leaders). However, God corrects Abraham's misunderstanding that because leadership will be given to believers only, so will the necessities of life. These will go to both the just and unjust for it is on the Day of Judgement that we will receive our rewards or punishments.

225: CONSULTATION *(SHURA)* 42:27

And he listens to those who believe and act righteously, and gives them more of His bounty, but for the unbelievers there is a terrible penalty.

If Allah were to enlarge the provision for His servants they would indeed transgress, beyond all bounds through the earth; but He sends it down in due measure as He deems best. For He is well acquainted and watchful with His servants.

Allah rewards believers in this life and in Paradise. He will always turn to us when we ask Him, but He knows best what we need. It may seem to us that we have acted righteously and deserve to have our prayers answered when, and as, we ask, or that disbelievers are benefiting from His bounty unfairly. But we have neither the wisdom nor the goodness to make such assessments. Allah does not seek to harm us, but He may test us as he tests the disbelievers. And it may be that our desires will harm another although we do not realize it. Only He knows how to balance the different needs of all Creation and how to guide us.

226: THE FAMILY OF IMRAN (AL-I-IMRAN) 3:128–129

Not for you (but for Allah) is the decision whether He turn in mercy to them or punish them; for they are indeed wrongdoers.

Allah owns all that is in the Heavens and on Earth. He forgives whom He pleases and punishes whom he pleases, but Allah is Oft-forgiving and Merciful.

These verses delivered after the Battle of Uhud against the pagan Makkans remind us that the Muslim defeat there is as much a Sign from Allah as was the victory at the earlier Battle of Badr. It is an important lesson to us that we must never presume Allah's help will automatically come to us because we think ourselves better than our enemies. Allah's Mercy will come only if we are faithful and righteous in all we do, but if we fail, as happened at Uhud, when greed overtook some of the Muslim soldiers, then we cannot control Allah's punishment nor how He chooses to bring our enemies to repentence. Nor should we see such incidents as Allah's ultimate rejection of us, for in His mercy he allows us the opportunity to be guided even after we have transgressed, provided we sincerely repent.

227: THE FAMILY OF IMRAN (AL-I-IMRAN) 3:145

Nor can a Soul die except by Allah's leave, the term being fixed as by writing. If any do desire a reward in this life, We shall give it to him; and if any do desire a reward in the Hereafter, We shall give it to him. And We will swiftly reward those that (serve us with) gratitude.

Fleeing from death whether in battle or in peacetime is of no avail, for each of us has a preordained time to live which can neither be cut short nor increased by so much as a second. The point therefore is not how to survive for as long as possible but how to live life in the best possible way. Do we wish to benefit from worldly riches of our short stay on earth or do we wish to benefit from the eternal riches of the Hereafter? Those who put their all into achieving wealth in this life will surely succeed in this, while those who spend their time and money for the good of others and the cause of Allah are the ones who sincerely desire to be rewarded in the next life – and Allah will reward them justly.

228: THE FAMILY OF IMRAN
(AL-I-IMRAN) 3:146–147

How many of the Prophets fought in Allah's Way and with them fought large bands of godly men? But they never lost heart if they met with disaster in Allah's Way, nor did they weaken (in will) nor give in. And Allah loves those who are firm and steadfast.

All that they said was: 'Our Lord, forgive us our sins and anything we may have done that transgressed our duty. Establish our feet firmly and help us against those that resist Faith.'

These verses were a timely warning for the followers of Muhammad ﷺ because after their defeat at Uhud the hypocrites and the Jews began to chip away at their faith, asking how they could possibly have suffered a defeat if Muhammad ﷺ really was the Prophet of Allah. But Allah's Knowledge is Absolute. It is to be expected that our limited perception cannot understand His grand Design. We should remember that the prophets stood firm even when they faced great hardship and apparent setbacks which later proved to be examples of Allah's Wisdom. Certainly the defeat at Uhud reaped long-term benefits – the Muslims learnt that their greed could jeopardize their own lives, their souls and the Mission. Although they had failed, their Faith was in the end strengthened by their repentence and they were able to renew the Mission with greater resolve. Such is the Wisdom of Allah.

Uhud should be a lesson to us when we are buffeted by great changes and setbacks in our lives and feel we have lost sight of Allah. We must remember that He never loses sight of us and it is only our blind clinging to the temporal rather than the eternal which weakens us.

229: HADITH
MUSLIM (*An-Nawawi's Forty Hadith* 27)

> *Consult your heart. Righteousness is that about which the soul feels tranquil and the heart feels tranquil, and wrongdoing is that which wavers in the soul and moves to and fro in the breast even though people have vindicated it again and again.*

Right and wrong are not social dictates to be redefined with every new cultural development. They are absolute and unchanging because they are determined by the Will of Allah. This is the knowledge Allah has given humanity which raises us above all other creatures. Even when an entire society has strayed from the Path, and new generations are only taught false values and ways, they are still accountable for any evil practices because they have been given the innate ability to differentiate right from wrong.

The root of the word 'Islam', *slm*, embraces the concepts of submission, purity and peace. When we obey Allah and behave righteously, when our thoughts and deeds are pure, then we experience peace and tranquillity.

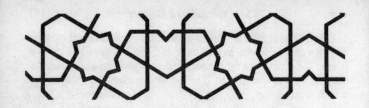

9   Knowledge and Purification

230: THE COW *(BAQARA)* 2:269

*He grants wisdom to whom He pleases and whosoever is granted
wisdom is rich indeed. But none will grasp the Message except men
of understanding.*

All knowledge belongs to Allah. Everything we learn, from the
first recognition of our own self as an individual to the
recognition of Allah, is granted by Him. Knowledge comes to us
when and how Allah wills. It may be a sudden flash of realization
(see 74) or it may be knowledge that we take for granted, such as
our own language. Yet the startling rapidity with which a child
grasps and masters its first language – an ability which it will
never have again to the same extent in its life – is an example of
how Allah can bestow knowledge on any mind no matter how
underdeveloped or untrained it is. Just as every child is born in
Islam (see 18) and therefore open to Allah's gifts of social and
moral knowledge, every adult can become open to His gifts of
deeper spiritual knowledge by continuing to follow Islam's
teaching or returning to them if he or she has strayed.

231: MYSTIC LETTERS TH *(TA HA)* 20:114

*High above all is Allah, the King, the Truth. Do not be in a rush
with the Qur'an before its revelation to you is complete, but say:
'O my Lord, advance me in Knowledge'.*

Just as the unfolding of the Qur'an to the Apostle 鬯 and his
people was a gradual process, so it is for any individual who

approaches it. True knowledge can never be grasped all at once by anyone other than Allah. So we must be patient, allowing the meaning and purpose of the Qur'an to unveil itself according to our own capacity and Allah's Will. We must be humble in the realization that our knowledge can never be complete; there is no end to what we can learn from it, the complete Revelation and final Revelation of Allah.

232: THE CLOT (*'ALAQ*) 96:1-5

Read in the name of your Lord and Cherisher

Who created man from a clot of blood.

Read and your Lord is most Bountiful

Who taught to write with the pen,

Taught man what he did not know.

All knowledge comes from Allah, it is one of his bounties, one of the ways in which he cherishes us. Knowledge is an instrument of Faith. It feeds our intellectual capabilities so that our ability to acquire knowledge grows and with increasing knowledge comes a deeper understanding of the True Faith.

This is the first sura of the Holy Qur'an to be revealed to the Prophet ﷺ. It was delivered in his fortieth year after he had lived and prayed for some years in the cave of Hiraa, near Makkah. The Angel Gabriel spoke the word *iqraa* (read or recite) three times before going on to reveal to Muhammad ﷺ his mission – to read out the Eternal Book; its readership – mankind; its Author – the Creator and Cherisher of Man; the instrument of the mission – the pen as the servant and symbol of Knowledge.

233: THE WOMAN WHO PLEADS (*MUJADALA*) 58:11

Allah will raise to high rank those of you who believe and are granted knowledge.

HADITH
BUKHARI: Book of Knowledge (*Kitab Al-'Ilm*) 10

The Prophet ﷺ said: 'Whomsoever Allah intends to do good, He gives right understanding of religion . . . knowledge is maintained only through teaching.'

Leadership in Islam is based on knowledge – knowledge that comes from spiritual insight and is grounded in the Qur'an. All people are equal citizens in the kingdom of Allah with the same basic rights and duties, but with knowledge and the consequent strengthening of faith come the extra responsibilities of leadership. It is the duty of those who have been granted knowledge to spread it as widely as they can through teaching and the example they set as leaders in the community.

234: HADITH
MUSLIM: Book of Prayer (*Kitab Al-Zakat*)

Abu Mas'ud said: 'The Messenger of Allah ﷺ said: "The man who knows most the Book of Allah shall act as Imam of a people; and if there are people equal in their knowledge of the Qur'an, then he who has greater knowledge of the Sunnah (Hadith), then he who is first in hijrah (immigration from impious society); and if they are equal in hijrah, then he who is older in years . . ."'

HADITH
BUKHARI 10:54

'Ibn. 'Umar said when the first emigrants came to 'Usbah, a place in Quba, before the coming of the Messenger of Allah ﷺ, the slave of Abu Hudhaifah used to act as their Imam and he had the greatest knowledge of the Qur'an.

Knowledge is such an important attribute for a leader that it even takes precedence over the virtue shown by emigration to escape religious oppression – or, by analogy, any act of sacrifice performed in the Cause of Allah. Seniority bears on the choice only if knowledge and virtue are equal between two men. Class or race have no bearing at all, as can be seen by the selection as *Imam* of a slave whose class indicates he would also have belonged to a racial minority.

235: HADITH
IBN.-I-MAJAH 224

> *The Messenger of Allah* 🕮 *said: 'The seeking of knowledge is obligatory upon every Muslim.'*

HADITH
TIRMITHI 39:19

> *The Messenger of Allah* 🕮 *said: 'The word of wisdom is the lost property of the believer, so wherever he finds it he has a better right to it.'*

These hadith lay down the principle of mass education for all – women and men, children and adults. It is a right and a duty for us to seek knowledge and it is therefore incumbent on an Islamic state to provide free education for all. Satan's strength lies in our ignorance, so it is with education that we can protect ourselves and our children. The arts and sciences can teach us much. The more we know about His Creation the more we know about Him, but they bring us to a Truth we already know even if we have forgotten. Knowledge of Our Creator and His Laws is in our soul from birth.

236: HADITH
BUKHARI: Book of Knowledge (Kitab Al-'Ilm) 35

> *Abu Sa'id Khudri said to the Prophet* 🕮 : *'The men have got an advantage over us in approaching you, therefore appoint for us a*

day with you.' So he promised them a day on which he met them and he exhorted them and gave them commandments.

In this tradition the Prophet ﷺ endorses women's equal right to knowledge at the same time as recognizing that the differences between the sexes may require that special arrangements be made to ensure this right is upheld. The dominant nature of men allows them to benefit, at the expense of the women, in a learning environment. The solution adopted by the Prophet ﷺ was to provide segregated tuition. Although mixed education is not unlawful, Islamic society favours segregated education in the interests of fairness.

237: HADITH
MUSLIM: Book of Purification (*Kitab Al-Taharah*)

The Messenger of Allah ﷺ said: 'When a bondsman – a Muslim or a believer – washes his face, every sin he contemplated with his eyes will be washed away from his face along with the water, or with the last drop of water; when he washes his hands, every sin they wrought will be effaced from his hands with the water, or with the last drop of water; and when he washes his feet, every sin towards which his feet have walked will be washed away with the water, or with the last drop, with the result that he comes out pure from all sins.'

The true Muslim must be pure in body and soul. The power of the Islamic way of life is in its understanding of the inextricable link between body and soul, worldly experience and spiritual experience, life in this world and life in the Hereafter. The nature of the one inspires and reflects the nature of the other. They are as practice is to Faith. Thus by purifying our body we inspire and reflect our soul's purification.

238: REPENTANCE OR IMMUNITY
(*TAUBA OR BARAAT*) 9:108

There is a mosque whose foundation was laid from the first day on piety; it is more worthy for you to stand there. In it are men who love to be purified and Allah loves those who make themselves pure.

In Islam, piety is synonymous with purity. Therefore when we endeavour to be pious we must purify ourselves. Allah wishes us to be pure in body and soul. The very act of turning to Him is an act of purification, for His love cleanses us of sinful deeds. We turn away from the spiritually polluting effects of Evil. When a person prepares himself for prayer he indicates to Allah his desire to be pure in Faith by ritually washing (see 149) his body. This is also a sign of reverence. To appear before anyone in a dirty state is disrespectful and inconsiderate. How much greater an offence it is to appear so before the One who is Pure and Perfect.

The particular circumstance of this verse was an attempted subversion of Islam by its enemies in Madinah. When the Prophet ﷺ first came to the city he founded a mosque, which is the one referred to here. Some hypocrites of Madinah, in league with those who had fought the Muslims at Uhud (see 226), constructed a rival mosque espousing the cause of Islam but in truth intending to create division amongst the Muslim community. Allah made it clear that there was neither piety nor purity at such an ill-founded mosque.

10   The Hypocrites

239: THE WOMEN *(NISAA)* 4:137–138

*Those who believe, then reject Faith, then believe, and reject
Faith, and go on increasing in disbelief – God will not forgive
them, nor guide them on the Way.*

*To the hypocrites, the tidings are that there is a grievous penalty
awaiting them.*

The temptations to hypocrisy are great whenever there are
conflicting beliefs and power. For many Muslims, it is a fact of
life that they live in a society in which power and prestige are in
the grip of non-Muslims. Occasions arise when immediate
material benefits might be gained by underplaying their Faith.
But the Muslim who capitulates to such temptation ceases to be a
good Muslim.

The evils of hypocrisy were never more apparent than in the
early years after the Muslims had migrated from Makkah to
Madinah when this sura was delivered. As the strength of Islam
grew in the community, so did the virulence of those who
opposed it, escalating the tension to war. It was in this context
that hypocrisy burgeoned, as the disbelievers swung back and
forth between the two camps according to which side looked
likely to triumph. Lacking Faith, they were blind to the Signs of
Allah's Invincible Power and relied on the illusory evidence of
military force, rank, wealth and rumour. They did not realize
that, whatever the outcome of the military struggle, they were
lost, for Allah's Mercy does not extend to those who repent when
it is expedient to do so.

240: THE WOMEN *(NISAA)* 4:139-140

Indeed, to those who take disbelievers for friends, rather than believers: is it honour they seek among them? No – all honour is with Allah.

Already he has sent you Word in the Book that when you hear others defying or ridiculing the Signs of Allah, you are not to remain with them unless they turn to a different theme. If you did, you would be like them. For Allah will collect the hypocrites and those who defy Faith – all in Hell.

We do not have to be in as extreme a situation as Muhammad 🕌 and his followers to encounter hypocrisy or to feel ourselves being drawn into it. All too often in our daily lives, we find ourselves in situations where our Faith is not common currency and, in fact, this may result in our being ostracized or even personally attacked. But a true Muslim does not bow to social pressure, for our obedience is to Allah alone. To obey anyone else is to stray from Islam and to condemn our souls to Hell. While a Muslim should always be courteous and considerate to everyone, whether or not they are Muslim, we should protect our own souls by avoiding those who not only do not believe but actively seek to engage us in disbelief.

241: THE COW *(BAQARA)* 2:8-10

Of the people there are some who say: 'We believe in Allah and the Last Day'; but they do not really believe.

They seek to deceive Allah and those who believe, but they only deceive themselves and do not realize it.

In their hearts is a disease and Allah has increased their disease, and grievous is their penalty, because they betray themselves.

Those who pay lip-service to Allah and think they have fooled Him, or indeed, fooled their fellow men, delude themselves. The duplicity of a hypocrite is soon detected and will dishonour them in this life and in the Hereafter. As with all who choose evil, Allah facilitates their progress in that direction. He may allow them some superficial success from their two-faced behaviour which will further convince them of the benefits of their hypocrisy, and so they will sink deeper into their own doom. When they realize their folly it will be too late.

242: THE COW (*BAQARA*) 2:14–18

When they meet those who believe, they say: 'We believe', but when they are alone with their evil ones, they say: 'We are really with you: we were only joking.'

Allah will throw back their mockery on them and give them rope in their traspasses, so they will wander back and forth like the blind.

These are the ones who have traded guidance for error, but their trade is profitless, and they have lost true direction.

The parable for them is of a man who kindles a fire. When it has illuminated all around him, Allah took away their light and left them in utter darkness so they could not see.

Deaf, dumb and blind, they will not return.

Allah will not get in the way of the hypocrites but allow them to be blinded by their own mockery. The parable tells of the disbelievers who were brought the Light by the Prophet Muhammad ﷺ but then turned away. Allah took the Light from them because that was their choice and He will help us to our choice whether it be to the Light or the Darkness. As the Prophet said: 'Actions are but by intention and every man shall have that which he intended' (An-Nawawi).

243: THE COW (*BAQARA*) 2:18–20

Or their likeness is of a rain-laden cloud from the sky. In it are zones of darkness and thunder and lightning. They press their fingers in their ears to keep out the stunning thunderclap, all the while they are in terror of death. But Allah is ever around the rejecters of Faith.

The lightning all but snatches away their sight. Every time the light helps them, they walk within it, and when the darkness grows on them, they stand still. And if Allah willed, He could take away their faculty of hearing and seeing, for Allah has power over all things.

This parable describes the type of hypocrite who is not so much double-faced and calculating as he is weak in Faith. He is easily made doubtful and wants no trouble. Islam comes as life-giving rain to refresh the parched spirit of the world, but with it come trials, tribulations and clashes as the powers of Darkness go onto the attack. This hypocrite tries to block his eyes and ears to the problems and the great flashes of light are almost beyond his comprehension. He fears death as any man does who is not secure in Faith. When the trouble recedes, he uses the Light of Islam to continue his life, but when darkness comes he freezes on the path, neither progressing nor straying from it. If He wanted, Allah could take away all Guidance, but for a time he may allow this weak man a little Light so that he may strengthen his Faith.

244: THE COW *(BAQARA)* 2:204–205

There is the type of man whose speech about this world's life may dazzle you and he calls Allah to witness about what is in his heart, yet he is the most contentious of enemies.

When he turns his back, his aim is to spread mischief through the earth and to destroy crops and cattle. But Allah does not love mischief.

How often we see and hear people, not least our politicians, who declare that they work in the Cause of Allah, that He is on their side, when in fact their every action is for their own ends. These hypocrites attempt to exploit the sincere Faith of others, knowing that the believers' dearest wish is the advancement of

Allah's Cause. Such hypocrites wreak havoc for themselves and society. An evil heart can do no good, no matter how silvery their words.

245: THE WOMEN *(NISAA)* 4:145–46

The hypocrites will be in the lowest depth of the Fire, no helper will you find for them.

Those who repent, mend their ways, hold fast to Allah and purify their religion in Allah's sight, they will be with the believers. And soon Allah will grant the believers a priceless reward.

Hypocrites are amongst the greatest sinners because by their duplicity they dishonour the name of Allah and represent it falsely to others. But Allah is Most Merciful and forgives the worst sinner if he sincerely repents so that his every thought and action is in the Name of Allah. True repentance bears no relation to the here-today-gone-tomorrow 'submission' of the impenitent hypocrite with an eye to the opportunity of the moment.

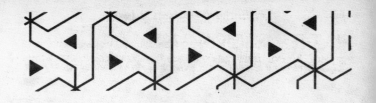

11 Jihad

246: THE BEE (NAHL) 16:125

*Invite all to the Way of your Lord with wisdom and beautiful
preaching and argue with them in ways that are best and most
gracious. For your Lord knows best who have strayed from His
Path and who receive Guidance.*

In this simple but beautiful verse all Muslims are commanded to
pass on the Message of Islam eloquently and in terms that are
most relevant to the listener. With the help of Allah it will touch
the listener's soul in ways we might not even realize at the time.
Such teaching, without threat or dogmatism and with the
example of the gentle, honest life that Muslims lead, has been the
international image of Islam – not the wars we have been forced
to undertake. *Jihad*, a word much bandied about amongst non-
Muslims, means to exert ourselves in repelling what is evil and
establishing what is good, that is – the Cause of God. First and
foremost, our efforts must go to communicating the Message of
Islam. The popular misconception – that *Jihad*, translated as the
'Holy War', is the principle of conversion by force – is the
complete opposite of its true principle besides being patently
absurd. The Peace of Allah is not communicated by war.
Physical violence may bring about a verbal capitulation from its
victim, but can never induce sincere belief, which is the essence
of Islam. It is only in the affairs of men that outward signs of
submission are accepted. In religion, where a man's innermost
secrets are as visible to Allah as his face, expedient capitulation
only counts against him.

247: THE COW *(BAQARA)* 2:256

Let there be no compulsion in religion. Truth stands out clear from error . . .

JONAH *(YUNUS)* 10:99

If it had been your Lord's Will, they would all have believed – all who are on earth. Will you then compel mankind against their will to believe?

The free will Allah has given us is the free will to worship as we please. It is to Allah alone that we must account for our choice. Men and women of Faith must endeavour to persuade the Faithless to submit to Allah, but we do not have Allah's permission to force anyone against his or her will to believe. Indeed, it is a contradiction in terms. If He had willed it, Allah would have created us without free will, but the merit of Faith is that it is arrived at through the individual's efforts and use of the abilities Allah has given to him to see the Truth. Faith imposed by physical fear, social or financial pressure is not Faith but hypocrisy (see 239–245), for which both the false convert and his converter are guilty.

248: THE PILGRIMAGE *(HAJJ)* 22:39–40

To those against whom war is made, permission is given to fight, because they are wronged, and truly Allah is most Powerful for their aid.

They are those who have been expelled from their homes in defiance of right – for no reason except that they say: 'Our Lord is Allah.' If Allah did not check one people against another, there would surely have been monasteries, churches, synagogues and mosques pulled down in which the name of Allah is celebrated frequently. Allah will certainly aid those who aid His cause, for truly Allah is full of Strength, Exalted in Might and Power.

The natural relation between Muslim and non-Muslim is one of mutual understanding and friendship, but when the Cause of Islam is attacked the Muslim is asked to defend his Faith and his home.

The delivery of these verses was the first occasion on which Allah permitted the Prophet Muhammad 🕮 and the Muslim community to take up arms. In the course of the Prophet's preaching at Makkah the believers met first intimidation and then outright persecution from the ruling Quraish tribe. However, they were directed by Allah to continue peacefully and with forbearance while the Prophet 🕮 continued his work.

After the Muslims migrated to Madinah the disbelievers of Makkah continued to persecute them. It was then that permission was given to fight in their own defence. The principle of freedom to worship Allah, and indeed to live, was now at stake. Allah revealed in these verses that, in such circumstances, military action becomes an act in accordance with His Will – as it has been in the past for the People of the Book. Our guardianship of our own species may take the form of war when Allah chooses us to blockade the spread of evil.

249: THE COW *(BAQARA)* 2:251

> *By Allah's Will they routed them and David slew Goliath; and Allah gave him power and wisdom and taught him whatever He willed. And if Allah did not check one people by means of another, the earth would indeed be full of mischief. But Allah is full of bounty to all the worlds.*

There are many lessons in the story of the young Israelite shepherd who felled the fully armoured Philistine giant with his sling-shot. In the context spoken of here, the essential point is that we must fight for the preservation of our Faith, no matter how overwhelming the odds may seem. In fact, if we fight for Allah with courage and unshakable belief it is our foes who face overwhelming odds, for Allah has promised He will aid us (see 2). Allah loves all His Creation, but, to protect the ones who obey Him, He will use them to curb those who would abuse His beneficence and bring chaos to the world.

Furthermore, He will reward those who fight in His Cause.

David was given the power and wisdom to use the simple means available to him to stun Goliath and then wield the giant's own sword against him. Allah's gifts to David of power, learning and wisdom were lifelong. He became a great prophet.

250: THE COW *(BAQARA)* 2:190

Fight in the Cause of Allah those who fight you, but do not transgress limits, for Allah does not love transgressors.

After thirteen years of bearing with fortitude ostracization, torture, eviction from their homes and murder, the believers were commanded to fight those who had fought against them so virulently. This led to the Battle of Badr as the first in a series. But with the injunction came the admonition to behave humanely. The Prophet ﷺ later spelt out the forbidden transgressions, including the killing of women, children, the elderly, the disabled and those in monasteries, and the mutilation of dead bodies (*Kitab Al-Jihad*, Muslim and Bukhari).

251: THE COW *(BAQARA)* 2:193

And kill them wherever you catch them, and turn them out from where they have turned you out. For tumult and oppression are worse than slaughter, but do not fight them at the Sacred Mosque unless they fight you there. But if they fight you, kill them. Such is the reward of those who suppress Faith . . .

And fight them on until there is no more tumult or oppression and justice and faith in Allah prevail. But if they cease, let there be no hostility except to those who practise oppression.

Oppression of anyone, whether Muslim or non-Muslim, for holding views contrary to those prevailing at the time is an offence against Allah, for it is He alone Who is the Judge of our beliefs. Man has not been given licence to rule man in these matters. Although killing between men is a terrible thing, it becomes the only course of action if the alternative is that people should suffer for exercising the right, given by Allah, to practise their own Faith as they will. But as always, warfare is a last resort, when the enemy has allowed no other choice. As soon as they have ceased in their heinous actions, believers should also cease to fight them.

It is understood from the words 'let there be no hostility except to those who practise oppression' that, once the fighting is over, there should be a general amnesty and efforts to establish cordial relations, except in relation to those who were excessively cruel and venomous in their assault on freedom. Forgiveness is a virtue, but it is not mandatory, and in the case of impenitent brutality it becomes necessary to punish. After the Battle of Badr, only two of the prisoners of war were sentenced to death on this basis by the Prophet ﷺ. After the final conquest of Makkah, only four of the worst persecutors of Muslims were executed.

252: THE COW *(BAQARA)* 2:194

> *The prohibited month for the prohibited month, and so for all things prohibited – there is the law of equality. If then any one transgresses the prohibition against you, transgress against them in the same manner. But fear Allah and know that Allah is with those who restrain themselves.*

Allah's Justice is applied on earth as the law of equality. We are not to instigate violence, but if it is perpetrated against us we may respond in kind. These verses were in response to a question that arose due to fighting during the four sacred months of the Islamic year dedicated to pilgrimage. Ever since the days of Abraham, all crimes were forbidden in these months, not simply as crimes against humanity, but as crimes against Allah. It was sancrosanct that the pilgrims should be allowed to come and go from the Ka'ba without fear of robbery or personal harm. The non-Muslims had begun shifting these months around to their convenience so they might attack the Muslims at will. Allah therefore gave the Muslims permission to fight back in these months, as He had also given them permission to fight in the Sacred Mosque if they were set upon there (Surah 2:191; see 251 above). This is always bearing in mind that he who restrains himself or others in their aggression is beloved by Allah.

253: SPOILS OF WAR *(ANFAL)* 8:61

But if the enemy inclines towards peace, then you should also incline towards peace, and trust in Allah, for He is the One that hears and knows all.

Should they intend to deceive you – truly Allah is sufficient to you. It is He who strengthens you with His Aid and with the believers.

The root of the word Islam means, amongst other things, Peace. To incline towards peace is to incline towards Allah. War is at times an unavoidable step to peace. It is the price we pay for free will, for it is the ultimate expression of conflicting wills. But whenever there is a possibility of peace with our enemies we should take it, rather than continue fighting out of fear or suspicion. If, indeed, it is a trick by our enemies, then Allah and the solidarity He has given us amongst ourselves will come to our aid.

254: THE COW *(BAQARA)* 2:195

And spend of your earnings in the Cause of Allah. And do not make your own hands contribute to your destruction, but do good, for Allah loves those who do good.

Jihad includes giving our material wealth in the Cause of Allah. We cannot promote the Cause of the Spirit if we are bound by material priorities. To give financially is to unfetter the spiritual power tied up in material concerns. To cling greedily to our money will not only contribute to the destruction of the Islamic brotherhood, but to our own souls, for we will be called to account on the Final Day (see 90–131).

255: HADITH
IBN. KHUZEIMAH: *Collection of Sound Traditions*
4:881:3074

> *When one of the women asked the Prophet* ﷺ *: 'Are we allowed to
> participate in the fighting, or is there any* Jihad *upon women?' he
> said: 'There is a* Jihad *where there is no fighting or bloodshed.
> That is* al-Haj *(pilgrimage) and* al-Umra *(small pilgrimage).'*

Jihad is a duty of every Muslim, but it may take many forms, for
we are all different in our capabilities and encounter different
circumstances. The Cause of Allah begins with the Five Pillars,
including pilgrimage. In early Islamic history the women also
participated in the battle, bringing water and medical aid to the
wounded.

12 Marriage

256: THE CRITERION *(FURQAN)* 25:54

*It is He Who has created man from water: then He established
lineage and marriage, for your Lord has power over all things.*

Blood ties and marriage are the binders of society, created by
Allah as soon as He had created man as an individual. They are as
fundamental to human life as our main physical ingredient,
water. Our continuing life as a species and our moral and
religious life depend upon the ties of blood and marriage which
between them create the family. These are the bonds strong
enough to build lasting mutual relations of shared responsibility,
care and love. In Islam, to marry and raise a family is to follow
the Prophet's act and to obey Allah's Will.

257: THE BEE *(NAHL)* 16:72

*And Allah has made for you mates of your own nature and,
through them, given you sons and daughters and grandchildren,
and provided the best sustenance for you . . .*

Wives and children are a blessing from Allah. The continuity of
generations, an integral feature of Allah's Creation, is one of the
vital functions of marriage. Therefore, in Islam, celibacy is of no
benefit to society and – given that Allah has created us with
instincts contrary to this – of no benefit to the individual.
Through marriage, the instincts Allah has given us are put to
their lawful use.

Allah has given us wives of our own nature. In other words,

aside from their biological differences, they have a similar share of abilities and failings as men, and the same religious and moral rights. They are given to us not as servants or lesser partners but as companions and equals.

258: THE ROMANS *(RUM)* 30:21

And among His Signs is that He created mates for you from among yourselves, so that you may dwell in tranquillity with them, and He has put love and mercy between your hearts. Truly in that are Signs for those who reflect.

The gift of marriage is also the gift of companionship, and of sharing one's life. There are many benefits from a religious point of view. It trains a person to rule himself, containing sexual desires within the love and stability of a marriage. Responsibility, patience and endurance in the face of difficulties must be learnt, but with these come the rewards of peace and security of family life. Within the family, everyone helps, so the burden does not fall on any particular person.

It is specified that our partners can be found 'among yourselves', that is, among our own community, because marriage in Islamic society is not simply a matter of a personal relationship between two people but of a wider social relationship. Marriage is the cement of a community, bringing entire families together and providing a network of support and love. Naturally, the two who are to marry must be compatible, and this is more likely if they come from similar backgrounds and culture and can make their decision to marry on the basis of being properly informed about each other and each other's family.

259: THUNDER *(R'AD)* 13:38

We sent Apostles before you and appointed wives and children for them . . .

The almost unanimous choice, by the Prophets known to us, to marry and have children indicates that this is what Allah wishes

of us. It is an essential part of Prophethood that those appointed
live a lawful human life. In doing so, they set an example for us to
follow, and are able to understand and relate to the problems of
everyday life.

Jesus was one of the Prophets who did not have his own family.
We revere Jesus as one of Allah's Prophets, chosen for his time
and people. However, he died a young man after a mission of
only three years, which did not attempt to deal with the complex
questions of family, community and state. That task was left for
the last Prophet ﷺ who was to bring the Universal Message.

The fact that there were Prophets such as Abraham and
Zachariah, who were given children as a reward from Allah (see
47), despite their old age and barrenness, is evidence that not
only is family life Allah's Will, it is also a blessing from Him. This
is of course self-evident to those of us who have been so favoured.

260: REPENTANCE *(TAUBA)* 9:71

> *The Believers, men and women, protectors one of another; they
> enjoin what is just and forbid what is evil . . .*

The moral rectitude of a society is the responsibility of both men
and women. Marriage plays a vital role in this, with each partner
caring for the other's spiritual well-being and protection from
evil – that is the nature of love rooted in commitment and
compassion, not romantic fantasies.

261: HADITH
MUSLIM AND BUKHARI (Agreed): Book of Marriage *(Kitab Al-Nikah)*

> *All young people, whoever is able to marry, let him marry, for this
> will keep him chaste and lower his gaze, and wherever it is not
> possible let him fast, for surely fasting is going to reduce the sexual
> drives.*

In Islamic society, we do not believe that natural sexual desires
should be suppressed, but that they should be controlled and

used as Allah intended them within the sanctity of marriage. We do not prescribe a set age for marriage. As soon as a young man feels sexual drives it is best for his family to arrange his marriage.

As a religious duty, marriage should be fulfilled, but as with all religious duties, Allah does not require of us what we are not capable of. If for some physical or financial reason – these days it is often academic studies – a young man is unable to marry when he feels the need, he should fast to lessen his sexual drives.

262: LIGHT *(NUR)* 24:32

Marry those among you who are single, or the virtuous ones among your slaves, male or female. If they are in poverty, Allah will give them means out of His grace, for Allah encompasses all and knows everything.

If these is no suitable partner within our social circle, there is no shame in marrying people of lower social station, exemplified in the time of the Prophet by the slaves. It is virtue, not wealth, which should be the main criterion for choosing a partner. Nor should we despair if we think we are too poor to marry. Allah's beneficence is great towards those who pursue family life. It is better to marry when we feel the need, than to wait until we feel financially well off.

263: HADITH
IBN.-I-MAJAH: Book of Marriage *(Kitab Al-Nikah)* 2518

There are three people Allah has undertaken to help – the person wishing to marry to keep himself away from life's sensuous attitudes, the slave who wishes to buy his freedom and the person who is fighting for the establishment of the Word of Allah.

In the Islamic view, marriage is the fortress of chasity. Through commitment to one partner we can protect ourselves from falling into forbidden sexual practices. This tradition of the Prophet informs us that those who wish to marry will be as blessed by

Allah's beneficence in the same way as two categories of people it is known He greatly favours. All three are working in the Way of Allah. The first seeks freedom from impure sexual desire, the second seeks freedom from unjust social structures which deny the equality of all men in the eyes of Allah, and the third seeks freedom for the souls of all human beings.

We should take note that those seeking family life have priority in Allah's eyes not given to those seeking help in education or careers. Although schooling and work are of course important in life, the warm, strong, sharing relationships of family will bring us closer to Allah than pursuing aspirations in the outside world.

264: THE COW *(BAQARA)* 2:187

> *Permitted to you on the night of the fasts is the approach to your wives, they are your garments and you are their garments...*

Our husbands and wives are like our clothing, they protect us, they are as close to us as anyone can be, they adorn us, they establish our dignity and respectability in the community. This analogy, applied to both partners in a marriage, conveys the equality and mutual benefit of the relationship.

265: HADITH
MUSLIM: Book of Charity *(Kitab Al-Zakat)* 2181

> *Allah's Messenger* 🌸 *said: 'Of the dinar you spend as a contribution in Allah's Path, or to set free a slave, or as a* Sadaqa *given to the needy, or to support your family, the one yielding the greatest reward is that which you spent on your family.*

All human beings are guardians of one another. That is why we speak of the Brotherhood of Islam. But none of us can be responsible for all the world. Allah has given us a social structure best suited to ensuring care for everyone. Our first duty is to our family, then to the local Muslim community, then to the Islamic community at large, and finally to the worldwide population. Care is ensured for the greatest number of people when charity begins at home.

266: THE COW *(BAQARA)* **2:221**

> *Do not marry unbelieving women until they believe. A slave woman who believes is better than a unbelieving women, even though she attracts you. Nor marry your daughters to unbelievers until they believe; and a male slave who believes is better than a believer, even though he attracts you. Unbelievers only beckon you to the Fire. But Allah beckons by His Grace to the Garden (of Paradise) and to forgiveness, and makes His Signs clear to mankind. Celebrate His praise.*

As an act of living in the way of Allah, it is not possible to marry someone whose thoughts and deeds contradict Allah's Will. Sincere belief is the most important criterion to look for when choosing a marriage partner. Even on a practical level, marriage between believers and unbelievers is doomed – such a fundamental difference cannot be the basis for the companionship, sharing and tranquillity which are elements of a happy marriage.

267: THE TABLE SPREAD *(MA'IDA)* **5:5**

> *It is lawful for you to marry not only chaste women who are believers, but also chaste women among the People of the Book revealed before your time – provided that you give them their due dowries and live honourably with them, neither taking them in casual relationships nor as mistresses . . .*

Muslim men are permitted to marry women from among the People of the Book (Jews and Christians), for they also believe in Allah and the Hereafter. Such women are allowed to continue in their own Faith while their husband continues in his. However, it is not permitted for Muslim women to marry Jewish or Christian men until the man has become a Muslim, i.e. declared belief in Allah as the one and only God and in all His Prophets. Muslim women are prohibited from marrying People of the Book for their own protection. Because the husband is responsible for providing for all her needs, she moves into his society and may live with his family. In such circumstances she would be deprived of the constant support of her own faith and vulnerable to pressures which may lead her astray.

Casual relationships out of wedlock are declared unlawful. Such relationships are not founded on commitment and social responsibility. For these reasons Muslim teenagers are not allowed to date or 'go steady' and be drawn into the loose sexual morals that so afflict Western society. They are brought up to honour family life and look forward to marriage sanctioned by Allah, their own family and the community.

268: HADITH
MUSLIM and BUKHARI (Agreed): Book of Marriage (*Kitab Al-Nikah*)

> Allah's Messenger 🌸 said: 'A woman may be married for four reasons: for her property, her status, her beauty and her religion; so try to get one who is religious; may your hand be smeared with dust.'

HADITH
MUSLIM: Book of Marriage (*Kitab Al-Nikah*) 3465

> Allah's Messenger 🌸 said: The whole world is a provision, and the best object of benefit of the world is the pious woman.

Worldly considerations can all too easily take precedence over religious considerations when we make our choices in life, particularly in a decision such as marriage which so directly affects the material conditions of our daily life. But we must never forget that the charms of worldly well-being can quickly be our undoing, both in this world and the next. Without piety, a woman may fall prey to ill-temper and immoral acts that will shame her, her husband and her family. Property without serenity, status without dignity, beauty without morality will afford us no real happiness while we live on this earth, and may well drag us into unlawful ways leading to the Fire.

269: LIGHT (*NUR*) 24:3

> Do not let a man guilty of adultery or fornication marry anyone

other than a similarly guilty woman, or a disbeliever. And do not let anyone other than such a man marry such a woman. To the Believers such a thing is forbidden.

Permissiveness is not acceptable in Islamic society. The stability of the family and the community it helps knit together is based on commitment and responsibility. Men and women who do not control their sexual desires are a danger to their family. Such people only deserve one another outside the Islamic community, amongst those who share their promiscuous values.

270: THE WOMEN (*NISAA*) 4:22–23

And do not marry women whom your fathers married from now on – it was shameful and odious, an abominable custom indeed.

Forbidden to you (for marriage) are: your mothers, daughters, sister; father's sisters, mother's sisters, brother's daughters, sister's daughters; foster-mothers, foster-sisters; your wives' mothers; your step-daughters under your guardianship, born of your wives to whom you have gone in – this does not apply if you have not gone in – previous wives of your sons proceeding from your loins; and two sisters in wedlock at one and the same time – from now on; for Allah is Most Forgiving, Most Merciful.

This list of relatives forbidden to marry one another is more or less agreed by most peoples of the world. Sexual relations between members of the same family is in fact contrary to the nature of man, and can only lead to degeneracy – moral and genetic. Decency between family members is therefore strictly maintained in Islam. The age-old sin of incest, and all its accompanying evils of child-molesting, domestic violence, rape, etc., plague modern society despite the general taboo, and will continue to do so as long as punity, modesty and respect for family members are shrugged off as outdated virtues.

271: THE WOMEN (*NISAA*) 4:19

O Believers, you are forbidden to inherit women against their will . . .

HADITH
MUSLIM: Book of Marriage *(Kitab Al-Nikah)* 3303–3308

> *Allah's Apostle* ﷺ *said: 'A woman who has been previously married has more right to her person than her guardian. And a virgin should also be consulted, and her silence implies her consent.'*

In Islam, marriage is a social contract between two individuals as well as two families. The marriage of a virgin is arranged by her father or male guardian with the father of the chosen son-in-law or, if he is a mature man, the prospective husband himself. This is certainly not a denial of the woman's rights. The father of a family has within his prescribed duties utmost care for the women and children and the management of the financial and external affairs of the household. He is therefore required to arrange the contractual aspects of marriage for his children. But as can be seen from this Qur'anic verse and hadith, it in no way denies a woman's personal freedom. The Prophet ﷺ advocated the rights of women, differentiated from men's only according to the needs arising out of sexual differences. No one must be forced to marry against his or her will, but nor should he or she be abandoned to organize the foundation of his or her adult life with no experience whatsoever in this area. In the case of a woman who has already been married, she has run her own household and has the experience in nuptial matters necessary to choose another husband wisely.

272: HADITH
MUSLIM: Book of Marriage *(Kitab Al-Nikah)* 3286

> *Al-Mughira ibn. Shouba told the Prophet* ﷺ *that he was going to marry. The Prophet* ﷺ *said: 'Go and look at her, for this is sure to make life better between you.'*

It is a general principle of Islamic society that before a couple are married they should see one another with a chaperone. It is very important that both people involved feel happy with the arrangement. It is not acceptable for a man to refuse pointblank for his daughter to be seen by her prospective husband.

273: HADITH
MUSLIM: Book of Marraige *(Kitab Al-Nikah)* 3286

*Allah's Apostle ﷺ said: 'None among you should outbid another
in a transaction, nor should he make proposals of marriage upon
the proposal made by someone else.'*

As in all aspects of life, a Muslim should act so as to maintain
cordial relations and unity within the community. Marriage is
the great harmonizer, the promoter of love and peace, and should
not be started by sowing rivalry and resentment between
members of the community.

274: HADITH
IBN.-I-MAJAH: Book of Marriage *(Kitab Al-Nikah)*

*Announce the marriage and beat the drums. The difference
between what is lawful and what is unlawful is the singing and
beating of the drums.*

Marriage is partly an act of social responsibility. Therefore it
must be publicly announced. In this tradition *(hadith)*, the
announcement takes the form of singing and beating the drum.
The marriage ceremony itself is simple, only requiring the
presence of the prospective wife, her father or guardian, the
prospective husband and two male witnesess. The girl's father
says: 'I give you [girl's name] in marriage' and her intended
husband says: 'I accept.' The woman has to have given her
consent to the marriage. There are a few very exceptional
circumstances when this is not necessary – but otherwise, a
marriage contracted against the woman's will is not binding. The
family may chose to have an *imam* (religious leader) or any good
Muslim to conduct the marriage ceremony.

275: THE WOMEN *(NISAA)* 4:24

*... seek them in marriage with gifts from your property – desiring
purity, not lust. Seeing that you derive benefit from them, give
them their dowry at least as prescribed, but if, after a dowry is*

prescribed, you agree mutually to vary it, you are not at fault, and Allah is All-knowing, All-Wise.

THE WOMEN (*NISAA*) 4:19

Nor should you treat them (your wives) with harshness so that you may take away part of the dowry you have given them – except where they have been guilty of open lewdness . . .

When a man is to take a woman as his wife, he is instructed to give her a dowry. This, like the public announcement (see above), is an important element of marriage. As the woman is committing herself fully to the man, he makes a gesture of commitment on his part and of his ability to provide for her. Through this formal sign of respect, marriage is dignified as an act of contract rather than of lust. The dowry is the wife's, to do with as she will – to invest in business or to spend. This may include spending it on her husband or family, but it is entirely up to her.

No man is to be allowed to drive his wife out of his household through unkind treatment, so that he may repossess the dowry he has given her. The only circumstances for reclaiming the dowry are when she has been promiscuous.

276: THE WOMEN (*NISAA*) 4:19

. . . live with them (your wives) on a footing of kindness and equity. If you take a dislike to them, it may be that you dislike a thing and Allah brings about through it a great deal of good.

HADITH
TIRMITHI, ANA-S-I, AL-HAKIM: Book of Good Manners

Allah's Messenger ﷺ *said: 'The true Muslim in Faith is the one who is perfect in good manners and is good to his family.'*

Marriage is a partnership. It is the first duty of a husband to treat his wife or wives kindly and fairly, providing for them as best he can without favouring any or favouring his own needs. A marriage should be imbued with a sense of justice and sharing, comfort and compassion, love and respect, morality and, above all, love of Allah. This is not always easy, depending on the personalities involved. However, we should not immediately fall into enmity and quarrelling, but accept differences and difficulties as a challenge which may be overcome for the greater good of those concerned.

A Muslim should always remember that good manners and kindness in marriage are religious duties, and that Faith which is not transmitted into good actions rings hollow. True goodness to one's family, of course, means not only physical nurturing but, most importantly, spiritual nurturing. The one who introduces anything unlawful into the house, whether it is dishonestly earned money or irreligious ideas, harms his family.

276: HADITH
IBN.-I-MAJAH: Book of Good Manners 1625

> *The last words to be uttered by the Prophet* ﷺ *to his companions were: 'Remember your prayer. Do not burden your servants more than they can manage, and fear Allah, fear Allah concerning your womenfolk. They are under your care, in your hand. You have taken them as a trust from Allah, and they were made lawful to you in the name of Allah. Good manners with them does not simply mean not to harm and abuse them, but to bear any inconvenience, and to be patient and to follow the example of the Prophet* ﷺ .

Marriage is a responsibility for both men and women, but men have been given the physical strength to be the providers. This does not give them the right to rule women, in fact, as the Prophet ﷺ declares here, all allowances must be made for women and any inconvenience born. Furthermore, this must be done in a manner that is cordial and loving. The great importance of this is underlined by the fact that it is the final instruction the Prophet ﷺ gave to his companions.

278: HADITH
IBN.-I-MAJAH: Book of Good Manners 2697–2698

*His wives used to argue with him, and one might not talk to him for
an entire day, and he bore that. And one day there was an
argument between (his wife) A'isha and the Prophet 鬱, and Abu
Bakh (A'isha's father) intervened. Then the Prophet 鬱 said to
her: 'All right, will you talk, or shall I talk?'*

She said: 'You first, but talk only the truth.'

*Her father slapped her face, saying: 'How dare you say that to
him. He only speaks the truth.'*

The Prophet 鬱 said: 'We did not invite you to do that.'

*And one day A'isha said to him in anger: 'Well, you are the one
who claimed to be a Prophet.' He laughed, and didn't say
anything to her.*

In these traditions are examples for us all as to the best manner of
dealing with marital ill-temper. We see instances of the Prophet's
supreme patience. Not only does he admonish Abu Bakh for
showing impatience with his daughter's rudeness, on behalf of
his son-in-law, but he diffuses A'isha's anger with good humour.

279: HADITH
**MUSLIM and BUKHARI (Agreed): Book of Good
Manners**

The Prophet 鬱 used to say the best people were his wives.

*One day, A'isha saw some Abyssinian dancers in the mosque of the
Prophet. He said: 'Would you like to see?' She said: 'Yes,' and
put her chin on his shoulder, and went on watching until she said
'That's enough.'*

Affection and a sense of fun bring ease to a marriage. The
Prophet enjoyed a warm and often playful relationship with his
wives. Such lightness may seem like the sun glinting on the
surface of the water, but it does in fact shed a deeper and more
lasting light for times of hardship or difficulty.

280: THE WOMEN *(NISAA)* 4:3

If you fear that you will not be able to deal justly with the orphans,
marry women of your choice, two or three or four, but if you fear
that you shall not be able to deal justly with them, then only one,
or one that your right hand possesses (a captive). That will be
more sensible, to prevent you from acting unjustly.

Polygamy is not essential in Islamic society, nor is it particularly
encouraged, but it was widely practised in pre-Islamic times and
continues to be in both Muslim and non-Muslim societies –
whether it takes a legal form, or the hypocritical form in the West
of mistresses, prostitution and a succession of girlfriends or
common-law wives. It is a fact of life which, for various reasons,
Islam recognizes and organizes, so that there is neither hypocrisy
nor wrong done between human beings.

One significant reason for polygamy is, of course, war. This
verse was delivered immediately after the Battle of Uhud at
which the Muslims suffered a severe defeat, resulting in many
widows and orphans. As revealed here, no man must take in
marriage more women than he can provide for physically and
emotionally.

However, there are other situations where polygamy takes into
account the human need. For example, if the wife is barren, but
the couple do not wish to part, a second wife can bring the joy of
children to them all. Or if the wife is ill and needs another to care
for her, or if she is sexually cold, it is better that she does not feel
pressured. Another occasion these days when a man might take
more than one wife is due to living for a time in another country
where he is unable to take his wife, for instance, a young man
from Saudi Arabia studying in Manchester. It is better that he
marry another woman than fall prey to the lures of promiscuity
or prostitution.

281: HADITH
TIRMITHI: Book of Marriage *(Kitab Al-Nikah)*

Allah's Messenger 🕮 *said: 'He who has two wives, and is*
inclined to one more than the other, and does not deal justly with

them, he will come on the Judgement weakened on one side.'

Unfairness in the treatment of one's wives, who have been given as a gift from Allah to be loved and cared for, is a sin that will disfigure a man when he comes before Allah on the Day of Reckoning. The Prophet Muhammad ﷺ had nine wives, and despite the great demands of his work he was scrupulously just with them all, providing for them equally and visiting them on a circuit of nine nights.

For many in the West there is an attitude that polygamy is somehow wrong, despite the fact that it occurs amongst the prophets of the Bible as a matter of course. We would ask: is it wrong to give a woman the protection and dignity of marriage, but right to use a woman for your own selfish sexual desires without giving her the respect or commitment that is her due? Many non-Muslim men bounce from one lover to another, with false promises of security and love. Or, if they are married, they have affairs with their secretaries and then, when they have had enough or society catches them out, the secretary is disgraced and out of a job. This is not the way we treat our women.

282: THE CONFEDERATES *(AHZAB)* 33:4

Allah has not made for any man two hearts in his body.

THE WOMEN *(NISAA)* 4:129

You are never able to be fair and just as between women even if it is your fervent desire, but do not turn away (from a woman) altogether, so as to leave her hanging. If you come to a friendly understanding and practice self-restraint, Allah is Oft-Forgiving, Most Merciful.

These verses reveal the rather discouraging truth that, although we are required to be just to all our wives if we choose to have more than one, we will never be able to do so. It is the nature of the human heart that some will be dearer to us than others, and some will also be more emotionally demanding of us. However, no matter what our preferences, we must not brush aside a wife by denying her conjugal rights. In this we can and should be fair toward her.

283: THE CHILDREN OF ISRAEL (*BANI ISRA-IL*) 17:29

Do not keep your hand tied to your neck (like a miser's), nor stretch it out to its utmost reach so that you become culpable and destitute.

Islam is the way of the 'golden mean', that is, of moderation. While a man is required to be generous with his money, first toward his family and then toward the needy and Allah's Cause, Allah does not wish the financial or religious security of a household to be jeopardized by excessive spending, either altruistic or self-indulgent. The wife and her children have the right to be clothed, fed and cared for, within the means of her husband and in the manner to which she is accustomed.

284: THE CRITERION (*FURQAN*) 25:74

And those who pray: 'Our Lord, grant to us wives and children who will be the joy and comfort of our eyes, and give us the grace to lead the righteous.'

The main obligation of a wife is to ensure the blissfulness of married life. This she does by obeying the same codes of good manners as her husband. She must be faithful and trustworthy, with the modesty befitting a woman. She must not receive strange men in the home or accept gifts from them without her husband's approval. She should make herself attractive for her husband and be warm and loving toward him. These are the lawful (*halal*) obligations of the wife. Domestic chores do not fall into this category. Those she can do as an act of love and goodwill. There is a tradition of the Prophet which recounts a debate between one of his daughters and her husband over how they would share out the work. The Prophet ﷺ resolved it by saying to his daughter: 'All the work at home is yours and all the work outside is his.' However, this injunction is a matter of good manners, it is not legally binding on the wife. There is another tradition of the Prophet which says a husband should endeavour to bring the food cooked to his wife's table.

285: THE WOMAN (*NISAA*) 4:34

Men are the protectors and maintainers of women, because Allah has given the one more strength and responsibilities than the other and because they support them from their means. Therefore, the righteous women are devoutly obedient and guard in their husband's absence what Allah would have them guard.

Islam recognizes the equality of women and men, at the same time as recognizing their differences. Accordingly there are different roles for each sex, neither of which is considered inferior. They are complementary roles, equally important in the running of society for the benefit of all. Because of their strength and responsiblities, men naturally deal in the public realm in their role as family protector and provider. As the bearers and nurturers of children, it is practical for women to stay in the home. They must guard their purity, reputation and husband's good name, for without these family life would soon begin to crumble.

286: THE WOMEN (*NISAA*) 4:34–35

As to those women on whose part you fear disloyalty and ill-conduct, admonish them first, then refuse to share their beds and, lastly, beat them lightly; but if they resume obedience, do not maintain a grudge, for Allah is Most High and Great.

If you fear a breach between the two, appoint two arbiters, one from his family and the other from hers. If they wish for peace, Allah will cause a reconciliation, for Allah has complete knowledge and is acquainted with all things.

If there are difficulties between a couple, they should, if possible, sort it out themselves. In Islam, the first preference in all human interactions is for the parties concerned to resolve the situation to their mutual satisfaction. In the case of a wife behaving unlawfully, the internal process involves three stages: verbal warning, denying conjugal rights and finally a gentle beating. If the wife improves her ways, the husband must resume a convivial and loving relationship without any backlash of nagging, sulking or punishment.

If there are problems between people which they cannot sort out themselves, the preference is always to resort next to the family before drawing on the resources of the wider community. The families' love and understanding of the personalities involved qualifies them as the most suitable source of arbiters. If the couple have argued themselves into a corner and wish, in their hearts, to be reconciled, Allah will use the family arbiters to effect the reconciliation.

287: HADITH
AL-KHATTABI: *Reasons for Revelation*, vol. V

S'ad ibn Ar'abie had trouble with his wife Habibi, daughter of Zaid, so he slapped her. Then her father brought her to the Prophet 🌸 *saying: 'I wedded my honorable daughter to him and he slapped her.'*

The Prophet 🌸 *said: 'She must revenge herself upon her husband.'*

So she went out with her father to do so, but the Prophet 🌸 *called them back, saying: 'Gabriel (the Angel) has just come to me. He has given me this verse. We wished something, but Allah wished another thing.'*

And he delivered this verse: [see 4:34 opposite].

The permission to beat wives must be understood as a right not to abuse, but to gently admonish. It must never contravene the law of kindness to wives. There are numerous traditions which clarify what was meant by beating. When Ibn. Abbas asked what was the nature of the beating permitted, the Prophet 爨 replied: 'With your toothbrush,' indicating that it was in no way meant to cause physical harm, but simply to serve as a gesture of justified displeasure. Beating on the face is not permitted (Abu Dawud), nor is wanton beating. Muslim, Bukhari and Tirmithi all agree on the tradition of the Prophet: 'One of you goes and beats his wife as he beats his servants, then, at the end of the day, goes and sleeps with her – how can this be?'

288: HADITH
MUSLIM: Book of Marriage (*Kitab Al-Nikah*) 3467–3468

Allah's Messenger 爨 *said: 'Woman has been created from a rib, and will in no way be straightened for you; so if you wish to benefit by her, benefit by her while crookedness remains in her. And if you attempt to straighten her, you will break her, and breaking her is divorcing her. . . . He who believes in Allah and the Hereafter, if he witness any matter he should talk in good terms about it or keep quiet. . . . So act kindly toward women.'*

The Prophet 爨 uses the analogy of a rib to illustrate the differences in physique and temperament between women and men, despite the fact that they share the same essential nature and rights. The differences should be acknowledged, for it is the complementary relationship of men and women, sexually and temperamentally, that knits together the fabric of our society. Women should not be forced to think in line with their husbands. A man may not agree with a particular habit or act of his wife, but unless he can approach the matter in a positive, tactful manner he should refrain from comment. Women are of the greatest benefit to themselves, their husbands and families if they are allowed to develop according to their own potential, not to one imposed upon them. Naturally, if her behaviour is unlawful her husband must make a stand for everybody's sake, but even then he should avoid unnecessary harshness.

289: THE CHILDREN OF ISRAEL (*BANI ISRA-IL*)
17:32

*Nor come near to adultery, for it is shameful and evil, opening the
road to other evils.*

Adultery is a sin in itself, degrading to those guilty of it and
showing no concern for others. But its dangers are greater than
simply the downfall of the souls concerned. It strikes at the heart
of the family, threatening its stability, the best interests of the
children and, through this, the very fabric of society. Domestic
violence, feuds, divorce and even murder can arise from this
sinful act. Even the contemplation of committing adultery is a
destructive, inhuman and irreligious act, for the shift in attitude
of the would-be adulterer can arouse suspicions and fears in the
partner. These can take on a life of their own to eat away at the
marital bonds of love and trust.

290: HADITH
MUSLIM: Book of Marriage (*Kitab Al-Nikah*)

Allah's Messenger *said: 'By Him in Whose Hand is my life,
when a man calls his wife to his bed and she does not respond, the
One Who is in the heaven is displeased with her until he (her
husband) is pleased with her.'*

Sexual intimacy within marriage is a natural expression of the
love and commitment between man and wife. A wife who
withholds herself from her husband is acting to erode the marital
bond, and so displeases Allah. Allowance is, of course, made for
ill-health, and a husband should be sensitive to a wife's modesty,
so that the relationship is gratifying for both partners. When a
marriage is conducted with proper care and consideration on
both sides, Allah is well pleased with it.

291: HADITH
MUSLIM: Book of Marriage *(Kitab Al-Nikah)* 3369

Allah's Messenger 🌺 *said: 'The most wicked among the people in the sight of Allah on the Day of Judgment is the man who goes to his wife and she comes to him and then he divulges her secret.'*

HADITH
MUSLIM: Book of Marriage *(Kitab Al-Nikah)*

One day the Prophet 🌺 *was offering the prayer, and after finishing he remained sitting and turned to us and said: 'Is there any one of you who will go to his wife, close the door, pull the curtains, have sexual relations and then go and speak about what has gone on?' They were silent. He looked at the women and said the same thing.*

Then a young woman rose on her knees and said: 'Yes, by Allah, they do that.'

The Prophet 🌺 *said: 'Do you know what is the parable of this? Anyone doing that, it is as if they had met Satan in the middle of the road for sexual intercourse while people were watching.'*

The role of marriage as a bastion of purity and trust is attacked by those who prattle about their intimacy with their wives. They insult the modesty of their wives, and they create an atmosphere of lewdness that is the enemy of family life. Faithfulness to one's partners refers to words as well as deeds.

292: THE COW *(BAQARA)* 2:222

They ask you regarding menstruation. Say: 'It is unclean, and an indisposition. So keep away from women when they are menstruating, and do not approach them until they are clean. But when they have purified themselves you may approach them in any manner, time or place ordained for you by Allah. For Allah loves those who turn to Him constantly, and He loves those who keep themselves pure and clean.'

293: HADITH
MUSLIM: Book of Menstruation *(Kitab Al-Haid)* 578

*A'isha reported: 'When anyone amongst us (the Prophet's wives)
was menstruating, the Messenger of Allah 鷺 asked her to tie
waist-wrapper around herself when the menstrual blood was
flowing profusely, and then he embraced her'; and she (A'isha)
observed: 'And who amongst you can have control over his desires
as the Messenger of Allah 鷺 had over his desire?*

The restriction on contact during a wife's menstruation refers
only to sexual intercourse. Contrary to the Jewish practice of
segregating the woman as if she herself was unclean, the Prophet
鷺 encouraged cuddling and affection towards wives during
their periods. Indeed, this is a time when care should be taken
that the woman does not feel abandoned. There are many
traditions of the Prophet 鷺 reported by his wives telling how,
during their periods, they washed and combed his hair, lay
beside him and provided their laps as a headrest while he read
them the Qur'an. The uncleanliness refers directly to women's
menstrual blood. As with Allah's other restrictions relating to
women's menstruation, this one is primarily for the woman's
benefit. It ensures that her husband does not press himself upon
her at a time when she is physically and emotionally stressed.

294: THE COW *(BAQARA)* 2:223

*Your wives are as a fallow field to you; so approach your tilth
when or how you will, but perform a good act for your souls
beforehand; and fear Allah and know that you are to meet Him (in
the Hereafter), and give this good news to those who believe.*

Here, as elsewhere, the highest spiritual matters are dealt with in
conjunction with the affairs of daily life, for they are the ways that
Allah has given us. Sex is not treated as a bad or unhealthy thing,
but encouraged as a good and necessary part of married life. The
advice to perform a good deed first underlies the fact that it is the
attitude with which we conduct ourselves that matters – if we
perform some good deed before approaching our wives, we come
in a righteous frame of mind.

13   The Family, Divorce and Death

295: MARY (*MARYAM*) 19:2

*This is a recounting of the Mercy of your Lord to his servant
Zakariya.*

Behold he secretly cried to his Lord.

*Praying: 'O my Lord, my bones are ailing and my hair glistens
with silver, but I am never unfavoured by my Lord in my prayer to
You.*

*'Now I fear what my relatives will do after me, But my wife is
barren, so give me an heir as from Yourself –*

*'Who will truly represent me and represent the posterity of Jacob;
and make him, O Lord, one with whom you are well pleased.'*

*'O Zakariya, we give you good news of a son. His name shall be
Yahja. On no one of that name have we conferred distinction
before.'*

The story of the Prophet Zakariya (Zacharius) and the
circumstances of the birth of his son Yahya (John) reveals Allah's
key purpose in giving us children. In his wisdom, the Prophet
Zakariya recognizes that children are given as the heirs of Islam.
Zakariya was not a wealthy man, and the posterity of Jacob he
refers to was, of course, the religious heritage that Allah had
promised to Jacob's descendants (see 46). It was not for the joy
children bring, or security in old age, or even the moral discipline
for his own soul that such a responsibility gives, that prompted

Zakariya to pray for an heir. He saw that the people were worshipping false gods, and that the posterity of Jacob was in danger of being squandered. He asked merely for a son by name, an adopted son, appointed by Allah, but was blessed with a son by blood, for Allah is the All-Powerful Creator.

All children are born as Muslims (see 18), and it is our responsibility as parents to see that their spirits are nurtured and educated so they do not squander this heritage given by Allah.

296: HADITH
IBN.-I-MAJAH: Book of Virtue, Good Manners and the Joining of Ties of Relationship (*Kitab Al-Birr Wa's-Salat-i-Wa'l-Adab*) 3669

> *The Prophet of Allah said: 'If a man has three daughters and brings them up well, educates them and clothes them from what Allah has given, and gives them in marriage to decent people, they will become a shield to protect him from hell-fire.'*

> *They (his companions) said: 'What if he has only two daughters?'*

> *He said: 'Yes, even two daughters will protect him.'*

> *They said: 'What about one?'*

> *He said: 'Yes, even one.'*

Men are the protectors of their daughters in this life, but as in all relationships in Islam, there is reciprocity. A well-cared-for daughter will be to the benefit of her father in the Hereafter. The Laws of Allah are just.

297: CONSULTATION (*SHURA*) 42:49

> *To Allah belongs the kingdom of the heavens and the earth. He creates what He wills. He bestows sons or daughters according to His Will.*

Or He bestows both sons and daughters, and leaves barren whom He chooses, for He is full of knowledge and power.

Children, both daughters and sons, are a blessing from Allah given to us in accordance with His Grand Design. We should not allow the superficial freedom given to us by birth control methods to obscure the fact that we can neither prevent nor bring about the creation of a soul unless Allah intends it.

298: HADITH
MUSLIM: Book of Marriage *(Kitab Al-Nikah)* 3883

Jabir reported that a man came to Allah's Messenger 鬖 *and said: 'I have a slave-girl who is our servant, and she carries water for us, and I have had intercourse with her, but I do not want her to conceive.' He said: 'Practise 'azl (coitus interruptus) if you like, but what is decreed for her will come to her.' This person stayed back, and then came and said: 'The girl has become pregnant,' whereupon he said: 'I told you what was decreed for her would come to her.'*

Children are one of Allah's greatest gifts, therefore birth control is not encouraged in Islamic society. However, it is permissible and, on occasions, advisable, for example if the women's health is at risk. Allah does not wish us to harm ourselves for the sake of children. Financial limitations or academic commitments may also present the need for birth control. And, since it is the wife whose body will do the work, she must feel physically and psychologically up to it. It is better to postpone children than to foist motherhood on a young woman who fears the ordeal, the responsibility or the damage it may do to her looks. However, we must always keep in mind that creation ultimately lies in Allah's hands (see 202–218), so we cannot prevent a birth if He wills it.

299: THE CHILDREN OF ISRAEL *(BANI ISRA-IL)* 17:31

Do not kill your children for fear of want: We shall provide

*sustenance for them as well as for you. Truly, killing them is a
great sin.*

All children have an inalienable right to life. In the immediate
context in which the Prophet 🕌 spoke, economic hardship and
the demands of war resulted in some Arabs committing the
heinous crime of killing their children – in particular the girls,
who were seen as a disadvantage for a society at war.

In Surah 81:8–14, Allah warns that those responsible will be
called to account on the Day of Reckoning 'when the baby girl,
buried alive, is asked for what crime she was killed.' Indeed, the
very Earth itself will cry out against the crime.

The practice still occurs today, but there is a broader point
here, as well as the prohibition of infanticide. It is the duty of the
parent to preserve the child's life, that is, not to endanger it
through neglect or exposing it to life-threatening elements in
society.

300: HADITH
MUSLIM: Book of Marriage *(Kitab Al-Nikah)* 435

Allah's Messenger 🕌 *said: 'The two men, Sadb. Abu Waqqas
and Abd. b. Zama'a, disputed with each over a young boy. Sa'd
said: "Messenger of Allah, he is the son of my brother 'Utba, as he
made it explicit that he was his son. Look at his resemblance."
'Abd. b. Zama'a said: "Messenger of Allah, he is my brother, as
he was born on the bed of my father from his slave-girl." 'Allah's
Messenger* 🕌 *looked at his resemblance, and found a clear
resemblance with 'Utba, but he said: 'He is yours, O 'Abd,
because the child is to be attributed to he whose bed it is born on,
and stoning for a fornicator. . . .'*

It is the fundamental right of a child to have its father's name and
all the rights of inheritance which accompany this. Islam does
not subscribe to a notion of illegitimate children disenfranchized
from family rights. Even if a parent has sinned, it is not the child
of that act who should be punished. All children are born
innocent in Islam. Therefore, a child automatically takes the
name of his mother's rightful husband. Physical resemblance

cannot furnish decisive proof of birthright, and such a criterion would only create opportunities for adulterers to benefit from their sinful deeds and mischief-makers to sow doubts and suspicions between spouses. The primacy of the family unit is upheld by the law given here, alongside a warning to those who would threaten the stability of the family through their selfish, godless acts.

301: HADITH
AHMAD ANA-S-I: Book of Marriage *(Kitab Al-Nikah)*

Allah will ask every shepherd concerning those who are under his care whether he has looked after them or neglected them, and He will ask this of each man about his household.

HADITH
ABU DAWUD: Book of Marriage *(Kitab Al-Nikah),* Family Maintenance

It is sin enough that a person will not care for those he is responsible for.

Every child has the right to be fed, clothed and protected from harm by the guardian Allah has appointed for him on earth – in the first instance, his father. It is therefore the legal obligation of a father or male guardian to do this to the best of his ability. To neglect this duty is a sin, for which he will be called to account on the Day of Judgement. Likewise, we are placed in charge of those creatures who provide for us – such as sheep. If we fail to care for them, this will be held against us on the Day of Judgement.

302: THE COW *(BAQARA)* 2:233

The mothers shall breast-feed their children for two full years, if the father wishes the breast-feeding to be completed. But he shall bear the cost of their food and clothing on equitable terms. No soul shall have a burden laid on it greater than it can bear. No mother shall be treated unfairly on account of her child, nor father on account of his child. An heir will bear the same responsibilities. If, after due consultation, they mutually agree on weaning, they are not at fault. Nor is there any guilt if you decide on a wet-nurse for your children, provided you pay what you offered on equitable terms. But fear Allah and know that Allah sees well what you do.

This verse was delivered in the context of a Revelation about divorce arrangements, but the general principles it lays down are taken to apply whether the parents are in or out of wedlock. The mother is responsible for suckling the child for a maximum of two years. Financial provision for the well-being of the child lies entirely with the father. This in no way affects the mother's rights to the child if the parents are divorced. If the father dies, financial responsibility for the child passes to any adult heirs he may have. However, Allah does not ask of a person what they do not have to give. If the financial burden is too great for a man, it passes to his male relatives, and if they cannot manage, then to the Muslim community. Similarly, the women are not asked to bear a burden too great for them. It is permissible to wean before the child is two if both parents are agreed, and to pass the child to a wet-nurse or, by analogy, to bottle-feed.

303: HADITH
MUSLIM: Book of Gifts (*Kitab Al-Hibat*) 3970

Nu'man b. Bashir reported: My father gave me a gift and then brought me to Allah's Messenger ﷺ *for him to bear witness to it. He (the Prophet* ﷺ *) said: 'Have you given such a gift to every son of yours?'*

He said: 'No'.

Whereupon, He (the Prophet ﷺ *) said: 'Don't you expect virtue from them as you expect from him'.*

He said: 'Yes, of course'.

He (the Prophet ﷺ *) said: 'I am not going to bear witness to it (as an injustice)'.*

Ibn. 'Aun (one of the narrators) said: 'I told this Hadith to Muhammad 🌸 *(the other narrator) who said: "Truly, we narrated that he had said: 'Observe equity among your children.'"'*

The preservation of the family and the maximum development of children's physical, intellectual, emotional and spiritual potential rests on equality within the family. To deny one child in favour of another disadvantages the denied one personally and the family as a whole by sowing the seeds of resentment and envy; this will, at best, cause rifts and, at worst, tear the family asunder.

304: THE PROPHET HUD (*HUD*) 11:42–47

So the Ark floated with them on the waves like mountains and Noah called out to his son, who had separated himself: 'O my son, come on board with us and do not stay with the disbelievers.'

The son replied: 'I will take myself to a mountain. It will save me from the water.' Noah said: 'Today nothing can save anyone from the Command of Allah except those on whom He has mercy.' And the waves came between them and the son was among those overwhelmed in the Flood.

Then the word went forth: 'O earth, swallow up the water. O Sky hold back your rain.' And the water abated and the matter was ended. The Ark rested on Mount Judi and the word went forth: 'Away with those who do wrong.'

And Noah called upon His Lord and said: 'O my Lord, surely my son is of my family, and Your promise is true and you are the most just of judges.'

He said: 'O Noah, he is not of your family for his conduct is unrighteous. So do not ask of me that of which you have no knowledge. I give you counsel, lest you act out of ignorance.'

Noah said: 'O my Lord, I seek refuge with you lest I ask You for that of which I have no knowledge. And unless You forgive me and have mercy on me I should indeed be lost'.

Like all father's Noah loved his son dearly and was grief-stricken at his loss. In his distress, he asked why Allah took one of his family. But Allah's promise had been that he would save those of Noah's family who were believers. An idolatrous wife of Noah's was also lost in the flood which Allah sent. Noah quickly realized that he had spoken in ignorance of His words and submitted himself to Allah's Mercy. This is an example for us all. In the upbringing of our children we must try to ensure their spiritual safety, but in the end each soul is responsible for itself. No one can intervene for another.

305: THE CHILDREN OF ISRAEL (*BANI ISRA-IL*) 17:23–24

Your Lord has decreed that you worship none but Him and that you are kind to your parents. Whether one or both of them reaches old age in your life, do not speak a word of contempt, nor reject them, but address them in terms of honour.

And out of kindness, lower to them the wing of humility and say: 'O My Lord, bestow on them Your mercy even as they cherished me in childhood.'

Human relationships in Islamic society are based on mutual care and benefit, not least with the family. It is as important a legal duty for children to respect and obey their parents and to care for them when they become old and weak as it was for their parents to care for them when they were young and weak. This respect and honour in no way impedes our total submission to Allah. It is a command from him and a gesture of submission to Him.

Within the experience of selfless parental love and care is the echo of Divine Love which maintains and cherishes us and which we can never repay, but for which we can only try to show gratitude. It is a Sign to help us understand the relationship we have with our Guardian-Lord. If we cannot manage to show gratitude and honour to those on earth who have given us so much and love us so dearly, we shall surely fail in gratitude to Him whose love and care for us is above all and without limit.

306: HADITH
MUSLIM: Boof of Virtue, Good Manners and Joining the Ties of Relationship *(Kitab Al-Birr Wa's-Salat-i-Wa'l-Adab)* 6184

> *'Abdullah b. 'Amr reported that a person came to Allah's Apostle* ﷺ *and sought permission to participate in* Jihad, *whereupon he (the Prophet) said: 'Are your parents living?'*
>
> *He said: 'Yes.'*
>
> *Thereupon he (the Prophet) said: 'You should put your best efforts into their service.'*

As important as it is to fight for the estabishment of Islam in society, our first social responsibility in the way of Allah is to our family. Allah tells us this many times in the Qur'an, and the Prophet ﷺ never tired of stressing the importance of this. Scholars are generally of the opinion that the parents of the man in this tradition had no one else who could care for them, which is why they took precedence.

307: HADITH
IBN.-I-MAJAH: Book of Business *(Kitab Al-Buyu)* 2291

> *A man came to complain to the Prophet about his son, saying: 'I looked after him and maintained him when he was most in need until he grew up and became strong as I became weak. But now he will not give me any of his wealth to help look after me.' The man composed a small poem:*
>
> *'I maintained you when you were a babe*
> *And also when you became a strong young man,*
> *Spending out of what I was earning.*
> *Any night when you were sick or complaining,*

I stayed awake looking after you
As if I had been struck with the sickness myself,
My eyes flowing with tears.
And I carefully protected you from harm
Until you reached the age and strength
Where I expected you would look after me
And care for me.
My reward was roughness.
I wish, if you did not care for me as a parent,
You would care for me as a neighbour.
That is to open your house for me,
Support me as a good neighbour does.'

The Prophet ﷺ *told the son of the man: 'You and your wealth*
are the earning of your parents.'

The selfishness of youth described here has a familiar ring,
typical of the weaknesses of human nature which can be our
undoing and do not change. In fact, the cult of the individual and
of youth, which have flourished in modern Western society,
provide ample opportunity for Satan to increase his hold.
Parents are not only left in poverty after years of hard work for
their children, but their children are too busy pursuing their own
interests to provide the love and respect that is vital to personal
well-being. Not only do such children put their souls at risk in
the Hereafter, but by disregarding family ties they are creating
their own misery in their own later years.

308: THE WISE (*LUQMAN*) 31:14

And We have enjoined man to be good to his parents: in pain upon
pain his mother bore him and weaned him after two years. Hear
the command: 'Show gratitude to Me and to your parents. I am
your final Goal.

'But if they try to make you worship with Me those of whom you
have no knowledge, do not obey them, yet treat them justly in this
life and follow the way of those who turn to Me in love. In the End
you will all return to Me and I will tell you the truth of all that you
have done.'

Despite our unpayable debt to our parents, when the will of man conflicts with that of Allah, it is always Allah we must obey because only Allah's Will is perfectly just and good. This does not mean we should be rude or unkind to our parents or those in authority over us who urge us to transgress. We should treat them with the respect and love which is their due, while firmly maintaining our position of Belief. Indeed, it is out of love for them that we should explain why we must disobey them and that they too should follow Allah's Will for we all, parents and children alike, belong to Him and will return to Him.

309: HADITH
MUSLIM: Book of Virtue, Good Manners and Joining the Ties of Relationship (*Kitab Al-Birr Wa-s-Salat-i-Wa'l-Adab*) 6180

> *Abu Haraira reported that a person came to Allah's Messenger* 🕌 *and said: 'Who among the people is most deserving of a fine treatment from my hand?'*
>
> *He said: 'Your mother.'*
>
> *He again asked: 'Then who (next)?'*
>
> *He said: 'Again it is your mother.'*
>
> *He said: 'Then who?'*
>
> *He said: 'Again it is your mother.'*
>
> *He said: 'Then who?'*
>
> *Whereupon he said: 'Then it is your father.'*

This tradition highlights the care and gratitude Islam pays to women. While both parents should be loved and respected fairly, it is our mother who surrendered her own body to exhaustion and pain so it could serve as a vessel for carrying our soul into this world. Such an act epitomizes the principles of selfless love and

care for others which are at the heart of Faith. It is the first
encounter we have with Righteousness and it should be the first
for which we show gratitude. Futhermore, it is in the nature of
motherhood that a woman will be physically weaker and
economically dependent so she is more in need of good treatment
from us.

310: MARY (*MARYAM*) 19:42–48

*Behold, he said to his father: 'O my father, why worship that
which neither hears nor sees and cannot benefit in any way?'*

*'O my father, knowledge has come to me which has not reached
you. So follow me. I will guide you to a way that is straight and
even.*

*'O my father, do not serve Satan for Satan is a rebel against
Allah Most Gracious.'*

*'O my father, I fear that a penalty from Allah Most Gracious will
befall you so that you become a friend to Satan.'*

*His father replied: 'Do you hate my gods, Abraham? If you are
intolerant, I will stone you. Now get away from me.'*

*Abraham said: 'Peace be on you: I will pray to my Lord for your
forgiveness. For He is Most Gracious to me.'*

*'And I will turn away from you and from those whom you invoke
besides Allah. I will call on my Lord. Perhaps, by my prayer to my
Lord, I shall not be unblessed.'*

The Prophet Abraham's forfeit of his father's love reveals to us
how we should behave in that most painful of situations when
our own parent strays from Islam. We see in Abraham the
righteous son, with the best interests of his father at heart, trying
to dissuade him from worshipping false gods. He warns his
father that Allah punishes disbelievers by allowing their nature
to degenerate so it develops an affinity with evil. Abraham

addresses his father gently and with love. His tone is solicitous even when his father, his soul hardened by its alliance with Satan, threatens his life and then banishes him from his sight. He obeyed his father to the extent that it was in accord with Allah's will and left his homeland for ever. He continued to pray for his father's soul, as promised, until he realized that his father's soul was irrevocably lost. 'And Abraham prayed for his father's forgiveness, only because of a promise he had made to him. But when it became clear to him that he was an enemy to Allah, he dissociated himself from him, for Abraham was most tender-hearted and forbearing.' (9:114)

311: THE WOMAN WHO PLEADS (*MUJADALA*)
58:1–4

Allah has indeed heard (and accepted) the statement of the woman who pleads with you concerning her husband and carries her complaint to Allah; for Allah always hears the arguments from both sides as Allah hears and sees all things.

Women possess as much right to be heard by society and by Allah as men. We see both in the Qur'an and the Hadith that not only did women express their opinions and grievances openly and without prejudice against them, but their voices carried weight in discussions and debates they had with Allah's Messenger 🌼 and other Muslim leaders.

The particular circumstance lying behind the verses revealed here was the practice of Arab men divorcing women by declaring 'You are to me as the back of my mother.' This freed the man from conjugal obligations, while denying his wife the right to move out of his home or to remarry. A woman had come to the Prophet 🌼 when her husband discarded her in this manner, leaving her trapped and without means of support for her young children or herself. Subsequently Allah revealed this heartless practice was unlawful.

312: HADITH
ABU DAWUD: Book of Divorce *(Kitab Al-Talaq)*

> *Allah's Messenger* 🕌 *said: 'The most hated thing which is allowed by Allah is divorce.'*

HADITH
KASHF-UL-KHAFA: *Traditions That Are Common on the Tongues of the People*

> *The Prophet* 🕌 *said: 'Marry and do not divorce, for the throne of Allah is shaken when divorce happens.'*

Marriage is an institution of Allah. It is a blessing and a duty He gives to those who can manage it. It is the core of society and not to be taken lightly. Nevertheless, there is no value for anyone – Allah, man and woman, or society – in forcing two people to stay together if it becomes clear their temperaments will never be reconciled to one another. Such an imposition can only lead to a situation directly opposed to Islam. Anger, discontent, resentment, even hatred will destroy peace, contentment, goodwill and love.

313: THE COW *(BAQARA)* 2:226–227

> *Allah will not call you to account for thoughtlessness in your oaths, but for the intention in your hearts, and He is Oft-forgiving, Most Forbearing.*
>
> *For those who take an oath for abstention from their wives, a waiting for four months is ordained. If then they return Allah is Oft-forgiving, Most Merciful.*
>
> *But if they are set on divorce, Allah hears and knows all things.*

Divorce is not an immediate solution as soon as there are problems in marriage. It is a last resort to remedy a situation where people are tearing themselves apart and ruining their lives. Before reaching this point there are various stages to go through.

To begin the process, a couple in difficulty should remain in the same house but sleep in separate rooms and forgo all sexual contact for four months. This is a period for cooling down, reflecting and considering whether there is still a trace of love between them. If at this juncture they decide there is, they can resume relations without any formality. However, if the husband does not return to his wife's bed after this period, this is called a minor, revocable divorce. That is, they are no longer married. But if they change their minds, the man can seek his ex-wife in marriage and, if she agrees, they can remarry.

314: THE COW (*BAQARA*) 2:228–229

Divorced women shall keep themselves apart for three menstrual cycles, nor is it lawful for them to hide what Allah creates in their wombs if they have faith in Allah and the Last Day. And their husbands have the right to take them back in that period, if they wish to be reconciled. And women have rights similar to the rights against them, according to what is fair. But men have a degree of advantage. And Allah is Exalted in Power, Wise.

A divorce is only allowed twice. After that, the parties should either stay together on equitable terms or separate with kindness. It is not lawful for you (men) to take back any of your gifts (you gave to your wives) except when both parties fear that they would be unable to keep the bounds set by Allah. If you (judges) fear they would be unable to keep these bounds, there is no blame on either of them if she pays some ransom for her freedom . . .

The waiting period after divorce of three menstrual cycles ensures that if the woman is with child the husband will be aware of this, and it will influence his decision. Both parties have the right not to remain in a marriage that makes them miserable. However, the man is given a degree of power in the decision simply because he is the one financially responsible. Even then the revocable divorce is allowed twice. However, if the couple remarry and divorce a second and then a third time, the divorce is now irrevocable. This provision gives the couple opportunity to experience a wide range of emotions without allowing them an unlimited scope for behaviour that will dishonour the sanctity of marriage.

When a couple divorce, the woman takes with her what remains of her dowry and any gifts her husband has given her. The allowance for the two to come to some agreement other than this is to protect the woman against her husband refusing a divorce because he cannot afford it.

315: THE LIGHT (*NUR*) 24:6-9

And for those who accuse their spouses and have no evidence but their own, their solitary evidence (can be accepted) if they bear witness four times taking an oath in the name of Allah that they are solemnly telling the truth;

And the fifth (oath) should be that they solemnly invoke the curse of Allah on themselves if they are lying.

But the wife shall receive no punishment if she bears witness four times in the name of Allah that her husband is lying.

And the fifth oath should be that she solemnly invokes the wrath of Allah on herself if her accuser speaks the truth.

It is in the nature of adultery that there are unlikely to be many witnesses to it. In the case given here, where a husband or wife is making the accusation, their evidence alone can be taken as substantial proof, first, because such an accusation reflects badly on them as well and is therefore unlikely to be made if the accuser is not absolutely sure. No one likes to be cast as the cuckold and there are other, less degrading reasons for which divorce can be obtained. Secondly, the disputes lies between two people who are as close as any two individuals can be, so it is unlikely that they would make such a charge through misunderstanding. Thirdly, no true Muslim would wish to call the wrath of Allah upon his or her soul by lying.

316: THE FAMILY OF IMRAN (*AL-I-IMRAN*) 3:156–158

> *It is Allah Who gives Life and Death, and Allah sees well all that you do.*

> *And if you are slain or die in the way of Allah, forgiveness and mercy from Allah are far better than all they could amass.*

> *And if you die or are slain, it is to Allah that you are brought together.*

Death at a predetermined time is part of God's Design. If we are sincere believers we have nothing to fear – Eternal Bliss awaits us. For both these reasons, Muslims should face their own death, and that of their loved ones, with fortitude and hope. We should not live a cowardly life for ever trying to avoid death because, when the time decreed by Allah arrives, we will die no matter what we do. By the same token, it is a sin to take His Law into our own hands and seek our own death.

These verses were delivered after the Battle of Uhud when the casualties and the defeat had shaken the besieged Muslim community to its roots. At this time, with many loved ones slain and the menace of Arabian political power gathering its forces, Allah reminded them that to die in His Cause was the surest way of receiving His Mercy in the Hereafter.

Similarly, although it is natural that we should feel bereaved if someone dear to us dies, we should not allow these feelings to run away with us in excessive displays of emotion. It is a sign of mistrust in the Allah's Love and Mercy. If we believe, we know we will be reunited with those we love for ever in the Eternal Garden.

All return to Allah in death, so it is the duty of the deceased's family or community to prepare him for this occasion, purifying his body for the last time and praying for his soul.

317: THE WOMEN (*NISAA*) 4:7,11

> *From what is left by parents and close relatives, there is a share for*

*men and a share for women, whether the property is small or large
– a determinate share.*

> *... Allah directs you as regards your children: to the son a
> portion equal to that of two daughters; if you have only daughters,
> two or more, their share is two-thirds of the inheritance; if only
> one, her share is a half. For parents, a sixth share of the
> inheritance to each if the deceased left children. If there are no
> children and the parents are the only heirs, the mother has a third;
> if the deceased left brothers or sisters, the mother has a sixth. The
> distribution in all cases is after the payment of legacies and debts.
> You cannot judge whether your parents or your children are
> nearest to you in benefit. These settled portions are ordained by
> Allah, and Allah is All-knowing, All-wise.*

The founding of Islam was the founding of women's
independent rights to property. Not only do they have the right
and complete control of a dowry from their husband (see 275),
but they have rights and control of inheritance from their parents
and their children. Women receive a smaller portion than the
men, not as a reflection of society valuing them less, but as fair
recognition that the men have to support their wives and families
financially while women have the freedom to use the money
solely for their own benefit.

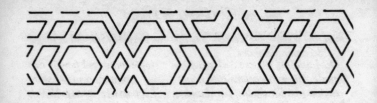

14   The Community

318: THE FAMILY OF IMRAN (*AL-I-IMRAN*) 3:104

> *Let there arise among you an* ummat *advocating all that is good, enjoining what is right and forbidding what is wrong. They are the ones to attain peace and prosperity.*

The word *ummat* is not easily translated as it embraces the concepts of brotherhood, community, nation, religion and way of life. The *ummat* is central to Islam as a religion that includes love of humanity in our love of Allah. Islam is not a religion of the hermit or the ascetic, cut off from his fellow men and daily life. Indeed, worship of Allah and work in His Cause is synonomous with community life.

319: THE COW (*BAQARA*) 2:143

> *Thus we have made you an* ummat *justly balanced that you might be witnesses over the nations . . .*

The Islamic community is not founded on race, locality, nation, political ideology, class or a human ruler. It is based purely and simply on belief and submission to Allah, his Apostles and His Books. Thus, the Islamic community is balanced, without the prejudices and fanaticism of sectarian interests. It must avoid excesses and extremes, but seek always the moderate way that does not alienate but embraces. The community is a witness to all peoples of the Truth through example and teaching.

320: THE INNER APARTMENTS (*HUJURAT*) 49:13

O Mankind, We created you from a single male and female and made you into nations and tribes so that you may come to know each other. Truly the most honoured of you in the sight of Allah is the most righteous of you. And Allah has full knowledge and is well aware.

Our treatment of our fellow human beings must always be in accord with our common humanity. This surah of this verse was delivered nine years after the migration to Madinah, at a time when the Muslim community was growing rapidly, drawing on the peoples of many different tribes. It was known as the Year of Deputations for by now representatives of diverse tribal and political interests were visiting the Prophet ﷺ in official recognition of Islam. It was at this time of Islam's increasing power that Allah enjoined us to remember that we are brothers and sisters, descended from the first man and woman He created. The importance of this injunction has continued to grow as Islam's role in the world has grown.

321: HADITH
BUKHARI: Book of Good Manners

The Messenger of Allah said: 'O Women of the Faithful, do not think it is a little thing which you give to your neighbour even if it is a small part of the leg of a goat.' (Abu Dawud included the addition:) 'Give gifts to each other for surely gifts take away ill feeling from the heart.'

A single act of generosity is like a pebble thrown into a pond creates widening ripples of goodness for ourselves and others. It establishes the spirit of mutual support and co-operation which is essential to Islamic society. Each individual is responsible for the welfare for others in the community and the community is responsible for him. The smallest gift is a reminder of this, fostering goodness in the soul of the giver and encouraging others to also act righteously.

322: THE WOMAN (*NISAA*) 4:135

O you who believe, stand out firmly for justice, bear witness for Allah, even though it is against yourself or your parents or your kin, and whether it is against rich or poor, for Allah can best protect both. Do not follow your passions lest you swerve; and if you distort or refuse to do justice, truly Allah is well-aware of all that you do.

In Islam, justice is not a system of complex laws and loopholes to be exploited only by a professional elite, varying from state to state and from year to year. It is unchanging and perfectly suited to all peoples of all times because it is the absolute Justice of Allah, which each one of us is responsible for upholding and to which we will be answerable on the Final Day. All acts are performed within the sight of Allah and He knows all secret thoughts and desires which motivate them.

No loyalty, whether it be for a beloved relative, a needy supplicant or a wealthy employer, should lead us to betray Allah's Justice. Nor should feelings of hatred or envy sway us to act unjustly towards them in the name of Allah. This applies at all levels because the Universal Justice crosses all boundaries of gender, class, race and culture. There must be no prejudicial treatment in personal, community, national or international relationships.

323: SHE WHO IS TESTED (*MUMTAHANA*) 60:8–9

Allah does not forbid you to deal with kindness and justice with those who have not fought against you for your Faith, nor driven you out of your homes, for Allah loves those who are just.

Allah only forbids you from turning in friendship toward those who fought you for your Faith and driven you out of your homes or supported others in driving you out. Those who turn to them do wrong.

We should pay non-Muslims the same respect and kindness we afford Muslims, unless they are working to destroy our Faith or our homes. This verse was delivered when Asma, a sister-in-law of the Prophet 	ﷺ, was expecting a visit from her mother, a disbeliever. Asma asked the Prophet 	ﷺ if she was allowed to entertain her mother and accept her gifts. He told her this was permitted and soon afterwards this verse was revealed (Muslim & Bukhari, *Explanations of the Qur'an*). The only limitations on relations with non-Muslims who wish us no harm are in regard to marriage and inheritance. Friendship or allegiance with those who seek to destroy Islam is itself, however, an act against Islam.

15   Food and Drink

324: THE COW (*BAQARA*) 2:172

*O believers, eat of the good things that we have provided for you
and be grateful to Allah, if it is Him you worship.*

The overwhelming majority of foods are lawful in Islam. Eating,
with gratitude, the pure and wholesome foods Allah has given us
is in itself an act of worship. In Islam, a moderate and healthy
diet is a religious responsibility as it is fundamental to the
physical, mental and moral health of the individual and
consequently to the health of his family and of his society.

325: THE BEE (*NAHL*) 16:67–69

*And your Lord taught the bee to build its cells in hills, on trees and
in hives.*

*Then to eat of all the fruits and flowers, and skilfully find the
spacious paths of its Lord. From its belly comes a fluid of varying
colour with healing qualities for men. Truly this is a Sign for those
who give thought.*

Like all nature, the bee obeys Allah's Laws perfectly. So when
we see it eating from the great range of foods the Lord provides,
we may take this as a Sign that Allah wishes all his Creations to
enjoy His Beneficence. One of His bounties was to inspire the
bee with instincts which provide us with a delicious health food.
We see yet again in the integrated design of the Universe
evidence of a Single Creator (*Tawhid*) who designed the earth so
it would serve humanity's needs.

326: THE TABLE SPREAD (*MA'IDA*) 5:90

*O believers, do not make unlawful the good things which Allah has
made lawful for you, but commit no excesses. Allah does not love
those given to excess.*

The excessive strictures on diet that had developed within the
Jewish tribes by the time of the Prophet 🕮 are immediately
relevant to this verse, but prohibition on food based on
superstition or neurosis continues today. It is ungrateful to
prohibit foods that Allah has given to us as wholesome nourish-
ment.

Islam advocates moderation in all things. Overindulgence in
lawful pleasure is a transgression, as is excessive abstinence. Our
body is a gift from Him and should neither be stuffed beyond its
needs nor starved in the misguided belief that this will please
Allah. Abstinence is not in itself a bad thing; on the contrary, it
can develop self-discipline and compassion for those who have
no choice but to go without. However, it should be moderated
abstinence, as, for example, the fasting at Ramadan.

327: THE COW (*BAQARA*) 2:173

*He has only forbidden you dead meat and blood and the flesh of
swine and that on which any other name has been invoked besides
that of Allah. But if one is forced by necessity without wilful
disobedience, nor transgressing due limits, then he is without guilt,
for God is Oft-Forgiving, Most Merciful.*

The Divine Decrees regarding food are in the best interests of
our health, as modern medicine has discovered. Dead meat refers
to carrion – that is, an animal that dies of natural causes – and
meat which has not been lawfully killed for human consumption
with Allah's name pronounced over it. Instances of dead meat
include '... that which has been killed by strangling, or by a
violent blow or by a headlong fall or by being gored to death; that
which has been (half) eaten by a wild animal, unless you are able
to slaughter it (appropriately)' (Surah 5:4). In each case, the
point is that it becomes dead meat because the blood congeals

before being taken out of the body. However, if it can be slaughtered appropriately, that is, if the blood is still flowing and the prescribed method of slaughter (see below) can be performed in the name of Allah, the food becomes lawful and eatable.

Swine are unhealthy on various counts. They are of course renowned for their filthiness – living on offal and rotting foods – with flesh which is prone to disease and very fatty.

Of course, no believer should eat food that has been killed or prepared in the name of a false god.

Surely, Allah does not demand of us that which will do us more harm than good. If we have no choice than to starve or eat prohibited foods, we should choose the latter.

328: HADITH
MUSLIM: Book of Games and Animals That May Be Slaughtered and Animals That May Be Eaten (*Kitab-Al-Sayd Wa'l-Dhaba'ih Wa Ma Yu'kalu Min Al-Hayawan*) 4810

> *Allah's Messenger* ﷺ *said: 'Truly, Allah has enjoined goodness to everything, so when you kill, kill in a good manner and when you slaughter, slaughter in a good manner. So every one of you should sharpen his knife and let the slaughtered animal die comfortably.'*

Every effort should be made to slaughter an animal with compassion. This is done by slitting the throat with a knife that is as sharp as possible so that the animals's death is quick and relatively painless. The animal should not be shown the knife nor should it witness or have its death witnessed by another animal. It should be transported comfortably to the place of slaughter and its body should be left free to toss about as it bleeds (*An-Nawawi*, vol. II, p. 152).

The tradition refers not only to slaughtering but to all instances of lawful killing. There are crimes, such as pre-meditated murder, for which the punishment in Islam is death. But even the perpetrators should be put to death swiftly and cleanly.

329: THE TABLE SPREAD (*MA'IDA*) 5:5

They ask you what is lawful for them (to eat). Say: 'All things good and pure are lawful to you.' And you have taught your trained hunting animals in the manner Allah directed you. Eat what they catch for you, but pronounce the name of Allah over it and fear Allah, for Allah takes account swiftly.

The question of meat caught by trained beasts and birds of prey arises given that the quarry is not killed in the prescribed manner of slaughtering (see above). But Allah reveals that the training of animals to hunt for humans was ordained by Him and therefore constitutes a lawful form of slaughter so long as it is done in His Name. Since the kill does not usually occur in the presence of the men, it is understood that the Name of Allah should be pronounced when the beast or bird of prey is released to the hunt.

330: HADITH
MUSLIM: Book of Games and Animals That May Be Slaughtered and Animals That May Be Eaten (*Kitab-al-Sayd Wa'l-Dhaba'ih Wa Ma Yu'kalu Min Al-Hayawan*) 4748

Allah's Messenger 🕌 *prohibited the eating of all fanged beasts of prey and all the birds having talons.*

The general rule about animals is that the flesh of those which live on plants is lawful. Those which kill for their food are by definition constituted of dead meat, so we become indirect consumers of carrion if we eat such beasts. Furthermore, many scholars are of the view that there is a connection between the food we eat and our temperament. Some would argue that the ruthless nature of beasts of prey can infect the disposition of a man who eats their flesh.

331: HADITH
MUSLIM: Book of Games and Animals That May Be
Slaughtered and Animals That May Be Eaten *(Kitab-
Al-Sayd Wa'l-Dhaba'ih Wa Ma Yu'kalu Min Al-
Hayawan)* 4816

> *Ibn. 'Umar happened to pass by some young men of the Quraish
> who had tied up a bird to shoot arrows at it. Every arrow that
> missed became the possession of the bird's owner. As soon as they
> saw Ibn. 'Umar they left, whereupon Ibn. 'Umar said: 'Who has
> done this? Allah has cursed him whoever does this. Truly Allah's
> Messenger* 🕌 *invoked a curse on anyone who made a living thing
> a target.'*

Allah has given us the bounty of the earth to serve our needs, not
to provide callous fun. It is a sin against His Creation to play with
the lives of animals or inflict suffering upon them simply for
sport. Our role as viceregents (see 207) entails care and
compassion for all Allah's creatures. What is more, cruelty
towards animals perverts our attitude towards fellow human
beings.

332: THE TABLE SPREAD *(MA'IDA)* 5:90–91

> *O believers, intoxicants and gambling, idols and divining arrows
> are an abomination devised by Satan. Eschew them so that you
> may prosper.*

> *Satan's plan is to arouse enmity and hatred between you with
> intoxicants and gambling and prevent you remembering God and
> Prayer. Will you not then abstain?*

The successes of Satan are all around us. No socially responsible
person could argue in defence of products and activities that lead
to crime, violence, mental disability, death and the breakdown of
family life, to name but a few of the effects of gambling and
alcohol.

333: THE BEE (*NAHL*) 6:67

And from the fruit of the date-palm and the vine you get wholesome food and drink. Behold, this is also a Sign for those who are wise.

The date-palm and vine provide fresh fruits, date honey and vinegar. Yet from the rotten, fermented fruits come the intoxicants which destabilize individuals and communities. Allah's bounty is everywhere in Creation, but as part of our test on earth, he allows Satan to try to lure us from the straight way through misuse of His bounties. We have free will. The choice is always ours.

334: HADITH
TIRMITHI: Book of Drinking (*Kitab Al-Ashriba*)

A man who was a Bedouin and friend of the Prophet 鑑 came to stay with him and brought a large bottle of wine as a gift. The Prophet 鑑 said: 'Didn't you know that Allah has prohibited it?'

Then the man said: 'Shall I sell it?'

The Prophet 鑑 said: 'He who prohibited it prohibited selling it.'

The man said: 'Should I give it as a gift to the Jews?'

The Prophet 鑑 said: 'He who prohibited it prohibited giving it as a gift.'

The man said: 'What shall I do with it then?'

The Prophet 鑑 said: 'Throw it away.'

HADITH
AHMAD: Book of Drinking (*Kitab Al-Ashriba*)

... 'Let him not sit in a place where intoxicants are being served.'

The Prophet ﷺ cursed ten categories of accomplices in the advocacy of alcohol, from distiller to drinker. Any complicity whatsoever is a sin, for we are all guardians of one another. Yet governments all around the world continue to allow and indeed profit from the sale of alcohol. Such is the greed of these governments that they compound their sin and insult the followers of Islam by selling of alcohol in their embassies in Muslim nations. It must be added that, for all the avarice motivating the encouragement of these evils, the cost to national economies through crime, illness, accidents and civil disorder is far greater than the short-term gain.

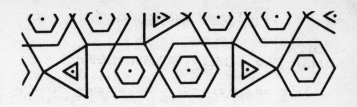

16   Business

335: THE WOMEN (*NISAA*) 4:29

> *O believers, do not consume your property amongst yourselves in deceits, but trade and traffic together by mutual goodwill; and do not kill yourselves, for truly Allah has been most Merciful to you.*

Good business is a result of goodwill. It cannot arise from fraud, coercion or taking advantage of someone's desperate straits to benefit yourself to his or her further disadvantage. The Lord encourages us to trade as stated in Surah 62:10–11, where we are told to cease business for our Friday prayer, but to disperse once it is completed to continue seeking His Bounty. It is apparent that business conducted in a spirit of mutual benefit is not only lawful but beneficial in cementing community relations. However, it must be transacted without breaking the few, but immutable, prohibitions.

The instruction not to kill ourselves can be taken at face value as an injunction against suicide, but is generally believed also to relate to the previous warning, therefore indicating that unlawful business practices and greed will lead to our destruction, personally and as a society.

336: THE HEIGHTS (*A'RAF*) 7:85

> *Give just measure and weight, and do not withhold from people that which is their due; and do not create mischief on the earth after it has been set in order – that will be best for you if you have Faith.*

DEALING IN FRAUD (*TATFIF*) 83:1-7

Woe to those that deal in fraud –

Those who, when they have to receive by measure from men, exact full measure,

But when they have to give by measure or weight to men, give less than due.

Do they not think that they will be called to account?

On a mighty Day,

A Day when mankind will stand before the Lord of the Worlds?

No, Surely the Record of the wicked is (preserved) in Sijjin.

And how do we explain to you what Sijjin is?

It is a Register marked with names.

One of the great unbalancers of personality, society and nature is man's greed, which contrives to derive more than a just share, more than is due. The Creation is just because it was created by He Who is Just (see 15). To act unjustly unbalances the order of Allah's Universe, and is a sin that will not go unnoticed. Whether we are caught by a human judiciary system or not, we can be assured that we will be called to account on the Day of Judgement. *Sijjin* refers to a prison in hell, and may refer to the place where the record is kept or where the transgressors themselves will go.

337: HADITH
TIRMITHI: Book of Business (*Kitab Al-Buyu*)

Allah's Messenger ﷺ was asked to fix prices. He said: 'It is Allah who has the power to raise and reduce, and I wish to Meet Allah without transgressing. I do not want the burden of anyone on my shoulders.'

It is a basic principle of Islam that everything Allah created is free for the use of humanity. There are many Qur'anic verses which say that Allah made the Universe subservient to the needs of human beings (see 9). Therefore, it is against Allah's Just Laws to interfere with the freedom of the market, where prices find their own level according to genuine demand and ability to buy. Internal manipulation of the market as a means of furthering profit also goes against Allah's Just Laws. Monopolies commissions, cartel agreements and the stock exchange are all examples of intervention and control which Islam stands against. To those who play the stockmarket, the Qur'an's warnings against gambling should be heeded, for that is what such behaviour actually is, and its reward of punishment in the Hereafter is recorded.

338: HADITH
TIRMITHI: Book of Business (*Kitab Al-Buyu*)

One day the Prophet ﷺ was going to prayer and he saw the people buying and selling. He called to the merchants and traders, so they looked up. The Prophet ﷺ told them: 'Traders will be resurrected on the Day of Judgement as sinners, except those who are honest and righteous.' And the Prophet ﷺ continued: 'The honest businessman will be resurrected on the Day of Judgement among the Prophets, the most truthful and the martyrs.'

From this tradition about the Prophet ﷺ we know dishonesty in business will bring us retribution as if we were disbelievers, but that fair trading is an act so pleasing to Allah that those who practise it will be amongst the ranks of Allah's most beloved.

339: FAMILY OF IMRAN (*AL-I-IMRAN*) 3:180

And do not let those who hoard the gifts which Allah has given them think that it is good for them. No, it will be the worse for them. Soon the things which they hoard will be tied to their necks like a twisted collar on the Day of Judgement. The heritage of the heavens and the earth belong to Allah, and He is well aware of all that you do.

HADITH
IBN.-I-MAJAH: Book of Business *(Kitab Al-Buyu)* 2153

> *The Messenger of Allah* ﷺ *said: 'The one who brings food to the market, Allah will help him provide well for his family, and the one who hoards is cursed by Allah.'*

Allah wishes us to work and sell the fruits of our labour honestly, and to trust in Him that our needs will be met. We can see for ourselves how important it is for our own souls that we do not become attached to our worldly possessions. They will hang around our necks like a slave's collar and be our undoing on the Day of Judgement.

In this earthly life, we can also see the importance to the community of a freely flowing economy, where the money is not siphoned off into financial stockpiles, seen at its ugliest in the form of a Swiss bank account.

340: THE COW *(BAQARA)* 2:198

> *It is not crime on your part if you seek the bounty of your Lord (during Pilgrimage). Then when you pour down from 'Arafat, celebrate the praises of Allah and the Sacred Monument and celebrate His praises as He has commanded you, even though you had previously gone astray.*

Anas Aburi *(Reasons for Revelation)* reports that this verse was revealed after some traders who sold provisions to pilgrims came to the Prophet ﷺ asking if they were allowed to conduct business while they were on the *Hajj* (Pilgrimage). Others had claimed that they should receive no profit if they were to consider themselves valid pilgrims. The Prophet ﷺ asked if they said their prayers regularly and dressed themselves appropriately for the Pilgrimage. They replied yes, and this led to an affirmation from Allah that the profits of fair trade, 'His bounty', could be sought. In this, as in the injunction to return to seeking His bounty after the Friday prayer assembly (see 153), we see that business is encouraged by Allah as being both lawful (if the prohibitions are observed) and beneficial to the community.

341: THE COW (*BAQARA*) 2:275

Those who devour interest will not stand, except as one who has been driven mad by the touch of the Evil One. This is because they say: 'Trade is like usury.' But Allah has permitted trade and forbidden usury. Those who desist from the practice after receiving direction from their Lord shall be pardoned for the past – their case is for Allah to judge; but those who re-offend are companions of the fire; they will dwell there for ever.

Here is an indisputable prohibition from Allah on usury. In this life the money-lender's passion for money makes him as a man possessed, distorting both his values and intelligence. In the Hereafter, the punishment is far greater still.

While there is no dispute that the Qur'an forbids usury, there is some difference of opinion over its definition. Quite simply, usury is any loan which draws benefit. It means selling £1 for £1.20. The difference of opinion arises in relation to the twentieth-century economy, where lending is done by large institutions. Do the economics of seventh-century Arabic society, where individual loan-sharks exploited the hardship of others, not differ from the modern system of banking? Is it wrong, for instance, for an individual to lend his money to a large, powerful bank in return for interest which the bank can well afford to pay? The answer to both questions is yes. Yes, they do differ in scale and complexity, but bank interest is still wrong when the full picture is considered. Those banks can well afford to pay interest to the individual customers, because they are able to charge exorbitant rates of interest elsewhere, not least in underdeveloped countries that are caught in a rising debt spiral because of the rate of interest. The issue of profit without honest work at the expense of others remains the same. Allah's Wisdom is not limited by current affairs – nor are His Prohibitions.

Of course, this is not without its difficulties for the Muslim homebuyer or businessman in the modern world, and has led to the establishment of Muslim banks which do not function on an interest basis. They operate by honest investment in business ventures on behalf of the customers, who all share in the profits and losses. Even in these early days of this development there has been considerable resistance from Western institutions.

342: HADITH
TIRMITHI: Book of Business *(Kitab Al-Buyu)* 1206

> *The Messenger of Allah* 鬱 *cursed the person who devours interest, and the person who pays the interest, and the two persons who are witnesses, and the person who writes the document.*

This tradition of the Prophet is a warning against any collaboration whatsoever in usury. It is binding on the Islamic community to see that no person is ever in such a desperate predicament that he or she cannot find an alternative to borrowing at a rate of interest. Gifts or loans without interest from the family, the community or the state should be arranged to help those in need.

343: HADITH
BUKHARI: Book of Business *(Kitab Al-Buyu)*

> *Al-Bukhari reported that a man came to him and said to him: 'I earn my living with my hands and I draw.' Ibn. Abbas said to him: 'I will tell you what the Prophet told me. Anyone drawing pictures will be punished by Allah until he blows the spirit into that picture, and he will never be able to blow the spirit into it.' The man became angry and Abdullah said to him: 'Why don't you go and draw things that have no spirit.'*

It is forbidden in Islam to draw or shape figures and animals. Allah alone must be worshipped, not His Creation nor our pale imitations of it. Once a person starts trying to copy Allah's Creation, the sense of true worship of Allah will be closed to him. He will be preoccupied with his own role as creator, and may even begin idolatrous worship of the articles.

Furthermore, artistic expression which is not strictly relevant to religious life contravenes the principles of simplicity essential for righteous living. The concerns underlying the prohibition of usury and gambling apply to the excesses of the art market. Today we can see these even more clearly, as speculative buying and selling of art reaches a scale not known to those Muhammad 鬱 addressed. Millions of pounds are spent, largely to the benefit of dealers who manipulate the prices without regard to genuine needs or worth.

344: THE COW (*BAQARA*) 2:219

They ask you concerning wine and gambling. Say: 'There is great sin in them and some profit for men; but the sin is greater than the profit.'

Allah is the Most Just, so the Message of Islam is based on balance, whether in balancing each soul's good acts against its transgressions and judging them accordingly, or in balancing the advantages and disadvantages of a particular object or activity. He tells us here that, although there is some benefit of pleasure in alcohol and gambling, it is far outweighed by the damage to our souls and society.

Gambling refers to profiteering without honest work. It is the use of chance, and in some instances fraud, to benefit some to the disadvantage of others. Allah prohibits any transactions that do not have fixed terms of conditions and payment (see 347). For the Arabs of Muhammad's time this verse referred to fairly easily identified situations, for instance, dicing, betting and casting lots, using marked arrows, for random portions of a slaughtered animal. Today the same principles of gambling have developed more subtle forms – for example, insurance. There is no insurance in Islamic states. Insurance is a gamble with no fixed amount of remuneration to the insured. It is based on the premise that the proprietors or shareholders of the company will benefit through a system of taking a person's money and lending that money out on an interest basis to benefit themselves. Such systems do not obey the Laws of Allah and should be eschewed. This does not apply, of course, to state-organized insurance such as health, where there is no profit, but simply a sharing of the expenses for everyone's benefit. As with banking, the Islamic world is developing its own forms of co-operative insurance, where costs are shared fairly by the insured without profiteering by an outside party.

345: THE COW (*BAQARA*) 2:219

They ask you how much they are to spend. Say: 'What is beyond your needs.'

Of what benefit is hoarding, to ourselves or to the community? We should use wealth according to our and our family's needs without being mean, and then we should sell our goods, invest in honest business ventures, spend for the benefit of others and contribute to Allah's cause. It is a sign of distrust in Allah's Beneficence to hoard for fear of a rainy day. 'And He gives you all that you ask for . . .' (Surah 14:34). The Creation provides for the needs of all (see 203). It is only our own greed and dishonesty that upset the balance.

346: THE GATHERING (*HASHR*) 59:7

What Allah has bestowed on His Apostle from the people of the townships belongs to Allah and to kindred and orphans, the needy and the wayfarer; so that it does not simply circulate among the wealthy. So take what the Apostle assigns to you, and deny yourselves what he withholds from you, and fear Allah, for Allah is strict in punishment.

These verses were delivered at the time when Jews of Madinah were expelled, after betraying the treaty made with the Muslims and plotting to kill the Prophet ﷺ . The Muslims and their allies, the Ansar, who had invited the Prophet ﷺ to Madinah, were now in possession of the Jewish land and property. But Allah exhorts the people not to be greedy, but to follow his Guidance delivered to the Prophet ﷺ for distributing the wealth so that it will circulate widely for the benefit of all. This principle of sharing according to needs, and in the knowledge that all belongs to Allah, is as relevant to us today as it was to the Muslims of Madinah.

347: HADITH
MUSLIM: Book of Business *(Kitab Al-Buyu)* 3661

Hakim b. Hizam (Allah be pleased with him) reported that Allah's Messenger ﷺ said: 'Both parties in a business transaction have the right to annul it so long as they have not separated; and if they speak the truth and make everything clear they will be blessed in their transaction; but if they tell a lie and conceal anything the blessing on their transaction will be blotted out.'

HADITH
TIRMITHI: Book of Business *(Kitab Al-Buyu)* 1311

The Messenger of Allah ﷺ said: 'Whoever is making such contracts, let it be in a well-defined measure and well-defined weight to a well-defined timetable.'

In all business transactions, it is Allah's Will that all be honest, clear and mutually agreed. Contracts should be drawn up with care to avoid misunderstandings, and of course to ensure there is no dishonesty. For this reason, Allah enjoins us not to be casual in our contracts, even though it may be with friends or even relatives. Indeed, in such circumstances, ambiguous terms can lead to even greater ruptions, as the hurt is that much greater.

348: HADITH
MUSLIM: Book of Business *(Kitab Al-Buyu)* 3906

Ibn. 'Abbas (Allah be pleased with him) reported than when Allah's Messenger ﷺ came to Madinah and the people were paying in advance, he said to them: 'He who makes an advance payment should not make advance payment except for a specified measure and weight (and for a specified period).'

The traditions of the Prophet agree that undefined transactions are not acceptable in Islam. The sale of fruit before it is ripe enough to identify its condition can lead to the buyer paying an unjust price if the fruit is blighted. Likewise, the sale of animals too young or as yet unborn can result in unfair pricing.

Future contracts (*salam sale*) are lawful in relation to goods that can be defined exactly, such as a length of cloth. There is some difference of opinion over these traditions in regard to animals. Some argue that *salam sale* is always unlawful in the case of animals because the quality and quantity lie beyond our control. Others argue that the conditions can be set out in the contract.

349: HADITH
MUSLIM: Book of Business (*Kitab Al-Buyu*) 3913

Abu Huraira (Allah be pleased with him) said he heard Allah's Messenger 卿 say: 'Swearing produces a ready sale for a commodity, but blots out the blessing.'

It is a common enough ruse now, as in the Prophet's time, to swear in the Name of Allah that our goods are worth their price. But whether the oath is true or not, it degrades the Name of Allah. We are not to use His Name to give the impression that we are honest and sincere. We should give that impression through our own deeds.

350: HADITH
MUSLIM: Book of Charity (*Kitab Al-Zakat*), 263, 2266, 2271

Hamza, son of 'Abdullah, reported on the authority of his father that the Apostle of Allah 卿 said: 'When a man is always begging from people, he will meet Allah with no flesh on his face.'

Abu Huraira reported Allah's Messenger 卿 as saying: 'He who begs the riches of others to increase his own is asking only for live coals, so let him ask a little or much.'

Qabisa b. Mukhariq al-Hilali said: 'I was in debt and I came to the Messenger of Allah 卿 and begged from him regarding it. He said: "Wait till we receive Sadaqa, so that we can give that to you." He then said: "Qabisa, begging is not allowed except for three categories of person: one who is in debt, for him begging is allowed until he pays it off, after that he must stop; a man whose property has been destroyed by calamity, for him begging is allowed until he obtains what will provide him with a reasonable subsistence; and a person who has been impoverished, the genuineness of which is confirmed by three intelligent members of his community, for him begging is allowed until he obtains what will provide a reasonable subsistence. Qabisa, except in these three circumstances, begging is forbidden, and one who indulges in it devours that which is prohibited."'

The first tradition cited here uses an Arabian idiom to indicate that the beggar will have no dignity by the time his life has ended and he comes to Judgement. This is not strictly to prohibit begging for those who are in great need, as specified in the third tradition cited. However, it does make clear that the act, in any circumstances, is a degrading one.

The second tradition is a more severe warning to those who beg to increase their wealth, rather than as an immediate way of surviving. They are breaking the Laws of Allah which require charity from all who are not impoverished. The fire of greed that now burns them will become the fires of hell.

351: HADITH
MUSLIM: Book of Charity *(Kitab Al-Zakat)*

Abu Huraira is reported to have heard the Messenger of Allah 🕌 *as saying: 'It is better for one among you to bring a load of firewood on his back, and give charity out of it (and satisfy his own need), and be independent of people, than that he should beg from people whether they give him anything or refuse him. Truly the upper hand is better than the lower hand, and begin (charity) with your dependents.'*

The dignity of earning your own living – however meagre – is to be sought and is infinitely to be preferred to begging. Even the poorest gain in both esteem and heavenly reward if they honestly earn their own income and contribute to charity. How can a man not seek to earn an income to maintain his own family? After all, charity begins at home, by providing the essentials for sustaining family life.

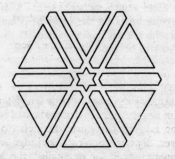

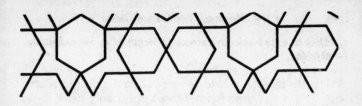

17   Crime and Punishment

352: THE TABLE SPREAD (MA'IDA) 5:44–45

*It was We who revealed the Law (to Moses) in which was guidance
and light . . .*

*We ordained for them in it: 'Life for life, eye for eye, nose for nose,
ear for ear, tooth for tooth, and wounds equal for equal.' But if
any one remits the retaliation by way of charity, it is an act of
atonement for himself. And if any fail to judge by what Allah has
revealed they are no better than the wrongdoers.*

Islamic law, like all the religions of the Book, protects five
essential things: the blood of every person, his wealth, his honour
(on account of his wife and daughters), his religion and his
intellectual capacity. In the first category, the law of equal
punishment applies. Every person who is injured or is a relative
of a murder victim has the right to demand equal retribution for
the criminal. The injured party has the right to mitigate the
sentence. However, anyone appointed as judge who dispenses
prejudicial treatment either for or against the accused is as
culpable as a criminal.

353: THE TABLE SPREAD (MA'IDA) 5:41–42

*As to the thief, male or female, cut off his or her hands: a
punishment by way of example from Allah for their crime: and
God is Exalted in Power.*

But if the thief repent after his crime and amend his conduct,

Allah turns to him in forgiveness; for Allah is Oft-forgiving, Most Merciful.

Theft falls into the second category of punishment in Islamic law. This is the area of punishments specifically stated in the Qu'ran. Fornication, accusing someone of adultery without proof, taking intoxicants, stealing, apostasy and waging war against God through thuggery and banditry, all fall into this category. The rationale behind the punishment is deterrence. To this end, there is considerable attention paid in the Hadith to the value of a stolen item and to the circumstances of the crimes warranting a hand being cut off. Stealing food to eat is not a crime. If the person committing theft does so out of great need, rather than greed, then the principle of deterrence is beside the point, and it is up to the discretion of those who are wronged to forgive the transgression, and even to find who is at fault for allowing this person to go hungry. A tradition of the Prophet relates how one of his followers was robbed of his cloak while praying in the mosque. He caught the thief in the act and took him to the Prophet ☙ , but when the Prophet ☙ ordered his hand to be cut off the follower became most distressed, realizing the man was needy. He immediately gave the man his cloak as a charity. The Prophet asked: 'Why didn't you do that before bringing him here?' (*An-Nawawi's, Forty Hadith*).

While a criminal or any sinner can be saved from eternal punishment by sincerely repenting before Allah, this does not apply in relation to punishment dealt out by humans for crimes against another human. Allah has ordained these punishments be executed out of justice for those wronged. Whether or not the criminal receives Divine Forgiveness in the Hereafter does not bear on the earthly sentence.

354: HADITH
MUSLIM: (*An-Nawawi's Forty Hadith*)

Whoever sees any evil action let him change it with his hand, if he is not able to do so, then with his tongue, and if he is not able to do so, then with his heart – and that is the weakest of Faith.

Islam is a religion of Faith in Practice. We do not relegate our beliefs to a sacred building or a special day. They are the way we live our lives. As Muslims it is incumbent on us to act on behalf of Righteousness. Evil deeds may necessitate we act within the third area of punishment in Islamic law, which is meted out according to discretion. It may simply be a box around the ears or it may mean going into battle. If we cannot change an evil practice through action, we should at least voice our disapproval, and if this has no effect then we should at least hope and pray that it changes. We fail ourselves and Allah if we begin by hoping and praying but go no further.

355: THE PROPHET HUD (*HUD*) 11:88

. . . and my success in my task can only come from Allah. In Him I trust and to Him I turn.

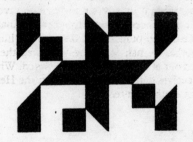

Bibliography

Qur'an & Hadith

Abdullah Yusuf Ali (trans.), *The Holy Qur'an*, Shaikh Muhammad Ashraf, Lahore.

Sahih Al-Bukhari (Hadith), Al-Maktab Al-Islamia, Istanbul, 1915.

Kashf-ul-Khafa, *Traditions That Are Common on the Tongues of the People*, Maktab Al-Turath Al-Islami, Halab, Syria.

Ibn. Khuzeimah, *Collection of Sound Traditions* (ed. M.M. Al-Aazami), Al-Maktab Al-Islami, Damascus and Beirut.

Sunnan Ibn Majah, Dar-ul-Fikr, Beirut, 1954.

Mishkat-ul-Masabih, (trans. 'Abdul Hamid Siddiqui), Kitab Bhavan, New Delhi, 1980.

Sahih Muslim, (trans. 'Abdul Hamid Siddiqui), 4 vols., Sh. Muhammad Ashraf, Lahore, 1976.

An-Nawawi's, *Forty Hadith* (trans. Ezzeddin Ibrahim & Denys Johnson-Davies, The Holy Koran Publishing House, Damascus, 1976.

Sunnan Al-Tirmithi, (trans. Al-Hatabi), Cairo, 1937.

GENERAL

The following works were consulted during the preparation of this volume.

Hammudah Abdalati, *Islam in Focus*, American Trust Publications, Indianapolis, 1975.

Maulana Muhammad Ali, *A Manual of Hadith*, Curzon Press, London and Dublin, 1944.

Maulana Muhammad Ali, *The Religion of Islam*, S. Chand, New Delhi.

Mahmud Shukri Al-Alusi, *Ruoh Al-Maani*, Darahya Al-Turath Al-Arabia, Beirut.

Abdullah Muhammad Al-Ansari of Cordova, *Al-Jami'li-Ahkam Al-Qur'an*, National Egyptian Library, 1967.

Ahamd Bahnasi, *Punishment in Islam – A Comparative Study*, Dar-ul-Orouyiah, Cairo, 1961.

S.M. Darsh, *Islamic Essays*, Taha Publishers Ltd, London, 1979.

Al-Fakhrurazi, *Tafsir*, Dar-al-Fikr, Beirut.

Shems Friedlander and Al-Hajj Shaikh Muzaffereddin, *Ninety-nine Names of Allah*, Wildwood House, London, 1978.

Al-Ghazizali, *Revivification of Islamic Thought*, Royal Printing Press, Cairo, 1887.

Gulzar Haider, Gardens of the Viceregent, *Inquiry*, March 1987.

Ibn. Hajar, *Fathul-Bari*, Dar-ul-Fikr, Beirut.

Ibn. Hazm (Dhahiri Fiqh), *Al-Muhalla*, Maktab Al-Gumhuria, Cairo, 1967.

Ibn. Hisham, *Seerat*, Moasasat-L-Risalat, Kuwait, 1981.

Sayad Nasr, *Ideals and Realities of Islam*, Unwin, London, 1975.

Thomas Ballantine Irving, Khurshid Ahamd and Muhammad Manazir Ahsan, *The Qur'an – Basic Teachings*, The Islamic Foundation, Leicester, 1979.

Ahmad Mustafa Ak-Maraghi, *Tasfir Al-Maraghi*, Dar-Ihya Al-Turath Al-Arabia, Beirut.

Sayad Abdul Alla Maudoodi, *Meanings of the Qur'an*, 10 vols., Lahore.

Ibn. Qudamah, *Al-Mughni*, Maktab Al-Gymhuria, Cairo.

Al-Qaradawi, *Al-Halal Wal-Haram Fil-Islam*, Al-Maktab Al-Islami, Beirut, 1967.

Ibn. Roshd Al-Qurtobi (Maliki Fiqh), *Bidayat-al-Mugtahid*, Maktab Al-Kulliat Al-Azharia, 1974.

Sayad Qutb, *Fi Dhilal-l-Qur'an*, Dar-Al-Arabia, Beirut.

Ibn. Aabidin (Hanafsi Fiqh), *Radd Al-Muhtar*, Dar-Al-Fikr, Beirut, 1966.

Ghulam Sarwar, *Islam Beliefs and Teachings*, Muslim Education Trust, London, 1984.

Arrow Health

☐ The Alexander Principle	Wilfred Barlow	£2.95
☐ The Zinc Solution	D. Bryce-Smith	£3.50
☐ Goodbye to Arthritis	Patricia Byrivers	£2.95
☐ Rosemary Conley's Complete Hip and Thigh Diet	Rosemary Conley	£2.99.
☐ No Change	Wendy Cooper	£2.99
☐ Day Light Robbery	Dr Damien Downing	£3.99
☐ The Biogenic Diet	Leslie Kenton	£3.99
☐ Ageless Ageing: The Natural Way to Stay Young	Leslie Kenton	£3.95
☐ Raw Energy: Recipes	Leslie Kenton	£3.99
☐ Joy of Beauty	Leslie Kenton	£6.99
☐ Sexual Cystitis	Angela Kilmartin	£3.99
☐ PM System: Preventive Medicine For Total Health	Dr JA Muir Gray	£5.99
☐ Women Who Love Too Much	Robin Norwood	£3.50
☐ Fat is a Feminist Issue	Susie Orbach	£2.99
☐ Callanetics	Callan Pinckney	£6.99
☐ Love, Medicine and Miracles	Bernie Siegel	£3.50

Prices and other details are liable to change

ARROW BOOKS, BOOKSERVICE BY POST, PO BOX 29, DOUGLAS, ISLE OF MAN, BRITISH ISLES

NAME...

ADDRESS..

....

....

Please enclose a cheque or postal order made out to Arrow Books Ltd. for the amount due and allow the following for postage and packing.

U.K. CUSTOMERS: Please allow 22p per book to a maximum of £3.00.

B.F.P.O. & EIRE: Please allow 22p per book to a maximum of £3.00.

OVERSEAS CUSTOMERS: Please allow 22p per book.

Whilst every effort is made to keep prices low it is sometimes necessary to increase cover prices at short notice. Arrow Books reserve the right to show new retail prices on covers which may differ from those previously advertised in the text or elsewhere.

A Selection of Arrow Books

Prices and other details are liable to change

ARROW BOOKS, BOOKSERVICE BY POST, PO BOX 29, DOUGLAS, ISLE OF MAN, BRITISH ISLES

NAME..

ADDRESS ....

....

....

Please enclose a cheque or postal order made out to Arrow Books Ltd. for the amount due and allow the following for postage and packing.

U.K. CUSTOMERS: Please allow 22p per book to a maximum of £3.00.

B.F.P.O. & EIRE: Please allow 22p per book to a maximum of £3.00.

OVERSEAS CUSTOMERS: Please allow 22p per book.

Whilst every effort is made to keep prices low it is sometimes necessary to increase cover prices at short notice. Arrow Books reserve the right to show new retail prices on covers which may differ from those previously advertised in the text or elsewhere.

Bestselling Non-Fiction

☐ Complete Hip and Thigh Diet	Rosemary Conley	£2.99
☐ Staying off the Beaten Track	Elizabeth Gundrey	£6.99
☐ Raw Energy: Recipes	Leslie Kenton	£3.99
☐ The PM System	Dr J A Muir Gray	£5.99
☐ Women Who Love Too Much	Robin Norwood	£3.50
☐ Letters From Women Who Love Too Much	Robin Norwood	£3.50
☐ Fat is a Feminist Issue	Susie Orbach	£2.99
☐ Callanetics	Callan Pinckney	£6.99
☐ Elvis and Me	Priscilla Presley	£3.50
☐ Love, Medicine and Miracles	Bernie Siegel	£3.50
☐ Communion	Whitley Strieber	£3.50
☐ Trump: The Art of the Deal	Donald Trump	£3.99

Prices and other details are liable to change

ARROW BOOKS, BOOKSERVICE BY POST, PO BOX 29, DOUGLAS, ISLE OF MAN, BRITISH ISLES

NAME...

ADDRESS..

....

....

Please enclose a cheque or postal order made out to Arrow Books Ltd. for the amount due and allow the following for postage and packing.

U.K. CUSTOMERS: Please allow 22p per book to a maximum of £3.00.

B.F.P.O. & EIRE: Please allow 22p per book to a maximum of £3.00.

OVERSEAS CUSTOMERS: Please allow 22p per book.

Whilst every effort is made to keep prices low it is sometimes necessary to increase cover prices at short notice. Arrow Books reserve the right to show new retail prices on covers which may differ from those previously advertised in the text or elsewhere.

Century Travellers

☐	Wild Wales	George Burrow	£4.95
☐	Ride to Khiva	Fred Burnaby	£4.95
☐	Two Middle Aged Ladies in Andalusia	Penelope Chetwode	£3.95
☐	Equator	Thurston Clarke	£4.99
☐	Zanzibar to Timbuktu	Anthony Daniels	£3.95
☐	Thousand Miles Up The Nile	Amelia B. Edwards	£4.95
☐	Fragile Eden	Robin Hanbury-Tenison	£4.99
☐	A Ride Along The Great Wall	Robin Hanbury-Tenison	£4.99
☐	Sultan in Oman	Jan Morris	£4.99
☐	Cameroon With Egbert	Dervla Murphy	£4.99
☐	Muddling Through In Madagascar	Dervla Murphy	£4.99
☐	On A Shoestring To Coorg	Dervla Murphy	£4.99
☐	The Waiting Land	Dervla Murphy	£4.99

Prices and other details are liable to change

ARROW BOOKS, BOOKSERVICE BY POST, PO BOX 29, DOUGLAS, ISLE OF MAN, BRITISH ISLES

NAME...

ADDRESS...

....

....

Please enclose a cheque or postal order made out to Arrow Books Ltd. for the amount due and allow the following for postage and packing.

U.K. CUSTOMERS: Please allow 22p per book to a maximum of £3.00.

B.F.P.O. & EIRE: Please allow 22p per book to a maximum of £3.00.

OVERSEAS CUSTOMERS: Please allow 22p per book.

Whilst every effort is made to keep prices low it is sometimes necessary to increase cover prices at short notice. Arrow Books reserve the right to show new retail prices on covers which may differ from those previously advertised in the text or elsewhere.

Century Travellers

☐	Eight Feet in the Andes	Dervla Murphy	£3.95
☐	Full Tilt	Dervla Murphy	£3.95
☐	In Ethiopia On A Mule	Dervla Murphy	£3.95
☐	Where The Indus Was Young	Dervla Murphy	£3.95
☐	South	Sir Ernest Shakleton	£4.95
☐	Beyond Euphrates	Freya Stark	£4.95
☐	Lycian Shore	Freya Stark	£3.95
☐	Traveller's Prelude	Freya Stark	£4.95
☐	Jerusalem	Colin Thubron	£4.99
☐	Mirror To Damascus	Colin Thubron	£4.99
☐	Venturesome Voyages Of Captain Voss	J.C. Voss	£3.95
☐	Letters from India	Lady Wilson	£4.95

Prices and other details are liable to change

ARROW BOOKS, BOOKSERVICE BY POST, PO BOX 29, DOUGLAS, ISLE OF MAN, BRITISH ISLES

NAME..

ADDRESS..

....

....

Please enclose a cheque or postal order made out to Arrow Books Ltd. for the amount due and allow the following for postage and packing.

U.K. CUSTOMERS: Please allow 22p per book to a maximum of £3.00.

B.F.P.O. & EIRE: Please allow 22p per book to a maximum of £3.00.

OVERSEAS CUSTOMERS: Please allow 22p per book.

Whilst every effort is made to keep prices low it is sometimes necessary to increase cover prices at short notice. Arrow Books reserve the right to show new retail prices on covers which may differ from those previously advertised in the text or elsewhere.